THE
COUPLES
COMMUNICATION
Handbook

*The Skills You Never Learned
for the Marriage You Always Wanted*

RAFFI BILEK

HeartZig Press

First edition 2024

www.TheCommunicationBook.com

Published by HeartZig Press

Table of Contents

Introduction

"We need help with communication."

This is the single most common problem couples come to me with. They say it in different ways, with different words, but they often mean the same thing.

"We have communication issues."

"We're always arguing."

"We never talk anymore."

If any of these sound like you, you're not alone – not by a longshot! Few people are lucky enough to be taught good communication skills as they grow up. In school we learn things like how bees make honey or how to calculate the cosine of an angle, but day-to-day skills that will help us live happy lives somehow tend to get overlooked.

The good news is there's still time. You can learn and benefit from improved communication skills, starting right now. Communication is at the heart of all relationships, and marriage[1] all the more so. How else do two people who do not share a single brain manage to live in sync? Getting messages from one brain to another is critical. You may be all too familiar with some of the consequences of failures in communication:

- Constant arguing or fighting
- Silence and disconnection

---

[1] I'm going to use the words "marriage" and "relationship" in this book to mean some kind of long-term, committed, intimate partnership, whether it's a formal marriage or some other arrangement. I'll also use the words "spouse," "partner," and "significant other" interchangeably to mean your long-term romantic partner. Language is limited, so we'll just have to do the best we can with the words we have available. And I'm trying to keep it simple.

- Frequent misunderstandings about things that (you believe) ought to be simple
- Tasks that need to get done around the house don't get done
- People are always tense at home, walking on eggshells
- The feeling that "we're just roommates" instead of intimate partners

This is not what you got married for, that's for sure.

Then again, you probably didn't get married in order to communicate. Heck, in today's world it sometimes seems like that's *all* we're doing between our phone calls, Zoom calls, text messages, Facebook, TikTok, Instagram, and whatever other new platforms are out there by the time this book goes to print.

So what do people mean when they say they need help with communication? I think we're all looking for some of the following:

- We know how to address issues that come up in our marriage.
- We feel like we're on the same page most of the time.
- We can get practical tasks done together.
- We enjoy being in each other's presence.
- We don't stay mad at each other for too long.
- We have a mechanism to fix our marriage when things go off track.
- We feel connected.

Do those sound like the results you're looking for? Good. That's what we'll be learning how to achieve in this book. This book is a practical guide to improving your communication and thereby your marriage as a whole. We won't spend too much time getting into the philosophical, psychological, or empirical underpinnings of marital success; this book is a roadmap to getting to the top of the mountain rather than a geological study of what mountains are.

BUSTING A FEW MYTHS

What is good communication *not* about? Let's do a quick run through of some common myths about communication and marriage. I could write an entire book on this section alone (hey, maybe I will!), but that's not the purpose of this one; we just need to get these out of the way so we can proceed with a clear perspective. Here are some of those myths:

1. **We have to communicate about everything.** I know this is a book on communication, but that doesn't mean that you need to use it on every issue at all times. You don't have to tell your spouse every thought that enters your mind. (In fact, that would be a really bad idea.) You don't have to "talk about it" every time one of you rubs each other the wrong way. If I'm hungry, I get irritated at people a lot more easily. Talking it out at that point is a lot less effective than just grabbing a handful of trail mix.

2. **If your marriage takes work, something is wrong.** This is definitely not the case. *All relationships take work.* Movies and TV make it look like good relationships just flow naturally and easily all the time. Those relationships are not real. They are contrived and scripted and acted. A good long-term relationship in the real world will take a lot of emotional sweat and labor. *If you want your marriage to work well, then you need to work hard.*

3. **If there's no excitement, something is wrong.** This is another movie-manufactured fairytale. On-screen love looks like thrills and butterflies and fireworks. Relationships do often start with those feelings, but no relationship sustains that for the long term – and that is perfectly normal. Long-term relationships look and feel a lot more like glowing embers than popping fireworks. There is a toasty, calm radiance that keeps you cozy for an extended period rather than a thrilling light show that fizzles out pretty quickly. It is a profound warmth that can be truly life-sustaining long after the novelty and excitement subside.

4. **Good marriages don't have problems.** They do. You and your spouse are different people, with different upbringings and backgrounds and preconceived notions. It's impossible that none of those parts of you will bump up against your spouse's. There will almost certainly be issues you have to face. Some of them won't have any really good solutions. And you can still have a great, lifelong partnership. Read on.

5. **We have to agree on how we see or do things.** Well, if you guys are different people, the odds of you adopting all the same perspectives on or approaches to every issue aren't all that high. *And this is okay.* Sure, you'd like to get on the same page about how you spend money, how you discipline the kids, how you celebrate [insert name of holiday]. That certainly

makes things easier. But you may not get all the way there, and that's not the end of the road for a marriage. (Research shows that *most* couples have *irreconcilable* differences!) Good communication can help you survive and thrive notwithstanding those differences.

INTIMACY AND EMPATHY

Nearly all of what we're going to discuss here can be applied to other relationships in your life – your mom, your friends, your coworkers – but I'm going to focus on marriage, since this is where people most commonly perceive their communication issues, and also since here is probably where the biggest potential for pain and pleasure is. Moving on from a dying friendship is hard, but probably not nearly as painful as moving on from a dying marriage. Moreover, with your spouse you can go deeper with communication and connection, and develop real intimacy. There's a commitment and an obligation there that doesn't exist in other relationships.

Intimacy is what distinguishes your spouse from the other people in your life that you're close to. Intimacy means knowing all the parts of your spouse's inner world – even the hidden parts, the dark parts, the embarrassing parts.[2] Intimacy is sharing all of that with your spouse. Because being in a marriage means giving in so many ways – helping with the household duties, contributing financially, giving your time and attention – but the most valuable thing you give to your spouse is your *self*. Everything else you can in theory outsource. But you can't outsource you.

Intimacy means you have access to who your partner really, truly is; there are no walls between you. Intimacy means you care about them as much as you care about you. Now, these of course are ideals we strive for; nobody ever gets there 100%. But it's important to know what the goal is so we know which direction to aim for.

We are going to discuss the mechanics of striving for these ideals in our communication via two major pathways – sharing about yourself with your partner in an open way, and listening to your partner in a way that demonstrates your care for them. You will do these, broadly speaking, by putting yourself in your partner's shoes (as much as is possible – again, you can never fully, 100% understand the

---

[2] Someone cleverly noted that intimacy means "into-me-see." I'm pretty sure that's not the actual etymology. It's cute though.

experience of another person). This is what we call "empathy." And empathy is actually the crux, the core, the *sine qua non* of this book.

The internet is full of attempts to define what empathy is, but for the purposes of this book, my definition of empathy is *the ability to understand and share in the feelings of another*. This is not the same as simply recognizing what someone else is feeling (although that's obviously an important prerequisite) or feeling pity for them (which doesn't require you to thoroughly consider their individual experience).

Empathy is the most critical ingredient in all human relationships. It requires you to care about people who are not you. It requires you to acknowledge that there are ways of seeing the world that are not the way you see the world. It requires you to transcend the natural self-centeredness that we are all born with and think deeply about what *that* person is going through in *that* situation. Empathy is not the easiest faculty to attain, but it may well be the most valuable.

We are not going to spend much time on how to develop empathy, but we are going to talk about how to sharpen and apply it. That is to say, if you actually don't care about anyone besides yourself, this book probably won't help you very much. But if you *do* care about other people – especially your life partner – then I think this book will help you a lot. It will help you communicate effectively about difficult (and not-so-difficult) things. It will help you feel connected to each other. It will help you lay the foundation for a lifetime of awesomeness.

The process we're going to use is something I've called *empathic dialogue*, which I use in counseling sessions with my clients as well as in my own life.[3] I must admit that I didn't invent it. Many relationship theories and couples counseling modalities use something similar. In Imago Therapy they use mirroring. In the PREP approach it's called active listening. The Gottman method uses the Gottman-Rapoport Intervention. These are all based on similar principles; I've packaged them a bit differently in a way that I believe will help you succeed, added a few new ideas, and given it a warm and fuzzy name. So if you already have a method that works for you, great. And if you've tried these other ones before and they haven't

---

[3] You will encounter many of the couples I've worked with in the pages below. The vignettes that start and end the chapters are made-up people having made-up conversations, but stories within the chapters are all true renditions of people I've worked with, with details changed to protect their privacy.

worked for you, don't throw your hands up – this approach still has something to offer. I'm going to hand you a crystal-clear method for better communication with your spouse: you'll have fewer fights, and when conflict does come up, you'll know how to use it as a vehicle for connection instead of pain and frustration. You'll finally feel *heard*.

But don't take my word for it. Turn the page and see for yourself.

Chapter 1

Timeout

Rob and Denise are having a good day. They spent time at the aquarium with the kids, and for once, nobody cried, nobody got lost, and nobody threw up. It's a bit of a milestone for them. Now that they've gotten the kids in bed, they're planning to chill out on the couch together and watch a movie. Rob's got the remote. Denise goes to the kitchen to get the popcorn from the microwave. Suddenly, Rob hears a loud groan from the kitchen:

Denise: *Rob! The sink is still full of the dishes from dinner!*

Rob: *I know – I said I would do them later!*

Denise: *No, we agreed you'd do them before we started watching.*

Rob: *No, that's not—*

Denise: *What's wrong with you?! Why can't you ever think of anyone but yourself?*

Rob: *Why do YOU always have to have things YOUR way? If the dishes don't get clean at exactly the minute you want—*

Denise: *It's ALWAYS later with you!*

Rob: *WHY DO YOU ALWAYS HAVE TO DO THIS??? THIS IS NOT ABOUT ME!!!*

Denise: *IT'S ALWAYS ABOUT YOU, ROB, BECAUSE YOU ALWAYS MAKE IT ABOUT YOU!*

If there is only one thing you take from this book, it should be this:

TALK ABOUT IT LATER.

Of course, the night does not end with Netflix and chill.

Does this scenario have a familiar ring to it? Everything's going smoothly, but then one little thing goes wrong and then pretty quickly things heat up and turn into a nasty fight? If so, you're not alone. Many couples struggle with arguments that get out of hand. Fortunately, we're going to learn how to rise above that problem. But before we talk about how to communicate in a way that works, I want to talk about how *not* to communicate in a way that *doesn't* work. In fact, *if there is only one thing you take from this book, it should be this:*

TALK ABOUT IT LATER.

I am convinced that relationships everywhere would be vastly improved if people could implement this rule. It is totally normal to get hijacked by your emotions in a difficult moment; that's how our brains are wired. And it just means that we've got to be aware of that in order to avoid falling into the trap. How many times have you gotten into an argument where you:

1. solve nothing;
2. say the same things you've said in previous arguments;
3. say things you don't mean, wish you hadn't said, and can't take back; and
4. feel worse instead of better at the end of it?

Right, that's what I thought.

It's perfectly fair – and normal – to feel angry with your spouse. That does not mean it's a good idea to say or do whatever comes to your mind. As one of my mentors taught me, "You can get angry, or you can solve the problem, but you can't do both." Anger pushes us into fight-or-flight mode, pumping stress hormones into our body and gearing up our nervous system to respond to threat. "Respond to threat" and "work through a problem in your marriage" are very different courses of action.

I want to be clear again that there is nothing wrong with you if you find yourself in fight-or-flight when things get really stressful. You are human. This is the human brain's natural response system, one that kept us out of trouble back when the saber-toothed tigers came around looking for brunch.

Your spouse is not a saber-toothed tiger.

That's why we need to learn how to do things differently. I don't mean we should learn how to not feel stress. It's simply not possible to have an intimate relationship – or a life, for that matter – without some degree of stress and friction. What I mean is that we have to avoid getting into a situation where we're triggered into fighting with or fleeing from our partner. Once your brain goes into fight-or-flight, the frontal lobes shut down and the rear part of your brain, the "reptilian brain," lights up. Your whole decision-making apparatus is compromised. Trying to battle your way out of that is useless; your only hope for a decent interaction is not to get there in the first place, or to back out as soon as you can when you find yourself there. "Talk about it later" is your key.

BEFORE YOU GET INTO IT

The first way you can implement this talk-about-it-later principle is to *avoid bringing things up in the moment.* It is extremely rare that you will encounter a situation in your marriage that is an actual emergency that needs to be dealt with on the spot (and you'll probably know when it *is* an emergency because someone will be bleeding heavily). In the story above, Denise was upset (on the face of it, at least) that Rob hadn't done the dishes. She has every right to feel unhappy about this; maybe there is even an ongoing problem in their marriage with Rob ignoring Denise's requests. Denise can and should feel free to discuss this issue with him.

NOT. NOW.

Right now Denise is indignant about the dishes. Her emotions are jacked up. It is a very good bet that things are going to go sideways if she tries to deal with this on the spot (as in fact they do). Consider how the evening would have turned out differently if Denise had internally acknowledged her frustration, put it aside so they could enjoy the movie, and dealt with it the next day. I frequently tell my clients, *"Strike when the iron is cold."*

> Strike when the iron is cold.

When the iron is hot, you are bound to make bad decisions. Wait on it. I promise you will get better results.

Now, this doesn't mean that you can sweep problems under the rug and they'll just go away. Don't be a rug sweeper. You've got to address the things that are bothering you in your marriage or you will just build up resentment and anger and eventually the whole thing will come tumbling down. We're going to talk extensively about how to do that. But the first step is the timing. Talk about it *later*.

I want to openly acknowledge that this can be really hard. I mean *really* hard. I cannot tell you how many times I've stared down the barrel of this internal conflict myself. It goes something like this:

Me: I can't believe my wife just did that. So not okay! I'm going to give her a piece of my mind.

Me: Wait. This is not going to go well. I'll tell her tomorrow.

Me: No, it's fine. It's just a little thing! I'll say this one piece of it and then we'll have a whole conversation later this week.

Me: That is so not a good idea.

Me: But I really need to say something about this right now.

Me: But you really don't.

Usually the trump card that wins it for Good Raffi is that I know I'm going to have to face my clients the next day and if I don't follow my own advice that's really lame. You may have to find a different winning argument for yourself. Trust me, it's worth it. You do not need to talk about it *now*. If you're afraid you'll forget about it, definitely go ahead and write it down, or make a note on your favorite app, or however you want to record it. Remember, this is not about sweeping it under the rug; it's about dealing with it at a time that will actually work (which, again, is not now).

What you'll find is that about half the things that bother you in the heat of the moment turn out to be totally trivial when you look at them the next morning. You realize you were hungry or tired or stressed and whatever your spouse did was a bit irritating but nothing that is really significant at all. And you can unreservedly let go of the whole thing and move on.

But then you have the other half of things, which are absolutely issues you need to talk about. You will. *Not now!*

Some of you may be thinking of a well-known axiom that seems to be in conflict with what I'm saying here. Ever heard the idea that you should "never go to bed angry"? I think this is terrible advice. You know full well what happens when you try to go this route. Something happened that upset you and you and your spouse are getting ready for bed, silently stewing. It's midnight, you want to get to bed, but you decide to listen to your grandma who told you never to go to bed angry, so you tell your spouse how upset you are. What happens? Now it's 3 a.m. and not only are you both still angry, you're also dead tired, and you're a wreck in the morning to boot. Right?

> Ever heard the idea that you should "never go to bed angry"? I think this is terrible advice.

I have never had a couple tell me that no, actually they fix everything then and there at midnight and the next day is gumdrops and jellybeans. It's okay not to force it. Give yourself permission to be angry at your spouse. Do that thing where you both face opposite directions in bed and it's clear everyone's ticked off. Is it awkward? It's awkward. And it also won't kill the marriage – but enough 3 a.m. fights might do just that. Awkward is better than argument.

Sometimes your spouse doesn't even realize something happened, and they see on your face and in your body language that you're annoyed about something, and they go, "Is everything okay?" or "Are you upset?" You can take the bait and launch into it, but you know how that ends. I am not suggesting that you should put on a show and pretend everything is fine (which it's clear is not the case anyway). You can be honest! "I'm actually kind of angry at you right now, but I'm not in a place to talk about it. Let's discuss later." That's allowed!

Of course, it is helpful if your spouse is on board with this and does not go, "No, tell me what's wrong, tell me, you can't just be mad at me and not tell me! We have to talk about this!" and so on. If you both accept the principles we've been discussing so far, it will be a manageable situation – namely, that you're both allowed to have angry feelings; that holding off is a better path than getting into another ugly argument; and that you will talk about this at a better time. If they're reading this book as well, hopefully you're both on the same page here. But even if they haven't read this book yet, you can still pull this off: you say, "I know you want to talk about it, but I'm not able to talk about this nicely right now. We'll talk about it when I can do this well." Repeat yourself as needed, or simply excuse yourself from their presence. (See the pitfalls section below for more on this.)

There really is nothing wrong with being angry and dealing with it later. Yes, this could make for an uncomfortable Sunday if that's hanging in the air, but it sure beats a knock-down, drag-out fight. People sometimes think that if you're angry, you have to dwell in and give vent to your anger until things are resolved. Not so! You can be angry at each other and still carry on living – making breakfast for each other, picking up the dry cleaning, figuring out who's going to walk the dog. It can be a little distant and a little formal, but it won't kill you and it's not a sin. Actually, it's also possible to tuck it away for later (especially when it's not a massive issue at hand) and carry on *enjoying* each other as well. You can be angry at your spouse for making an inappropriate comment to your mother, but still recognize that overall they are a wonderful person and put the issue on the backburner (not under the rug) to deal with later on – and then still enjoy watching your show together, or going out for dinner, or what have you.

Sure, it would be nice if "have a mature and respectful conversation to deal with the problem" were an option at this point in time. If you are at a certain level of anger, that just isn't the case. *Talk about it later.*

WHEN YOU'RE ALREADY IN THE MIDDLE OF IT

The second situation where you need to implement "talk about it later" is when you realize you're already in a pot that is starting to boil. This might be because you failed to push off bringing up a topic right away[1] (or maybe you did manage to postpone it, but it's just a really tough subject, and even when you return to it in a calm time the conversation gets heated). Sometimes you're discussing a subject that doesn't even seem like a big deal at all until things get testy or even explosive (this is usually because some button got pushed that's connected to a deeper issue).

Normal! This is all normal. At this point what you need to do is take a timeout. Actually, you need to take a timeout *before* you get to this point if at all possible. Remember, once your frontal brain goes offline, all bets are off. You *must* disengage

---

[1] Good news! Even when you make mistakes, you can still maintain a great marriage. It's not like you have to follow every instruction in this book exactly, in every conversation, or you're headed for a breakup. Failure is normal! You pick yourself back up and try to do better at the next opportunity.

before you get there because once you're there, you simply can't make a good decision anymore, and you are likely to make the situation a lot worse.

> When a conversation begins to get heated, you take a break.

What this means is that when a conversation begins to get heated, you take a break. If either of you notices either of you getting escalated, it's time to call a timeout.[2]

Recognizing Your Feelings

One of the main challenges people can have when it comes to pulling out when they begin to feel escalated is that they don't even notice when it's happening. Emotional intelligence – the ability to understand and manage your own emotions (as well as recognize those of others) – has been gaining recognition in recent years as a key element of not only successful relationships but of happy lives.

It's important to be aware of how you're feeling. This is not just touchy-feely kumbaya stuff; it's in fact modern science. There was a fascinating study done of people with serious brain injuries to the emotion-processing centers of their brain. These people's emotional systems were essentially offline. And one of the consequences was that although they could intellectually function just as well as before, *they were incapable of acting*. They could tell you exactly what the right thing to do is in a given situation, but they couldn't *do* it.

Emotions are the engines which move us to act. (That's not just a cute metaphor – it's what the word *emotion* means. The "motion" part is not coincidental.) *We do what we do because of the way we are feeling in a given moment.* That's not to say that we're all just acting on whims and passing feelings. But research has shown time and time again that the decisions people make are a lot more influenced by their emotions than they might care to recognize.

---

2 Taking a timeout is not the same thing as "flight" (i.e., running away). When you are in fight-or-flight mode you are focused only on survival, you don't care about anyone else, and you have no intention to come back. A timeout is a measured plan to step away, calm down, and reengage later.

As we noted above, you need to notice when you're getting angry in order to be able to pull out before things spiral out of control. But if you don't generally know what you're feeling, developing a deeper awareness of this will absolutely improve your marriage, romantic relationship, family bonds, and really your life overall. Grab a self-help book, download an app, or find a therapist to help you do this vital personal work.

Calling Timeout

What does a timeout look like in practice? Here are the steps you need to go through:

1. Say you need a break.
2. Say you're coming back.
3. Go calm yourself down.
4. Come back and try again.

Let's break it down:

1. Say you need a break.

When you realize that things are starting to go south, you start by calling it out. But you have to do it without dumping on your partner – i.e., you don't accuse your partner of being angry and that's why you need a break. You know what happens when you do that:

You: *Calm down, you're getting angry!*

Your partner: I AM NOT ANGRY!!!

So don't go there. Don't point fingers at each other here. It's just more fuel on the fire. It's also a proven fact that never in the course of human history has anyone ever said to an angry partner, "Calm down!" with the result being that their partner actually calmed down. Therefore, do not say:

- "You're getting angry."
- "I see you can't handle this right now."
- "You're getting too heated."

These all put the blame on your partner. It won't work. Mind you, it's not that you aren't correct; you may very well be. But a key perspective you will encounter in this book is that I am a lot less interested in who's right and who's wrong and a lot more interested in what works. Instead of commenting on your partner's emotional state (right though you may be), here are some more neutral ways you can say it to get the point across, regardless of who is more escalated at the moment:

- "This conversation isn't going to go well."
- "I can't handle this right now."
- "This is getting too heated."

Of course, if you recognize that it's you that's getting ramped up, you can certainly own that: "I'm feeling angry and I can't do this well right now." We can only take responsibility for ourselves. If I am angry, I can say so and take steps to deal with it. But if *you* are angry, I cannot make you acknowledge it, own it, or do anything about it. And my trying to do so is only going to make you angrier. It is also more likely to elicit denial than agreement and change. So again, whether you are right or not isn't very relevant right now. What's relevant is what works, and what works is not telling your partner they're messing things up.

> If I am angry, I can say so and take steps to deal with it. But if *you* are angry, I cannot make you acknowledge it.

I do not recommend trying to achieve consensus here ("Do you think now is a good time for a break?"). I don't generally suggest taking unilateral action in a marriage, but this is one time when it's necessary. Your spouse doesn't know what's going on inside you, and they cannot judge whether you do or don't need a break right now or how close you are to crossing over the fight-or-flight line. On the flip side, it's possible they don't recognize how close *they* are to the line, and your taking the reins and calling a timeout might be the saving grace. Taking a timeout is something you need to do when you need to.

The truth is, it's not really a unilateral decision – you should agree on this plan of action beforehand. If your spouse isn't also reading this book (or even if they are), make sure to have a conversation ahead of time laying out the plan. That won't necessarily make it *easy* to pull off the disengage, but it will definitely make it *easier*.

The real struggle at this point is for the spouse who's being walked away from to allow it to happen. It can be a tough moment, but again, it's so necessary to preserve your marriage and ultimately work through whatever issues are at hand.

2. Say you're coming back.

After you've called it out that you need a break/timeout/whatever you want to call it, the next step is – and this is a really helpful piece that many people say has helped them with taking timeouts where they had failed before – *you say you're coming back to the conversation* (whether literally or figuratively): "I can't talk about this anymore right now. I'm taking a break. We can try again later." When you do this, you make it clear that this is a timeout and not a game over. (The team doesn't just head back to the locker room when they call a timeout! The goal is obviously to come back and get back in the game.)

When you walk away without saying that you intend to come back to it, the message that usually comes across is, "We're not going to talk about this" (and for many couples, that's exactly what happens). This is often experienced by your spouse as being blown off. They may feel not just angry but even panicky – like *there's a big problem and we need to fix it and you're running away and IT'S A CATAS-TROPHE!!!* Of course, it isn't; but it can feel that way – and this can lead to the very unhelpful behavior of one person following the other around the house as the latter tries to take a timeout. That is another wholly ineffective strategy which we will address more fully in just a bit.

If you're still reasonably calm when you call the timeout (which is ideally when you want to do this), you can get extra credit by saying *when* you're coming back – this way you're not just pushing the discussion off into the indeterminate future: "I'm going out, I'll be back in an hour," or, "Let's circle back to this on Sunday." Aim for something not too short or too long: five minutes is probably not long enough for both of you to cool down (unless you're really good at that); five years is probably overkill.

Of course, if you've got multiple kids, jobs, or any of the other things going on that make modern life so hectic, you may not be able to sit down within the next day or two and have this conversation well. You are much better off postponing it until you have the time and headspace rather than trying to push through the discussion when one or both of you simply aren't in a place to do it effectively. As you get better at communicating about difficult topics, you'll develop a confidence that the issue will get addressed (because it will), and even if no specific try-again time was stated you'll know that there *will* be a try-again time.

Often, by the time we call a timeout, we are too worked up to speak politely, let alone plan a try-again time. It's a good idea to have a predetermined time frame that is the default try-again time in such situations, or a set weekly time to revisit issues that have come up, or some other way of ensuring the subject doesn't just get dropped.

> **As you get better at communicating about difficult topics, you'll develop a confidence that the issue will get addressed.**

If you can pull off this step – especially if you have a spouse who is clingy, has abandonment issues, is prone to anxiety, etc. – it will help you both take a clean break as needed.

3. Go calm down.

After you skillfully call a timeout, the next step is – you leave.

When you leave, don't go sit in your office or your car and stew about the situation, or think up what you're going to say when you get back to really stick it to your spouse. That will definitely not help you make things better! (This applies both to the one who called the timeout and the one who didn't.) If you continue to think about the conflict, you'll come back just as hot as you left. That doesn't help much.

Go do whatever it is that will get your mind off the situation and help you settle back down. Go for a walk, play solitaire, do yoga, knit, play with the dog, bake a cake, exercise, call a friend – anything is fine so long as it helps you reset yourself. Talking with a friend doesn't count if you're just going to complain about your mate; exercising is a bad idea if you find yourself getting riled up imagining your spouse's head as the punching bag. You get the idea.

Another option to help you calm down during your timeout is to directly talk yourself down. If you're really escalated, you're probably better off distracting yourself as above; but if you're only mildly irritated at this point, you can try walking yourself through some of the ideas in the Mindsets chapter (chapter 11) to help you recenter yourself into a more productive frame of mind.

Relaxation Techniques

Many people find great benefit in using techniques explicitly designed to help you relax and bring down your stress levels. These are great approaches not just to call upon during timeout moments but also to implement regularly in your life, for the purpose of reducing your baseline level of stress. Here are a few simple methods with short descriptions (but feel free to hop on Google to find more information, guided videos, etc.).

- Deep breathing: research has shown that even pausing to take three deep breaths can have a measurable impact on your stress level. Really! That's it! Three deep breaths. Of course, if you're feeling ambitious, stop for a few minutes and take a whole bunch of them. It does a body good.

- Progressive muscle relaxation: in this exercise, you sequentially focus on the different muscle groups in your body – for example, your head, then your face, your neck, your upper arms, hands, etc. – and you tense them for a few seconds, then completely release. (Other takes on this method skip the tensing part and just have you relax the muscles while imagining all the tension flowing out of them.) Do your whole body from top to bottom and let the stress seep out.

Mindfulness meditation: there is a whole world of information out there, but let's just take a very simple approach to it. Sit in a comfortable position on the couch, or a recliner, or the floor, or whatever you like; close your eyes, and focus on your breathing. Just pay attention to the breaths going in and out. You can count them up to 5 or 10 if you like, then start over. When your mind wanders from your breath (it *will* wander), you simply bring your attention back to your breathing. It's important to be clear that a wandering mind doesn't mean you're failing at meditation; noticing your mind wandering and gently bringing it back to your point of focus is an integral part of the process.

4. Come back and try again.

After taking a time out, saying you're going to come back, and then leaving and calming down, the last step is to actually come back to the conversation. Bring it up again when things are calm. I know this can be scary! It will become less so when you get better at the communication skills we'll discuss in the rest of the book. If you have a regular relationship check-in time (see the sidebar that follows), that's great; otherwise, it's ideal if the person who called the timeout keeps an eye out for a good time and opens the topic back up (again, because that communicates to the other partner that the timeout was truly meant as a break and not a game over).

If you specified a time, come back when you said you would. This is true even if you're not really calm yet. It's critical to send the message that you're going to follow up, not blow it off. If you're still ramped up, you come back and you say so. "I'm back, but I'm still feeling really angry. Let's try again tomorrow after dinner." Don't make the mistake of skipping the come-back because you're not ready. That makes it harder to pull off timeouts in the future, because your partner will have learned from experience that you may not actually come back to deal with the issue. If you're stuck in traffic or something, give a call or a text, but don't just ignore the meeting time.

Once you are feeling ready to get back into the conversation, you'll implement the dialogue techniques we'll discuss later in the book. If you try to continue and things heat up again, take another timeout, or you won't have gained much. Getting through a conversation at an uncomfortably slow pace but without yelling and hurting each other's feelings is a far better option than charging through it with guns blazing and dumping out everything you wanted to say, leaving the marriage in tatters behind you. But hey, it's up to you.

Ken and Mia came in for marriage counseling after being married for just two months. They figured that the increasing squabbling that characterized their relationship in the year prior to the wedding was attributable to the stress of the planning and the complex family issues involved – Mia's parents were divorced and remarried to new spouses, and having all four of them together in the same room always went poorly; meanwhile, Ken had a sibling with a gambling addiction that was causing ongoing drama in his family.

The truth was that their relationship had a solid foundation to it, but their inability to deal with the stressful issues effectively was wearing away at it. They still felt very much in love, and they could identify and elaborate at length on what exactly they loved about each other. And it's not like these very difficult family issues were points of conflict for them; they largely agreed on how to handle them and were super supportive of each other when family issues flared up on either side.

The real problem was simply that when disagreements did happen, their commitment to "communication" led them to try to tackle every issue as soon as it came up. It was well-meaning but poorly executed. As I explained to them, it's simply not possible to deal with every issue in the moment. We might wish it could be so, but it isn't so.

When I gave them permission to not fix problems immediately, to allow things to be wrong for a while, and, critically, to be angry with each other for a bit, they both looked like a weight had been lifted off their shoulders. For them, little more was needed than the permission to talk about it later and a little guidance on how to practically execute that.

Making the Conversation Happen

Some couples are pretty good at not getting into it when they're mad – but then on the flip side they never get around to having the conversation at all. What this looks like is a pleasant and polite relationship that eventually explodes in a massive supernova argument when one or both parties can no longer keep their frustrations stuffed down. (Perhaps this sounds familiar to you.)

The challenge here is that once you've avoided an argument by not talking about something at the wrong time, it becomes very unpalatable to try to bring it up again later at the right time, because that's when everyone is happy and pleasant again, and raising the topic of something conflictual definitely doesn't appeal to anyone at that time.

But you have to.

If you never talk about the things that are bothering you, they will indeed fester in the marriage and then explode (or else just quietly strangle the marriage until it dies that way). Once you get good at empathic dialogue, this prospect won't seem so scary to you anymore; it will be a challenge you know you can power through and come out better and stronger on the other side. Part of making sure you get there is to ensure the difficult conversation does happen at some point. For some people the way to do that is to have a weekly set time where they sit down and address relationship issues. (This should be separate from date night or movie night or whatever other regular fun times you may have planned – if all your fun times get taken over by Serious Conversations, fun will rapidly disappear from your marriage.)

For other couples, a good way to address this is simply to schedule the conversation in the wake of a timeout – i.e., after you leave and calm down, you come back and offer some times to circle back to the issue. (Then put it in your calendar and make sure you do it!)

Whatever way you make it happen, *make it happen.* If you avoid all Serious Conversations, you may find your marriage in Serious Trouble. (Don't worry – you're going to get some very clear instructions on having those conversations in later chapters.)

PITFALLS AND HAZARDS OF TIMEOUT

Let's be clear: timeout is not always so easy to implement. We are emotional creatures, and getting a handle on our emotions rather than letting our emotions handle us can be tough. But I am confident that implementing this practice will make a big difference in your marriage. It's just going to take some effort and some practice. Let's take a look at some of the challenges to implementing this well.

It's hard to say what you have to say in the moment.

Sometimes you're so worked up that even saying "I think I need to take a break right now" might be beyond your ability. If you've gotten to that point, it can be sufficient to just call "timeout!" and bolt. Even if you can get a whole sentence out (politely), trying to come up with a number for how many minutes or hours you need can be taxing.

The best solution to this problem is to make sure you and your partner discuss the timeout method in a calm moment ahead of time, before you need to call upon it. That way everyone knows what the plan is and what it will (hopefully) look like. If you need to pull a one-word exit, it will already be a known technique. You can also come up with a default timeframe for when words or thoughts fail you – half an hour, or dinner that night or the next, or whatever suits you and fits your life and your schedule.

Your spouse still tries to say "just one more thing" when you call a timeout.

It is understandably very hard to disconnect from the conversation/argument when you feel very strongly about the subject. We've discussed at length why it's important to do so, but that doesn't mean it's easy. The good news is, the more you implement timeouts, the easier it will become to honor them and make a clean break when one is needed. (Like we said earlier, *easier*, not *easy*. It will probably never become super smooth and delightful to wrench yourself out of an escalating conversation. But the benefits you will reap will hopefully convince you to keep doing it when it's needed.) You and your spouse will both come to have experiences of disengaging and coming back to deal with the issue in a better way, and that will make it less uncomfortable to pull out in the middle of an important but increasingly contentious discussion.

> The more you implement timeouts, the easier it will become to honor them.

Additionally, as you get better at the communication skills we will shortly discuss, you will be more secure in your ability to have those difficult conversations, more confident that they will actually happen, and more skillful at postponing them, because you will not have that nagging pressure inside that tells you that if you don't deal with this *right now then you will never get a chance so you better say something RIGHT NOW.*

You feel like you are abandoning/being abandoned by your spouse.

It's been said that sometimes in order to get where you want to go, you've got to go in the other direction first. The taller you want to build the building, the further down you have to dig the foundation.

Leaving an escalating argument is not abandonment. It's a temporary withdrawal that is *in service of the relationship.* You are taking space in order to connect.

It's not necessarily a delicious feeling – in fact, timeouts are often quite uncomfortable for both of you in that moment – but it does a whole lot of good for you as a couple. When you or your spouse has to take a timeout, remember that it's for the benefit of the relationship. It will make the interruption more bearable.

> Leaving an escalating argument is not abandonment. It's a temporary withdrawal that is *in service of the relationship*.

Your spouse follows you around the house when you try to take a break.

This is a common dynamic some couples face. Many folks feel it's important to deal with the problem and not put it off, so they don't allow their spouse to "run away from the problem." A relationship problem is serious, after all, and we shouldn't let it fester, right?

The theory is totally correct. It just doesn't work.

I agree that your marriage is a priority and should be attended to in a timely fashion. But as human beings, we simply can't perform well under that kind of stress. When clients bring this dispute before me and ask me (explicitly or implicitly) to judge who's right, I always tell them I don't care what's right. I care what works. Right or wrong, trying to solve the problem *now* doesn't work.

If you are the one being followed: do your best to get some space between you and your follower. Don't take the bait and turn back into it. Go to another room. If you are followed, go to a room where you can lock the door and turn on some calming music. Better yet, leave the house, if your circumstances allow. Go for a walk around the block. Drive to a Starbucks and get an iced chai latte (if you're in control enough to drive safely). Anything that will give you the space for both of you to calm down. Again, the more successes you have with timeouts, the easier it will be for your spouse to let you go.

If you are the follower: you must recognize that this problem is not going to get fixed right now. I know you want it to. I know it can be really, really hard to sit with an unresolved problem. But the only other option to taking a timeout is to make the situation worse. That's what's on the menu. There's Take a Break, and there's Make It Worse. Come to a Mutual Agreement in a Loving Manner is, rightly or wrongly, not on the menu at this time, no matter how much you want it to be.

Of course, you don't need me to tell you this. Your experience bears it out. Have you ever gotten into the angry zone during a discussion-argument-fight, where things were really tense, maybe even nasty, and then clenched real hard, regained your composure, and came to a pleasant resolution? No, you have not. You may be saying, "Well, if only my spouse wouldn't yell/shut down/get defensive...!" But the point is, they cannot. They are in frontal-lobe shutdown (or they perceive that *you* are), and the only way out is to take a break and try again later. I'm sorry. I wish it were possible to make the problem go away now. I contend that it is not.

Abusing the system

One way that people can misuse the timeout concept is to spit out what they want to say and then call a timeout. They'll make their point, or worse, throw out a nasty barb, then hightail it. That is not fair play. If your goal is to discharge your emotions, get the last word, and stick it to your partner, hey, go for it. It's a free country. But I would not expect your marriage to get better. On the other hand, if your goal is to improve/fix/save your relationship, you would be wise to abide by a fair use policy: timeout is a tool to avoid and manage conflict, not to hit and run.

If you notice your partner doing this kind of thing, it's something to bring up at a later time and talk through like any other problem. But if this behavior becomes an ongoing pattern, it may call into question their commitment to making this marriage better for the both of you.

A lesser abuse of the system is using timeout as a way to get out of talking about an issue entirely. Timeout isn't about stonewalling. Like we said above, you don't end the game when you call a timeout – the goal is to come back and keep playing when you're ready. Of course, you need to develop the skills to come back and have a productive conversation; that's what we'll do in the rest of this book.

We also mentioned earlier that a lot of the issues that spark an argument turn out to be trivial and *don't* need further discussion – although you'd better check in with your partner before deciding the issue doesn't need to be addressed, because *they* might think it does! The point is, although not every little fight needs to be rehashed later, you should not use timeout as a way of getting out of discussing a topic. Not a winning strategy for the long term.

PUTTING IT INTO PRACTICE

So what does this look like for our discontented couple from the opening of the chapter, Rob and Denise? Let's replay this and see how it goes. Note that in any situation, there are usually multiple points of intervention – if you miss an opportunity to course correct, there are other ones you can still grab onto. In this scenario, the ideal point of intervention is immediately when Denise notices the dishes in the sink. She is displeased. The best thing to do is *strike when the iron is cold.* It will take a hefty act of willpower, but she can bite it for right now, remind herself that she can discuss it with Rob later, and enjoy the movie. "Overall, Rob is awesome," she can think to herself. "He messed up. We all do. Let's have a nice night anyway." She can choose to table the issue for now, then discuss it with him the next day over coffee.

But let's say she failed to do this and she went right into it:

Denise: *Rob! The sink is still full of the dishes from dinner!*

Rob: *I know – I said I would do them later!*

Denise: *No, we agreed you'd do them before we started watching.*

Rob: *No, that's not—*

At this point, Denise can recognize she's really ticked off and call a timeout. But let's say she flubbed that too:

Denise: What's wrong with you?! *Why can't you ever think of anyone but yourself?*

Here's where Rob can realize this is going off the tracks and call a timeout himself. The truth is, at any point from here on out, someone should call a timeout as soon as they spot what's going on.

Rob: *You know what, I need a timeout. I don't want the whole night to be shot. I'm going out for a walk. I'll be back in 20 minutes.*

Denise: *FINE!*

Okay, they got through the first gauntlet. Now they've got some space to themselves. Here are some ways they can talk themselves down from further conflict:

Denise: *Ugh! I can't believe he's avoiding the dishes again. This is like the bajillionth time. FINE. Look, it's just a small mess. I can live with a small mess. I don't need any dishes right now. And we'll talk about how annoying this is another time, when we're calm. I don't want to lose the whole night either. It's fine. Really. He's overall a great guy. He tends to be forgetful. I'm not going to let some bowls and spoons kill our date night. Let me check out what Kendra's up to on Instagram and get my mind off this.*

Rob: *She is SO ANNOYING about the dishes! Why does it always have to be done on her schedule??? We even agreed on it! Okay, fine, look, it doesn't even matter who's right about it. I'm going to walk it off. I'll apologize for misunderstanding what she wanted, and we'll chat later on about how she talks to me when she's upset, which is not cool. None of this is worth ruining the whole night over. Hey, there's Mr. Chung walking his dogs! I'm gonna spend a few minutes horsing around with them and then I'll head back inside.*

As I've said, I know this is hard, truly I do. Taking a break in the heat of the moment doesn't come naturally. It will take practice. And you'll get better at it. I can tell you this from personal experience. I still use timeouts when I need to. I'm human too. When my wife and I get annoyed at each other – which I fully expect to be a part of our marriage for the rest of our lives – we take a break and come back later. Nobody can manage conflict well when they're emotionally maxed out.

Don't give up. Appreciate small gains. If you have five opportunities in the next week to try this out and you succeed in walking away *one* time, *that is good news.* That's called progress. I don't work in miracles. I work in small change over time. That's the change that lasts. So cut yourself some slack if you're not perfect, and take pleasure in the small successes.

You can also make the most of your failures. If you have a blowup, you can think back and try to recognize the points of intervention where you could have done something different. (Focus on the points of intervention for *you*, not for your spouse. You're the only one you can change here.) Do that a few times, and you will probably notice that you're picking up on the flub sooner after the fight. Eventually, you'll spot it as it's actually happening – and you'll continue to fight anyway. But then one day, you'll catch the moment in real time, and *you'll actually manage to implement the timeout.* That will be a good day.

Working as a Team

Of course, relationship growth works best when you're doing it together. But taking a timeout is worthwhile even if your spouse isn't so on board, because you'll avoid things going further downhill. That said, when you're both in sync on bringing this into your lives, you'll likely see more success.

View it as a team effort. One effective way to do this is to reward yourselves for your wins. Put a jar out on the kitchen counter and call it the timeout jar (or some other more creative name, perhaps). Every time one of you pulls off a timeout, put $5 in the jar. (Research has shown that visual cues are a big boost to this process, so having an actual jar with actual bills in it is likely to boost your motivation more than just keeping a mental or even written account.)

Set a target amount and when you reach it, go out for a really nice dinner together (or go to a joint spa day, or whatever floats your boat). I recommend lots of high-fives and hugs along the way for added encouragement. Make it a joint goal, and enjoy the journey of reaching it together!

Like I said, if you take one thing away from this book, this should be it. *Talk about it later.* That means not starting a discussion on an issue in the heat of the moment when it comes up. It means taking a break when a moment gets heated. If you do, I can assure you that you will save a tremendous amount of wear and tear on your marriage, and you will both be happier for it.

Rob: *Babe? I'm back.*

Denise: *Hey babe. Look, I'm sorry about—*

Rob: *I know. It's no big deal. Let's hash it out later. Now let's just enjoy our movie, 'kay?*

Denise: *Yes! Please!*

Chapter 2

Exploring vs. Resolving

Naya: The car is still making that funny noise. Are you going to be able to take it to the shop this week?

Eric: Definitely. I said I'll take care of it, and I will. Not to worry.

Naya: Well, I know you said it, but you've said it a lot. And it's still not fixed. When are you going to take care of it already?

Eric: I said I'll do it this week, okay?! There's been a lot going on at work, I haven't had time.

Naya: You always have a lot going on at work!!! When are you going to deal with the stuff you need to at home also??? Where does your family come into play ever???

Eric: WHO DO YOU THINK I'M WORKING MY TAIL OFF FOR??? I'm trying to feed my family, for goodness sake!

Naya: YOUR FAMILY NEVER EVEN SEES YOU!!!

Eek. That didn't go well, did it? I suspect you've had conversations like this – ones that start out totally innocently and within a few sentences become a massive fight. What's going on here? And how do we do it differently?

THE ISSUE IS NOT THE ISSUE

The first step in making a change in this unproductive pattern is to recognize that the issue is not the issue. Couples almost never get into fights because of a disagreement on a factual point, like the car making a funny noise, or who left the milk out, or even the classic squeezing the toothpaste tube from the wrong end. They get into fights because of how they *feel* about what's going on. Feelings are what spur us into action (sometimes unhelpful action). If we were all totally rational actors, we would just keep discussing things calmly until we reached a resolution to the issue at hand. But we're not. We are powerfully influenced by our emotions, often in ways we're not even fully aware of (see sidebar "Recognizing Your Feelings" in chapter 1).

Here's an important key point to keep in mind when it comes to hashing out our issues: *you cannot solve a problem that you don't understand.* Sounds pretty obvious when you say it out like that, right? But so often we find ourselves trying to do exactly this – solve a problem before we even truly get what the problem *is*. Because the problem is not the clunkety-clunk noise you're hearing when you turn the steering wheel; the problem is how we both *feel* about that (such as that sinking feeling that you're about to cough up a lot of money for this) – and how we feel about the thoughts we have in response to that ("Why does this always happen to me?") and how we feel about how we communicate about that ("Why can't he ever just listen to me?"), and how we feel about a host of other things as well. The more we can get clarity on those feelings, the better we'll be able to find our way out of the problem we're facing. Not only that, but if we can share those feelings with each other, we'll have an experience of connectedness rather than combativeness through the process. After all, nobody is going to give you a way to remove all problems from your life. Difficulties will come up, from within your marriage and from without. A good marriage is one in which we handle those difficulties together and feel connected throughout, not one in which we have as few of them as possible.

> You cannot solve a problem that you don't understand.

So the first step in communicating about anything is going to be exploring the emotional terrain in which it's located. I'm speaking here about discussing things of substance, of course. You don't need to explore your feelings about passing the salt when your significant other asks for it – unless maybe there is some underlying issue there, which is certainly possible. You'd be surprised where underlying issues can pop up. I once worked with a couple where one partner had a neuromuscular disorder and the question of his dependence/independence around small physical tasks like being able to pass the salt was indeed a pretty emotional issue.

How do you know if there's an underlying issue? If a request to pass the salt ends up in a massive argument, there's an underlying issue. Any time a conversation becomes emotional or conflictual, you would be wise to consider that there might be something deeper going on.

> Geoff was not the neatest fellow you'd ever met. He admitted this openly at our first meeting. His ADHD made him terrifically creative, but also rather disorganized. He managed this quite well, but one habit that never seemed to go away was his tendency to leave his coffee cups all over the house (sometimes in very unexpected locations). It drove his wife Marie nuts and led to a lot of conflict.

> Of course, I could understand how annoying it is to find cups all over the place, and to not find them in the kitchen cabinet when you need them; Geoff understood it too, and regretted that he had such a difficult time staying on top of this. But I also asked Marie why this problem was so very enraging to her. Surely their children were also messy at times? Surely – I dared to suggest it – surely even she leaves a dish lying around from time to time? I assured her that I was not trying to convince her not to feel rage about it; I just wanted to understand more clearly what the rage was about.

> As we explored the situation together, we learned a good deal more about this problem. Marie acknowledged that coffee cups around the house were not a catastrophic situation. What really bothered her was that she had brought it up numerous times in the past, and nothing had changed; so now she just opted to say nothing when she saw a coffee cup. But that meant that every time she spotted a mug on the counter (or floor, or printer), she heard a tiny voice in her head saying, "Nothing I say makes a difference around here." That was enraging to her.

> This understanding was tremendously illuminating for Geoff (and for Marie as well). He had trouble understanding why one more cup in an already somewhat untidy house would make such an outsized impact. But he easily understood how painful it was for

Marie to feel silenced and impotent in her own home. This revelation led to an entirely different outlook on the issue for both of them.

What we're going to talk about isn't restricted to conflict resolution, by the way. It is super helpful to approach any conversation of significance in this way. If you are nervous about a promotion at work, or your spouse is worried about their aging parents, or you're wondering if it's time to redo the basement – these are great conversations to put through the process we're going to describe, even when there is no disagreement between the two of you. Perhaps you're familiar with the old stereotype of women wanting to talk about their problem and getting annoyed when men just want to fix it.[1] Of course, this is a generalization and not a universal rule. Sometimes that dynamic exists in the other direction, and sometimes it's not an issue at all for a couple, but I do witness this dynamic a lot with couples I work with, and it's frustrating for everyone involved. Remember, you can't solve a problem you don't understand – and people are more complex than can be expressed in a one-liner. That's why we need to open it up and talk about the issue rather than just throwing solutions at it. Whatever the problem is, if it's taking up more time and/or emotional energy than maybe it seems like it should – in fact, even if it's not – it's worth exploring.

> We need to intentionally separate our conversations into two separate phases: the exploration phase and the resolution phase.

In order to do this effectively, we need to *intentionally separate our conversations into two separate phases*: the exploration phase and the resolution phase.

EXPLORE FIRST, RESOLVE SECOND

The exploration phase is purely about exploring together what's going on inside each of you as far as the topic at hand is concerned – surveying the emotional terrain, as I put it before. And I can guarantee you that, especially when it comes to difficult or sensitive topics, there is a heck of a lot in there to survey, whether you're

---

[1] Check out the video at https://jasonheadley.com/INATN.html for a brief and excellent presentation of this point.

currently aware of it or not. Having a conversation with someone who cares about you – one that is not directed at finding a solution as quickly as possible – is a great way to unearth and learn about it.

The goal here is to understand as fully as possible what your spouse is experiencing. You are not judging it. You are not trying to decide how to handle the situation. You are not trying to make bad feelings go away. You are just aiming to learn what *is*. The upshot of this is that whatever feelings are being shared are allowed to be. They don't have to be fair, or rational, or realistic. The feelings are just *there*, and they cause a lot less trouble when we accept them as such. It's kind of like gravity: if you try to ignore or deny it, you are likely to find yourself in a spot of trouble. You don't have to like the feelings that are there, or agree with them, or encourage them. You just have to accept that they're around for the time being – because if you don't accept them and don't let them be as they are, they will not simply vanish or morph into the feelings you would rather be there. What they'll actually do is go into hiding and then pop back up in an argument about, say, passing the salt. This is not what you want. You want to bring them out into the open so that they aren't secretly sabotaging your marriage. That's why we're exploring.

> You don't have to like the feelings that are there, or agree with them, or encourage them. You just have to accept that they're around for the time being.

What happens if you don't explore before trying to resolve? Even if you do come up with a solution that both of you can agree to, it's likely that one or both of you aren't totally satisfied with it, and that it doesn't really address the actual problem (because you haven't even identified it). You've probably tried to implement solutions to questions and conflicts you've experienced in your marriage and found that they didn't work out so well or didn't stick. How could they? You weren't addressing all the elements of the situation, because you didn't even know what they were! How good is a solution that is based on a partial understanding of the problem? (Would anyone do this in a business situation? "I haven't really done much market research, but I'm betting we can increase sales by updating our logo." Not a winning plan.)

Imagine if Geoff and Marie had tried to throw a solution at the problem without exploring it first. (In fact, they did, numerous times, before coming to therapy.)

They would argue about the issue, then Marie would compel Geoff to put a reminder on his phone to clean up at night, or she would throw up her hands and say she was simply not going to wash the dishes anymore if he didn't put the cups in the sink. Well, firstly, these solutions rarely stuck for long, because consistency just isn't one of Geoff's strengths (of which he has many), and because Marie hated a sink full of dishes more than Geoff did. And Geoff was not super motivated to put his all into the problem because he just didn't understand the big deal about a stray cup on the couch.

But even if one idea were to work decently well at keeping the cups in the sink, does that solve the problem? If Geoff does the dishes now that Marie has forced his hand, does that help Marie feel like her needs mattered, like her voice was heard? It does not. She intuitively knows that next time they encounter an issue, she will be equally unheard. And so the conflict goes dormant until they encounter the next flashpoint, but it certainly doesn't go away.

Once Geoff understood what was really behind the arguments, he was not only in a position to make changes that would address the need, he was much more motivated to do so, because while he didn't mind terribly the thought of his wife living among scattered mugs ("What's the big deal, anyway?"), he *did* mind a whole lot the idea that his wife would think that her words and her needs weren't important to him.

Just having the conversation about possible solutions becomes easier once you've fully explored it: when do you feel more open to someone's suggestions, when they load you up with brilliant ideas, or when you feel confident that they've heard your concerns? I'm going to guess the latter. If you try to skip or rush through the exploration conversation to get to the resolution part, you're short-circuiting the process that actually gets you where you want to go.

> Just having the conversation about possible solutions becomes easier once you've fully explored it.

FACTS

I want to make something very clear here. The exploration conversation is *not a conversation about facts.* You are not trying to establish an accurate account of the events being described. You are trying to understand your spouse's *perception.* Therefore, *it is critical that you avoid arguing about what did or didn't happen, or who said what when, or which of you did what first.*

For starters, that kind of argument is just not going to get you anywhere. You know this is true, because you've had many such arguments, and they never get you anywhere. Right? So we have to abandon the let's-get-things-straight approach to dealing with disagreements. It is very common for members of a couple to differ about the facts of what happened *and yet they still have a good marriage!* Therefore, it must be possible to resolve issues without agreeing on the facts.

In most situations, you are never going to know for sure what actually happened. It's not common to have a video recording of the event in question – and if you did, it wouldn't help much. If you were ever in a situation where you actually had proof for your position and you successfully "won" the argument, you can probably attest that it did not result in everyone being calm and happy again, or in a closer, more satisfying relationship.

> It is very common for members of a couple to differ about the facts of what happened *and yet they still have a good marriage!*

Marvin and Chloe were a young couple from the inner city with a lot of passion and idealism. She consistently came to session wearing swag from her fledgling business; he was working for social good at his programming job. They wanted the best for their marriage, but repeatedly found themselves in arguments about minor (by their own assessment) situations, which became major arguments when they took to fighting about how the situation actually went down.

As I explained to them the total lack of value in establishing a factual account of what happened, they nodded their heads in agreement and confessed that they actually did have recordings of their arguments that they would turn to (their house was rigged up with security cameras). And indeed, they admitted that the recordings never helped.

In the most recent argument, Marvin had asked Chloe for an apology for something she had said. Chloe insisted that she did offer that apology, but Marvin disagreed. So they went back to the tapes, and lo and behold – she did in fact apologize exactly as he had asked! Do you think his response was to then apologize for his error, give her a big hug, and walk away whistling a merry tune? It was not. Instead, his response was, "Okay, you did say that, but the WAY you said it wasn't right!"

The reality is that facts do not change how we feel.[2] So we have to have a way to get out of this without having recourse to the facts. (A detailed description of that way is coming up soon.) We need to change our conversations from a discussion of who is right and who is wrong into something that puts us on the same

> ## We are not trying to establish who is right and who is wrong.

team. *We are not trying to establish who is right and who is wrong.* If that is your goal, you're going to have a rough ride in your marriage, because then the marriage is actually a zero-sum game. "If I am right, you are wrong. If I win, you lose." That is not a happy marriage. One person always has to be a loser! You probably don't want to be a loser, but it's also not great to be the winner – because do you really want to be married to a loser? You can't win as a team if one of you always has to lose.

Working as a Team, Part 2

Have you ever gotten into an argument with your spouse about whether you did or did not tell them some important piece of information? You know, the argument where you maintain you told your spouse you'd be home late, and they insist you did not? Or they swear they mentioned that they need you to pick up more herbal tea while you're at the store and you are dead sure they only mentioned getting milk, cheese, and a cantaloupe?

Of course you have. *I* certainly have. In fact, I have never asked this question to any married person and gotten a response in the negative. This is a

---

[2] Incidentally, this is also why politics is such a mess. There's a phenomenon called confirmation bias in which people (and this includes you and me) tend to discount facts that challenge their preexisting beliefs and only accept facts that confirm them. The facts that disagree with us simply don't change how we feel about the issue. The same thing happens in relationships – you and your partner are likely to zero in on different details of the story and argue endlessly about them – which is why I am strongly making this point about avoiding a debate around the facts.

classic example of a couple working at cross-purposes, fighting to establish who is correct. These arguments are often not even about what happened today but about data points that are entirely irrelevant to your actual lives, such as whether Eisenhower's favorite meal was in fact beef stew or fish chowder (answer: beef stew). The whole argument is an indication that we're not in team mode.

When we are on the same team, when we are one unit, it doesn't matter which one of us is right; it matters that we achieve our joint goals together. What's our joint goal here? Relationship. Harmony. Love. You don't get that by determining that in fact they did say something about buying herbal tea but you just didn't hear it because the TV was on too loud (which is so often what the reality is in these situations). You get that through grace and empathy.

A team approach to a situation like the I-told-you-no-you-didn't conundrum is to put yourselves on the same side of the figurative table and take into account everyone's experience together: "Boy, I know how frustrating it is when you're sure you told me and I didn't get the message. And it sure is frustrating for me to be held accountable for something I really don't recall you saying. We're both frustrated here, and we have no herbal tea to boot. What an annoying situation for both of us. Let's have a hug." Honestly, doesn't that sound like a better outcome? This is what I call "marital teamship."

If there's a physiological problem with someone's hearing or memory, you'll get that checked out. If your spouse has a pattern of not paying attention to your needs, that's a conversation you'll have down the road. But in that moment when an argument is brewing, seeing yourselves as a team and having empathy for both sides is a much, much better option.

There is a fun saying that "you can be right, or you can be married." You have a choice: you can aim for being right, self-satisfied, and smug, knowing that your way is the right one and your memory is better and you're just the rightest right person ever; or you can shoot for a marriage in which you feel connected, loved, and at peace. Those targets are in opposite directions. You choose.

I recognize that this concept is a huge hump for some people to get over. In our culture, there is an expectation that these people are usually men, who, according to the stereotype, are more "logical" and "rational" (though the truth is sometimes it's just the opposite). It's also tough for folks who are lawyers, auditors, researchers, analysts, and the like. They are used to dealing only in facts, and trying to achieve a goal without tapping into that part of themselves at all can be really tough. If you're one of those people, I'd like to remind you: this is an intimate relationship we are discussing, not a court of law or a policy debate. Business executives often say to me things like "I operate my business based on *facts*, not people's *feelings*." My response is that we're not trying to grow a profit here. We're trying to be in love. The requirements are pretty different.

I totally understand it can be uncomfortable to disconnect from facts, statistics, evidence, etc. as a guidepost to forward movement. If it's not resonating with you that we're talking about a totally different undertaking than legal analysis or market research, all I can say is, give it a try. You will be surprised at how much conflict can be soothed and how much connection can be built with this different approach. (You're also free to keep doing what you've been doing until now. But if that was working well, you probably wouldn't be reading this book.)

Therefore, when you find yourself in yet another argument about the facts, just stop. Reset. It is so compelling to try to get your side of the story out there, but I promise that arguing about what actually happened will not make the situation better and will not lead to a happier marriage. That train does not go to that station. The sooner you get off it, the sooner you'll be able to get to your true destination.

HELP ME UNDERSTAND

> Instead of "Let me explain this to you," your mindset should be, "Help me understand."

In order to be able to communicate effectively about whatever you guys need to talk about, it's vital to remember that you are aiming to *understand each other's perspectives and feelings* about the topic at hand, not win a debate. Instead of "Let me explain this to you," your mindset should be, "Help me understand." Understanding where your spouse is coming from is a critical first step to making any change in the way things are.

The Three Most Important Words

A lot of ink has been spilled on the topic of "The Three Most Important Words in a Marriage." The old school claimed that "I love you" sits at the top of the list. To be sure, "I love you" is a classic, a line that will always be useful and vital and indispensable for meaningful, long-term relationships. It is to marriage what Shakespeare is to literature. (I actually don't like Shakespeare at all, but you get the idea.)

The second generation of the Three Most Important Words took a slightly tongue-in-cheek approach with the choice of "I was wrong" (or "I am sorry"). Hey, I am all for apologizing and acknowledging our own mistakes. This can be very valuable, and certainly no relationship is going to make it very far if one or both parties can never apologize.

But I want to suggest my own Three Most Important Words. Acknowledging our mistakes is truly important – but you probably don't want your marriage to rest on a foundation of your mistakes. Instead, let's build a foundation of connection and mutuality. Try "Help me understand." You're unhappy about something? "Help me understand." What's that unhappiness about?

You're mad at me? "Help me understand." I don't see what I did wrong. Can you help me see how you see it?

You're having trouble with our son's attitude towards his sports team? "Help me understand." What bothers you about it? What do you wish? What other feelings do you have?

"Help me understand" will deepen your insight into each other; it will help you reduce conflict and disconnection in your marriage; and it will bring a richness to your marriage that you can't get to any other way.

I'm not saying that facts aren't *ever* important. You will certainly need facts in order to solve certain problems. Do we have enough money on hand to pay for that? What time do we have to be at the thing (you know, the thing?) and how long is it going to last? What *is* that clunking noise the car is making? You can't make decisions on these issues without those answers. But remember, in the exploration conversation, *we are not making decisions*. We are just *exploring*. The decision-making part comes *afterwards*.

Keeping this point in mind is critical to getting what you need out of this conversation. *No decisions are going to be made based on the exploration conversation.* Got that? If you say you really hate the color of the carpet, you and your spouse can explore the issue as much as you need, *and it doesn't mean you're going to change the carpet*. Maybe you will. And maybe you won't. That decision will be evaluated in the resolution phase. That's not now. That's later. Right now, it's just understanding what your feelings are. Maybe you are disgusted by the color. Maybe it makes you nostalgic because it reminds you of the carpet in your dad's home when you were a kid. Maybe you feel guilty about wanting to spend money on something you think is ultimately trivial. All those feelings need to come out and be put on the table, because they are going to drive how you engage with this issue. Again, if you try to solve the problem without attending to all this stuff, the solution will necessarily be imperfect.

This doesn't mean, however, that you must share every single thought and feeling you have about everything before taking any action. A lot of what we feel is buried deep down and often we don't even know what it is. Your spouse is not your therapist; you don't need to explore your entire psyche before making any decision on anything. But the more you do have out on the table, the easier it will be to come to a solution, and the better that solution is likely to be. If you're only dealing with 21% of the underlying issue, your answers aren't going to be very on target. If you've got 78% out in the open, what you come up with is going to be a much better fit!

Since you are not going to be making a decision in this conversation, it's important to agree that the things that are said "cannot and will not be used against you in a court of law" – meaning, if I say I hate the carpet, you are not allowed to hold me to that opinion when we later discuss renovation plans. Maybe I want to keep it anyway because I don't think it's worth the expense, or because I can't find an alternative I like better, or for whatever reason. Don't get stuck on the things that are shared in the exploration phase. It's an exploration. It can be tentative.

Likewise, if I accept and validate your opinion (see the later section on valida-tion), that doesn't mean I *agree* with you on what we're going to do. I can under-stand that you are attached to this particular carpet because your mother gave birth to you *right here on this carpet*, and I can openly appreciate how meaningful that is to you, and it *still* does not mean I'm agreeing to keep the carpet. That's a decision that has yet to be made (and it will depend as well on your hearing out *my* reasons for wanting to get rid of it).

Furthermore, if you are mad at me because you felt abandoned last night when I went out with the guys, I can accept that you feel that way and *care* that you feel that way, and I am not agreeing to stop going out with the guys, and I am *also not agreeing* that I am insensitive or insufficiently attentive or anything like that. There is no admission of guilt or apology or change of policy at this stage. There is simply an acceptance and an empathy for your experience as it is.

This leads us to an important upshot of this process: since we are not discuss-ing who is right and who is wrong, *there is no need to defend your position against your partner's*. Both positions can exist, and determining which one reflects the objective reality is not only unnecessary, it is also counterproductive. It is natural to feel an urge to defend yourself when you hear a narrative that seems to put you in a nega-tive light. Hear this: *defensiveness is the kiss of death for successful communication.* You have no doubt been in many arguments in your life where one or both parties are being defensive, and you can probably attest that they are excruciatingly ineffective and uncomfortable for everyone in-volved. It is normal to feel defensive; but allowing that to dictate the course of the conversation is ru-inous. We'll address how to handle those moments shortly; but for now, know that if you're engaging defensively, you are not engaging in communication that will better your marriage.

> Defensiveness is the kiss of death for successful communication.

SEPARATE CONVOS

In order for this approach to work well, it's important to remember *not to try to solve at the same time as you explore*. It's got to be two separate conversations. Those conversations may happen back-to-back, but there is a clear demarcation between the two.[3] This means that you may have to sit with a problem that you really, really want to solve while you and your partner move through all the thoughts and feelings surrounding it. That's hard. But also, so worthwhile. Marriages are not built on instant gratification or immediate change. They require maturity, patience, and dedication (among other things). This means waiting until the right time even when it's hard. Just as with timeout, sometimes you feel absolutely compelled to say something and you are called upon to hold back. It's worth the effort. Jumping in now with your solution, or your rebuttal, *will not get you where you want to go.* Unless where you want to go is to Rightville on a trip all by yourself.

You may actually have to do a couple of exploration sessions before you can take a stab at solving a significant problem. You might begin a conversation one day and continue it on another. If you need to talk about how you feel about visiting your in-laws over the holidays, that could be a big one. You probably won't resolve this issue in a half hour. Life isn't a sitcom in which you can put serious issues to rest in 22 minutes. Rather, for any given topic (certainly the bigger ones) you will likely need to have a series of conversations over time that do not end in a decision or a clear answer, until you are both truly ready to step into the resolution conversation. Good things come to those who wait, and all that.

It's worth noting that none of the *real* problems you will face in your life will have quick fixes. This recognition is important for successful marriages (and it will be absolutely critical if you will be raising children together: the struggles you will encounter with your children will get worked on and eventually solved over *years*, not days, weeks, or months). You are likely to face differences of a pretty fundamental nature – you're chronically punctual, she's consistently late; you're a strong disciplinarian, he's a big softie – these are not habits of character that will shift easily. Be prepared to have many exploration conversations over the course of a long timeframe, not One Big Conversation to rule them all.

It's also important to make sure that both of you are ready before giving the resolution conversation a shot. Being ready means that both of you feel heard and understood by your partner, and both of you are comfortable that you understand

---

[3] This is true at least for the big issues. For smaller questions, like "Where should we eat tonight?" you may have some feelings to explore, but unless there's a major issue hidden under the surface – and, as already noted, there very well could be, even about something that seems trivial! – it's possible to share a little and also pitch for the sushi place down the road more or less at the same time.

each other as well. If you are not confident that they really get you, or vice versa, then keep at it; finding a solution goes much better when you're both in that place of confidence. Remember, this doesn't mean your partner has to understand you to the deepest depths of 100% understandingness. Heck, *you* don't understand yourself that well. A grade of A– or B+ will probably do. Humans don't really do "perfect," but we can usually get to "pretty darn good."

As you go through this process it's valuable to cultivate the mental and emotional flexibility to switch back to exploration mode as needed. It is common to unearth more feelings and hangups while you're trying to resolve. You'll notice this either because something that comes up in the resolution conversation strikes a chord with you (or your mate), brings up a memory, or elicits strong feelings. This could be either in the content of what is being said or in the process of *how* it's being said. For example, maybe the discussion has triggered some baggage you've got around your parents, and there's important stuff to explore there; or maybe you don't like the way your spouse is engaging with you right now, and you need to stop and deal with that: "Could we stop for a minute and explore something else? I'm feeling a bit uncomfortable right now about the way you're talking to me."

It could also be that you *don't* notice something bothering you, but the conversation has become contentious and difficult again; you feel edgy, tense, or uncomfortable with how it's going. That's a good sign there's something under the surface here that needs to be explored, and you need to table the resolution process and go back to exploring.

My wife Chana and I were talking in the kitchen about a business decision I had to make. It seemed like a relatively practical matter. I was pondering my options, and she was pushing back with perhaps more force than was needed. The conversation was getting increasingly unpleasant, and I was feeling increasingly defensive and annoyed. Following my own advice, I called a timeout, interjecting with "I need to end this conversation right now." (Full disclosure: it was not successfully delivered in a particularly warm and fuzzy way.) It was a bit of a tense moment. But because we were able to back out before things got too bad, we were also able to return to the conversation relatively quickly. I asked if perhaps she was having some of her own feelings about the situation at hand that made this more than a simple resolution conversation, and that were leaking out in ways that I was being reactive to. She paused

for a moment, then acknowledged that this was probably true. So we restarted the
conversation as an exploration conversation, looking at her fears about and hopes for
our financial future (and mine as well), and it went much better.

CUE ME IN

In order to avoid missing the exploration phase and having your spouse run right
into resolution, it is really helpful – critical, even – to cue your spouse in that that's
what's going on. As we noted, men especially are famous for trying to fix their
spouses' problems when a fix is not at all the desired response. The key to avoiding
this is to *make sure to cue your spouse in beforehand.* In my house, we use the code
phrase "I'm just saying" as a preamble whenever we just want to share a thought or
a feeling without getting some kind of solution in response. If we want to sit down
for a full-on exploration session, my wife and I will say, "Hey, can we have a feelings
conversation about [such-and-such topic]?" This may be a bit too mushy for you.
That's fine. Find your own way to get the point across. "Exploration conversation"
or "empathic dialogue" works just fine. I've also had clients use terms like "a talky
talk," "one of those discussions," "a Raffi conversation"[4] – whatever works for you
to make sure you are both on the same page.

I want to underscore an important point here: I have been working with couples for over a decade. I teach people how to do this. And I *still* need a reminder
from my wife when she wants me not to solve a problem. So, to everyone, especially
to men: work on remembering that you don't need to solve the problem; you need
to listen first. And to everyone, especially women: don't expect your spouse to remember that they don't need to solve the problem – *cue them in* to what you need
instead of hoping they'll get it right.

I have also found that reminders peppered into the conversation can be a big
help. Either one of you can put it out there: "Just reminding us both that we're not
solving the problem here, right?" "Remember, we're just exploring right now." This
can help alleviate the pressure that can creep up on us and put us into a defensive
mode if we perceive that we're being blamed for something, or push us to try to
make the problem go away ASAP. For example, if your spouse is talking about how

---

4   I did not suggest this term, but I did find it flattering.

lonely they feel, and you've been working your tail off trying to be attentive and loving, you are likely to feel very frustrated, even angry. You might try to make the problem go away (thereby alleviating the discomfort you feel for being, or for having attributed to you, the cause of your spouse's loneliness). You might also get defensive in such a situation. These are completely understandable, but unhelpful, responses. If you can remember – and it can be helpful to say it out loud again – that you are just exploring the terrain and not accepting what is being said as the ultimate truth of the situation, it can make it much easier to get through those moments.

"I don't want to solve the problem right now but... I just can't do one more Thanksgiving with your family!"

"Yeah, let's have a talk about that..."

"I am really stressed about getting the house ready for the graduation party. This place really needs a new coat of paint."

"I hear ya. We're just exploring right now, right?"

If you are in an exploration conversation and you notice yourself wanting to defend yourself against something you heard or to push back against a solution that is being implied (or stated outright), check in and recall for both of you where you are in the process – exploring, not resolving. Be careful, however, not to use this as a passive-aggressive way of expressing your disagreement (see sidebar "Communication Styles" in chapter 6):

"I can't believe you forgot to book the tickets!"

"I know you're angry, but just reminding you, we're only exploring right now!"

What you're really saying here is, "I need to make it clear that I'm not actually wrong in this situation." It is defensive and will be taken as such. A better response might be "Whooo, you're obviously really angry right now. I get it. Can we put a pause on this and talk more about it later? I don't want this to turn into a big fight." (Remember timeout?)

BUT THEN WHAT?

Interestingly, you may discover that once you've gone through the exploration phase, *a resolution isn't even necessary.* Often, we already recognize that there is no great solution to a difficult problem. You probably can't avoid ever going to your in-laws again. You may not be able to afford to paint the house right now. But it helps a whole lot to bear the difficulty if your spouse is there to carry the load with you. People who go through challenging times together develop a strong bond. Talking about your problem is not a request to make it go away as much as an invitation to be together in that problem. You probably didn't get married/committed because you needed someone to take the car to the shop when it breaks down. More likely you were hoping to have someone to go through life with. Life often involves car problems. Weathering them together is what marriage is all about.

> You may discover that once you've gone through the exploration phase, *a resolution isn't even necessary.*

It is a surprise to many people (again, mostly men) that they are not being called upon to solve a problem. *When your spouse shares with you something that is not quite the way they wish it would be, they are likely asking you primarily to join with them in the situation, not to make it go away.* They are asking for your empathy. This is hard for a lot of folks to wrap their heads around, but once they do, it is a game changer. They can step out of the constant cycle of problems that weigh on the marriage and attempt solutions to relieve the pressure. Instead, there's a coexistence of problems with love and connection. The weight is borne jointly by the two of you, pulling you closer together rather than pushing you apart; and all this independent of whether you do or do not find a solution. That's good news.

That said, there are certainly many problems that *are* resolvable. Where should we go *next* year for Thanksgiving? What *can* we do if we don't have the money to get the car fixed right now? Once we understand the true problem on both sides, the resolution conversation goes much, much better. We can't come to a true resolution of the issue until I understand that you hate going to my parents because you feel ignored, and until you understand the tremendous pressure I get from them to go every year. Once we have those understandings, and once we can express our empathy for each other's concerns and experiences – then we are in a much better position to come up with a solution that adequately addresses them. And it is here that facts might become useful: How much does a new timing belt actually cost? How much longer can the Toyota be expected to last? How much do we have in the bank? Those are important points of information to have on hand when deciding what to do with your sedan; but these facts always sit in the context of how you feel about money, how you feel about Japanese cars, and all the other thoughts and feelings and perceptions that make up your inner world – which is why we *explore first, resolve second.* Remember, you can't solve a problem you don't understand. But once you understand the problem, finding a solution becomes much easier.

There is a further way in which exploration can sometimes obviate the need for resolution: sometimes the understanding that comes from exploring leads to a natural shift in the way you and your partner will engage:

> **Remember, you can't solve a problem you don't understand. But once you understand the problem, finding a solution becomes much easier.**

Chana and I had a little incident. We were expecting lunch guests and she was cleaning and setting up for their arrival. I grabbed a spare moment to sit down with two of my kids for a short installment of Bible study. Chana began calling for help from the other room, with a progressively more demanding tone. I increasingly resisted as I tried to get through a short passage. She called louder; I shut the door. Eventually I could no longer ignore her and I asked her (somewhat testily), "Would you like me to stop studying with my children and come sweep the floor?" I thought it was pretty obvious that the correct answer was "no." It turns out Chana did not agree on that point. She asked me to come sweep. I dutifully – but not cheerfully – went to sweep. And I was angry at her for the rest of the day for taking me away from something that was important to me and that I thought should be important to her. (I didn't yell or get snappy at her; I executed a decent timeout and just took some physical and emotional space.)

The next day, we discussed the issue. I told her I was angry at her. She heard me out and did not argue. Then she shared her own experience: she knows I am a little uptight about being punctual (fair point). I have in the past made comments about really wanting to start lunch on time (also fair). So she was feeling under pressure to get things ready to start on time. She had no idea that in my head I had already given up on being perfectly on time and had chosen to spend the time studying with my kids at the expense of punctuality. And she was irritated at me for asking a fake question as to whether I should sweep or study if I had already made up my mind what the "correct" answer was! I should have just told her what I wanted to do.

Through this conversation, I came to understand that she was feeling pressure to do what I wanted, namely, to be ready on time; she came to understand that I did in fact prefer a few minutes of studying with the kids in exchange for a few minutes of starting late. Now that we had a clearer vision of what the other person was going through, the resolution was already in hand: in the future, Chana could allow me to continue studying, because she would not feel pressured to start on time now that she understood I was okay with that outcome. And I would just tell her that I am choosing study over sweeping, knowing that she would be fully on board with that.

INVITATIONS

An understanding of exploring vs. resolving sheds some light on one of the most common traps couples get into. If you watched the video cited earlier in the footnote in the section "Explore First, Resolve Second" (chapter 2), you almost certainly recognized yourself in there to some degree, or at least the well-worn storyline: Woman has a problem. Woman shares problem. Man tries to fix problem. Conflict ensues.[5]

It is super frustrating for women (generally speaking) when they are trying to share a problem and the man clomps on in with a solution to fix it. And it is super frustrating for men (generally speaking) when they offer a solution to a problem that is bothering their woman – often a perfectly fine and appropriate solution! – and not only does the woman not appreciate the (brilliant) solution, but the man somehow finds himself in trouble to boot! What went wrong?

The answer is that *she* is in need of an exploration conversation, and *he* has jumped right to the resolution conversation. But she is not at this point looking for

---

[5] As I noted earlier, this dynamic can of course happen in any direction, regardless of gender, but both the Western cultural narrative as well as my own professional experience suggest that the direction I've represented here is the more common one. For clarity, I'm going to continue using this archetype to describe the situation.

a solution; she is looking to be *heard*. She wants to know that he *cares* about her problem. She wants to feel *connected*. Like we said above, that's really what a marriage is about, much more so than having someone around who can solve all your problems.

So if your wife walks in from a tough day at work and says, "I am so fed up with my boss!" – that is not an invitation to suggest how to better handle her jerk boss. It may truly sound like such an invitation to you. But it is not. It is actually an invitation for you to express and demonstrate to your wife that her problem matters to you – that *she* matters to you. That is what gets you to feel heard and connected, far more than offering up a solution that wasn't wanted to begin with.

The wrong response would be this: "Have you tried having a conversation with her?" Or this: "Geez, it's really time to start looking for a new job." Or, "Would you like me to come to the office and body-slam your boss for you?"

I suspect many of you have been in exactly this kind of situation – your wife complains about a problem, you offer a perfectly reasonable method of getting rid of said problem, and then she's mad at you. And you are totally bewildered. If you understand that this is about connection and not solutions, it makes a heck of a lot more sense.

The *right* response would be something more like, "Gaaah, is she driving you crazy about that TPS report again???" or, "You sound super stressed out." You are *sharing* in the problem, not *eliminating* it. We are in the exploration phase, not the resolution phase.

By the way, it doesn't even have to be a problem that's being shared. It could just be an arbitrary incident that happened today. "I ran into Judy today at the grocery store..." If you are a man and your wife says this when she walks in the door, your brain probably starts *racing* to figure out what you're supposed to do about this.[6] It's checking all its reference points. Does she hate Judy? Is Judy a weird person? Or someone she's been wanting to catch up with for a long time? Your brain is desperately trying to figure out what needs solving.

Nothing needs solving. What's needed is an indication that you care about what she's going through. And since you probably don't know what she's going

---

6   Most of the women I describe this to are a little incredulous about this. Honestly, ask your male partner if this represents his experience. I'd wager that, assuming he's reasonably self-aware, he'll agree that it absolutely is.

> You will get a lot more bang for your problem-solving buck if you stop to *really* understand your partner's experience before contributing your own two cents.

through – especially in a Judy situation – *it's time to get in and explore it*. All you need to do is ask. Often, you don't even need to do that – you just need to sit and listen while your wife *tells* you what she's going through without being interrupted by a doofus like you who's trying to solve something.

Important point: even when you think you *do* know what she's going through, the odds that you *fully* know what she's going through are slim (because people are complex, remember?). You will get a lot more bang for your problem-solving buck if you stop to *really* understand your partner's experience before contributing your own two cents.

A LITTLE Q&A

Q: Isn't it a sign of love to want to make my partner's problems go away?

A: It can be. But it can also send the message that you don't want to deal with the bad feelings they're experiencing as a result of their problem – that this part of them is unacceptable and unwanted, and that they have to suppress it. And maybe they do just that, accepting a quick solution that doesn't really address the depth of the issue, or simply turning a blind eye to the problem in order to pretend it's gone. Squashing our feelings or pretending they aren't there tends not to work well in the long run.

Trying to get rid of your partner's bad feelings can also actually be self-centered – you are uncomfortable seeing them stressed out, so you try to make *yourself* feel better by eliminating the stress; or you don't like that they're angry at you, so you offer a compromise right away to make the anger go away.

You will see much more success in your efforts at communication if you allow all these feelings to just *be*, uncomfortable as they are, and show that you care that these feelings are there, rather than trying to make them disappear. (In fact, much of therapy is about this exact process – helping clients feel their feelings rather than trying to ignore or deny them.)

Q: What if I really do have a good solution to the problem though?

A: Perhaps you do. So, first you go through the exploration – you make sure that you understand the issue at hand and *that your spouse also believes that you understand it.* If your spouse doesn't think you get it, they're not listening to your solution anyway. Teddy Roosevelt is credited with the brilliant saying "Nobody cares how much you know until they know how much you care." If your spouse doesn't *know* you care, your solution – your *good* solution – is going nowhere.

> "Nobody cares how much you know until they know how much you care."
> — Teddy Roosevelt

Once your spouse is convinced that you understand and care about their problem, *then* you can say something to the effect of, "Hey, I think I have a really good solution to this. Would you like to hear it?" It must be a genuine question. If your spouse says no, *do not give them your solution.* Even if it is an excellent solution – I mean one that is genuinely brilliant and will make the problem totally disappear, and possibly win you some spousal awards – don't offer it. You may find this difficult, and that is understandable. You love your spouse and want to eliminate that which is bothering them. Recall that you are in a marriage, and as a marriage partner you are not there to solve problems but to care and connect. It is a sign of caring, and of respect, to honor your spouse's boundaries and to give them the autonomy to deal with their problems however they see fit. It is *disrespectful* to demand they do things your way – even if your way is in their best interest. If you do insist on stating your brilliant solution even after they've made it clear they're not ready to hear it, then you are thinking about you and not about them. I can tell you where that will end up.

Q: But my spouse is suffering and I can help! Am I supposed to just do nothing?

A: If that is what has been asked of you, then yes. Yes you are. It will not benefit your marriage to replace their suffering with resentment (of you).

You can certainly let your spouse know that you have an idea you wish to share; if they don't want it, then your job is to sit on it, at least for the time being.

Q: But my spouse's choices affect me! Why should I sit by and deal with the consequences?

A: I'm not saying you have to let your spouse's choices ruin your life. I'm simply saying there is a way to have a conversation about this that leaves everyone feeling respected and heard. If you are frustrated that your spouse constantly complains about their boss but never does anything about it, and it's affecting you because they come home in a rotten mood every day, you absolutely can and should share that part in a *separate* exploration conversation (*not* at the same time your spouse is complaining about *their* problem!) in which the new topic is the problem *you're* having of a cranky spouse and how hard that is for you; and it will be incumbent upon your spouse to understand and care about *that* aspect of the situation as well.

Of course, you're welcome to coerce, cajole, pressure, strongarm, persuade, or bully your spouse into listening to or accepting your solution because really that's what's best for them. Let me know how that works out for you.

WHAT IS IT REALLY ABOUT?

Let's now go back and take a look at the conversation between Naya and Eric that started off this chapter. It didn't go so well. What's going on there?

What's going on is that there is a whole lot of stuff under the surface that is not being explored. They are launching right into the resolution of a problem without taking time to first understand what it's really about. And what it's really about is not a funny noise in the car – as becomes clear when things blow up.

What it's about is that Naya isn't feeling supported in the marriage. She often worries that if she doesn't stay on top of things, they won't get done. And she's exhausted from being in that position. What it's about is that Eric feels totally unappreciated by his wife, who never seems satisfied no matter how much he does –

and he is doing an awful lot, between working hard at a stressful job to pay their bills (including extra services for their special-needs son, dental work for their daughter, replacing the furnace that recently went bust, driving the kids around to their activities and appointments, managing the Airbnb rental they own, and more – and all he hears from her is, "When is the car getting fixed?"

What it's about is Naya's fear that the marriage is seriously deteriorating because of their inability to communicate, and Eric's increasing angry outbursts, and Naya's worry that she's no longer attractive, and Eric's fear that his marriage will end up just like his parents', and Naya's sadness about her son's disability, and Eric's embarrassment over the same.

And it's about a lot more than that too. Did you catch that in those few lines of dialogue? Of course you didn't. Naya and Eric didn't either. But in the coming chapters you are going to learn how to get to all of that (because it's there in your marriage too). Were Naya and Eric to recognize that they need to begin with exploring this stuff first, it would go a lot differently:

Naya: *The car is still making that funny noise. Are you going to be able to take it to the shop this week?*

Eric: *Definitely. I said I'll take care of it, and I will. Not to worry.*

Naya: *Well, I – You know what? I realize I'm feeling frustrated about this, and I think it's more than just the noise in the car. Can we sit down and have a feelings conversation about this?*

Eric: *Yeah, that sounds like a good idea. I think there's some stuff I'd like to get off my chest as well. Do you want to go first?*

Naya: *I would. Because I was thinking about it before, and here's what I think I'm really upset about here...*

Chapter 3

Speaking to Be Heard

Alex: *Can we have a conversation about something?*

Randy: *I guess. What's going on?*

Alex: *I feel like your family has been coming over a whole lot lately. We never get to hang out with my family. It's not really fair.*

Randy: *What are you talking about? Your parents were just here for Zack's graduation two weeks ago!*

Alex: *Yeah, and that was a disaster! You don't really make it so pleasant when my parents are here.*

Randy: *It wasn't a disaster! Meanwhile, I'm working my tail off to manage the kids and the house and the dogs and then your mom waltzes right in and starts criticizing! Of course that's not a pleasant interaction!*

Alex: *Maybe if you didn't spend so much time on the phone with your sister you'd have more time to manage all that stuff!!!*

Okay, let's roll up our sleeves and really get into the nuts and bolts here. How do you have this leave-the-facts-aside, talk-about-your-feelings conversation?

The first step is, make sure to pick the right time. You are not going to have a good conversation the night before a big work deadline, or when the baby is sick and screaming, or if your difficult in-laws are on their way over for a weeklong visit. You are also not going to have a good conversation if one or both of you are hungry, tired, or in physical pain. It's very hard to be your best self when your body is out of balance! (Of course, some things are more easily remedied than others. A quick snack or catnap might be enough to address your physical needs in the moment; a screaming baby is probably going to be asleep at some point. A crisis at your place of employment, on the other hand, might not be in your control and may offer few options aside from waiting it out.)

Likewise, you need to establish a context that works for connected communication – i.e., *turn off the phones!* Let the kids know you're busy for a little while. Reschedule your tennis game so you're not under time pressure. Do what you can to make this work in your favor. You may not be able to achieve a perfect scenario where there is no possibility of interruption, where you have as much time as you could possibly need and the world just stands still while you need it to; but you can do your best to get partway there. (By now you should be catching on to another important relationship principle that underlies successful communication and rewarding relationships – namely, that perfection is not necessary. Also, it's not nearly as valuable as effort. We'll touch on this more below.)

Does this mean you will be pushing off conversations and taking longer to satisfactorily deal with the issues you want to communicate about? Yes, it does. It will take patience (stop me if you've heard this before). I submit again that taking longer to do it well is probably a better option than doing it quickly and getting nowhere, but you can make your own choice about that. Remember, you

> Perfection is not necessary. Also, it's not nearly as valuable as effort.

should expect to have a series of exploration conversations, and they are not going to be over and done in a quick and convenient timeframe.

The truth is, depending on your stage in life, you may not have *any* time right now when the kids aren't screaming and your job isn't demanding and you're not a tired ragdoll of a human being. So what do you do? You do your best. This is life, my friends. Effort, not perfection. Try to get to bed an hour early if you can. Grab an apple before you try to sit down and talk. Stack the deck in your favor as much as possible. And just try to be realistic about whether you're in a position to do this well. Because if you're not, it's really not worth it to push through just to get into another fight. (If you are always tired, stressed, and miserable, there may be other things you have to put in order before your marriage is really going to see any progress anyway.)

Remember also that you need to strike when the iron is cold. If you're all worked up about how your partner just transgressed against you, that is also likely not a good time to try to do this. I know you really *want* to. And I know it's really hard to hold off. I promise you'll have a lot more success at this if you do, though. This is not to say that you have to be totally dispassionate and emotionless when you are sharing yourself with your partner – not at all! You certainly have to bring your emotions with you to this conversation; you just have to be in decent control of them when you do so. If you are so annoyed that you are making nasty, cynical comments, or so angry that you're losing your temper, or so worried that you're hyperventilating – you need to manage yourself a bit more until you're able to stay in control.

CUT IT

The next thing you need to do to make this work is to *cut the conversation in half*. By this I mean that *one* of you is going to be the speaker, and *one* of you is going to be the listener. The listener must put aside their own opinions, thoughts, and feelings for the moment – just for the moment! – and entirely focus on what's going on for their mate. When *both* of you try to get your point across at the same time, it quickly becomes a game of verbal ping-pong that escalates to a no-good place, as in the vignette above, and as you have no doubt experienced in your own life. Some people find it helpful to have an actual talking stick, or a conch shell, or whatever object it is to remind both of you who's in the speaker role at the moment.

You cannot attend to your own needs and someone else's needs at the same time – especially when they are in conflict. If you want to truly understand your spouse, you will have to *temporarily* put your own needs aside. If it helps, go ahead and take your brain entirely out of your head, and just put it on the table next to you. You can put it back in when it's your turn to be the speaker. While you're the listener, you are trying to adopt your

> When *both* of you try to get your point across at the same time, it quickly becomes a game of verbal ping-pong.

spouse's brain. You are trying to see the world as they see it. Soon you'll go back to having your own brain and your own thoughts and your own perspectives. For right now, you do not. When you are the listener, those are all sidelined while you enter into your spouse's universe.[1] We'll get more deeply into the listener's role soon.

The speaker, of course, has their own role to play here and their own best practices to keep in mind. One important principle to remember is that how you start the conversation will set the tone for the rest of it. We've already discussed timing above, which is part of how things start. We also mentioned previously that it's really helpful to cue your spouse in. When you sit down for an exploration conversation, you can remind them, "Remember, we're just exploring here. I just need you to hear how I'm feeling. We're not trying to solve anything." Something like that helps your spouse remember what you need from them right now.

> If you feel like you're in attack mode, you aren't ready.

Begin the conversation as calmly as you can. It is possible to be angry but also in firm control of yourself. If you feel like you're in attack mode, you aren't ready for this. Remind yourself that you and your spouse are not adversaries; if you start off with an attack (even a veiled one), you will soon find yourself in a fight.

The Sandwich Method

Some people recommend starting off with a compliment, or using the "compliment sandwich" approach (compliment-complaint-compliment). I have mixed feelings about this. On one hand, couching your not-so-positive issues in a context of love and positivity helps both of you remember that you're a team and are trying to work through something together as opposed to tearing each other down. On the other hand, I think more often than not it's simply

---

[1] I always think of the movie *Being John Malkovitch* when I discuss this idea. Remember the scenes where John Cusack would literally get into John Malkovitch's head and see the world through his eyes? That's kind of what we're aiming for here. Minus the creepy sci-fi bit, though.

not done genuinely. Rather, the speaker comes up with some compliments to try to soften the blow of the complaint, but the compliments are just perfunctory, the part they have to say in order to get to the part they actually care about. ("You make a killer apple pie. You're a disgusting racist. Nice shoes.")

If you are able to authentically focus on the positives of your spouse in that moment and want to make that part of the conversation, it can make a difference in how the whole thing goes. If you're doing it just as a tactic to get your real point across, I suggest you skip it; the lack of sincerity is likely to come through and scuttle your efforts.

HOW TO SPEAK

Okay, let's talk about how the speaker is going to speak. The fundamental principle of effectively communicating yourself to your spouse is to *talk about yourself.* You are going to describe what it is like to be you in the situation you're talking about. What is the experience you are having? What does it feel like? What goes through your mind? You want to help your partner understand you, see the world as you're seeing it.

You do *not* want to talk about your partner. This is a bit tricky – I don't mean that you must describe your life as if they aren't there somehow. You can refer to what they said or did, but only as a way of bringing attention to your own reaction, to how it impacts you. Fundamentally, you are trying to get your partner to understand your world, not to lay out an official History of Our Relationship.

Mark these words: *when you talk about your partner, you are inviting them to argue with you.* If you say, "You spent all night yelling like a maniac at the kids," you have just issued an invitation for them to disagree and say that's not at all what happened (or else to deflect and accuse you of something worse). Describing your partner, their behavior, their thoughts and intentions – this is a sure way to elicit defensiveness, which, if you

> When you talk about your partner, you are inviting them to argue with you.

will recall, I dubbed the kiss of death for communication. In order to communicate successfully, you need to keep the focus on yourself.

Again, you can't erase your partner from the situation you want to talk about, but you can minimize the potential for defensiveness in two ways: (1) Refer to what they said briefly and objectively. "Briefly" means you do not rehash the details of an hourlong sequence of events (see section below on Timelining). Don't run through every line your partner yelled; just note that yelling happened. "Objectively" means you try to stay away from judgmental language – adding "like a maniac" to the end of your comments is a judgment on what happened and will certainly trigger defensiveness. (2) Contextualize it by immediately bringing it back to you. You might say something like, "I heard you yelling over and over last night, and I feel really angry about it." See how this briefly states what I actually observed, couches it in my own perspective, and focuses on my reaction to the situation? Granted, your partner may still disagree that they yelled at all ("I raised my voice a little bit, that's not yelling!"), and part of the job of the listener is to avoid arguing back on things like that (we'll get to that in the following chapters). But if you focus on your own experience and not on prosecuting their behavior, this difference of opinion becomes secondary to the main point (how you feel about it) as opposed to the central focus of the discussion. Got it? Talk about *you*.

What this sounds like is a lot of "I-statements." These are a well-known and much-used tool in the therapy world to accomplish exactly what I am telling you, i.e., talking about yourself. I-statements start with the word "I," and then go to a feeling word, as in, "I feel hurt," or "I am angry about this." If you don't have a feeling word for what you're experiencing, do the best you can to describe it: "I don't know if I can keep up with this volunteering thing anymore. I feel kind of like... like I'm stuck in a box and I can't get out. And the box keeps getting smaller." (You can also Google "feelings wheel" for a helpful tool to get some suggestions of words that might fit what you're experiencing.)

You can stick in the part about your partner by tacking on another clause: "I feel very hurt *when* you make fun of my shoes." "I am angry about this *because* you woke the baby up after I asked you to be quieter." (And hey, you're allowed to switch up the order too: "When you eat my snack food, I get very irritated." But if your sentences are starting with the word "you," you are probably not on track.) Always remember that the point of mentioning your partner is not to center the discussion around them but rather to give a reference point for what's going on for *you*.

After you say your piece, you give your partner a chance to reflect back what they've understood from you. Make sure to chunk things down into pieces they can digest. If you try to describe how you feel distant from your partner and you speak for 17 minutes straight, they can't possibly take it all in. Describe one part of your experience, one part of how you feel, and let them capture that (in the process described in the coming chapters); then go on to the next part, and the next, until you've gotten out what you need to.

Gina and Dawson were both strong personalities. They both had a surplus of opinions to share with me right from the get-go about what the problems were in the marriage and why. I did a lot of nodding in the first session. Dawson was ex-military. Gina was a litigation attorney. Not a soft-spoken couple by any means.

One of the problems that quickly became apparent was the way their conversations turned into debates within a very short time after they began. Gina would unambiguously tell Dawson what he had done wrong in an incident of note from the past week, whereupon Dawson would defend himself vigorously and with conviction.

I spent some time teaching them the skills of empathic dialogue; they took it in with a mix of skepticism and hope. In our initial, stilted attempts, it seemed to work out okay; but at the next session they started back in with the same old pattern. I interrupted Gina as she was beginning to launch into her presentation of Dawson's misbehavior from the previous week: "I called you twice on Wednesday evening and you didn't pick up again. So how am I supposed to know when you're going to be home? You keep saying you're going to—"

I interrupted her. I urged her to drop the narrative and just tell him how she felt about what happened. She hesitated, thought for a moment, then turned to him and said, "When you don't call me to let me know you're running late, and I can't reach you, it is so frustrating to me."

Dawson said nothing for a moment. Then: "Oh. Well, that's a lot easier for me to hear." Gina was shocked. No debate ensued.

YOUR SUBJECTIVE EXPERIENCE

Your experience is by definition subjective. It's how you personally see and feel about things, not how things *are*, not how they *should be*. Remember that whole thing about not making this about facts? Facts are objective; what you are trying to get your spouse to understand is not. This is not a research paper, folks – this is your intimate relationship! If someone were to ask you how the marriage is going, you wouldn't answer by saying, "Well, we average about 1.6 arguments a week and spent 11 days on vacation last year, so it's going pretty good."

This is why we're relying on I-statements and feelings. If I tell you how I feel about something, it doesn't make a whole lot of sense for you to argue with me on that.

"I really like cats."

"No you don't!"

If I introduce some kind of objective standard, however, now you've got a place to argue.

"Cats are so much easier to deal with than dogs!"

"Are you kidding me? Dealing with a cat is like dealing with a moody teenager!"

And this reaction is pretty understandable, really. Because a call to objective facts is really a way of trying to be right, which we've discussed at length as Not a Good Way to Go. It's an attempt to compare your spouse to some supposedly empirical reality and thereby prove that they are not in accordance with it, which would (you believe deep down) compel them to change their mind and do something the way you want to be done.

The Merrick family was yearning for reconciliation. Adele reached out to me, desperate for help in dealing with her husband Ron's parents, whom she described as "terrorizing" her. Upon meeting them in a family session, the characterization wasn't far off. They were in her face, angry, and relentless. And they kept demanding an account of the facts. "What are the facts? What are the facts?" they would both insist. "The fact is, Adele refused to let the kids get on Zoom to speak with us. That's a fact."

I met with Mr. Merrick individually.

"What's your goal here, Mr. Merrick?"

"I want my son and his wife to be comfortable having us around." I tried to get him to talk about how it felt that his son and daughter-in-law were not currently comfortable having them around. He kept swinging back to facts and examples of what they had done and how he had tried to fix things.

"Mr. Merrick, you said your goal is to have your son and his wife be comfortable with you, right?"

"That's right."

"Let's say I get in there and convince them that you are correct, that your facts all check out, and they capitulate and admit that you're 100% right. What do you think will happen next?"

"Well, they'll see that they were wrong."

"And then once you've forced them into admitting they were wrong, do you think the result will be that they will joyfully welcome you into their home and feel comfortable having you there?"

Mr. Merrick was silent.

We already noted that people do not actually change their minds in response to facts and information. We easily dismiss data that contradicts our preconceived notions, or we try to tear it down. By turning to objective arguments, you are eliciting defensiveness and getting yourself stuck once again. (You see this happening briefly in Alex and Randy's discussion at the beginning of this chapter: Alex calls the event "a disaster," which opens the door for Randy to flatly disagree.)

In a discussion on economic policy or healthcare law, objective data is the way to go. In an intimate relationship, not so much. In fact, in a relationship, *being subjective is actually much more powerful.* Your spouse doesn't want

> By turning to objective arguments, you are eliciting defensiveness and getting yourself stuck once again.

to be pressured or shamed by you into doing what the "right" thing is, but they probably *do* want to make you feel loved; and this is probably the case even when you don't see eye to eye on a particular issue.

For example: let's say Valentine's Day comes and goes and you get a card but no chocolates. And you're disappointed. You believe chocolate is just what people are supposed to give on Valentine's Day. So you complain to your husband that he's "supposed to" get you chocolate on Valentine's Day. And he pushes back and says it's too expensive, or you're both on a diet, or whatever defensive maneuver it might be. Further irritated, you look it up online and find a statistic that says that the majority of couples do give chocolates on Valentine's Day and you show your husband. Does he now see the light and adopt your viewpoint? He does not. Instead, he goes and finds his *own* survey showing how chocolate is falling out of favor, and he tacks on a study about the ill effects of sugar to boot. This is not communication.

What if, instead of trying to strongarm your husband into buying you chocolates on the strength of empirical arguments, you simply said, "You know, it really makes me feel special when you buy me chocolates. Would you do that for me next year?" Which approach do you think is more likely to get you a box of pralines?[2] I know you have been taught to believe that the best way to make a case for yourself is with decisive, objective arguments. This works in debate class; it does not work in marriage. In marriage, you will get much farther with subjective sharing than with objective convincing.

I-statements are again of critical importance here: "I feel loved when you buy me chocolates," not "chocolates are the way to show love." Here are some ways we tend to botch that up:

- "Everyone knows you give chocolates on Valentine's Day!"
- "Any woman would want her husband to give her chocolates on Valentine's Day."
- "Ask any of your friends if they/their wives expect chocolates on Valentine's Day."

---

2   Answer: the second approach.

How do you feel when someone says something like this to you? You feel defensive, of course. You are being told you are in the wrong, and you feel compelled to prove yourself right. Not only that, but these kinds of statements are also somewhat demeaning. If "everyone knows" something that you do not, the implication is that you are stupid or ignorant. That does not go down smoothly.

But even more crucially, *it doesn't matter if this is the way "everyone" does it*. Should you and your partner respect each other's feelings only if they are "normal"? Let's imagine your partner calls you a nickname that others find cute, but you are hurt by it. Should your partner not care about your feelings because *other people* don't mind? If you would feel particularly loved by getting a box of paper clips for Valentine's Day – even if that's not what "most people" would want – should your partner ignore that because it's out of the ordinary?[3] This is why sharing your experience from a place of subjectivity is going to get you much farther. This is not about winning an argument. It's about being in love.

Remember to speak about your feelings as *your* feelings. "It's annoying when you leave on the kitchen light" is an objective statement: you are claiming that this action is by its nature something that annoys. Really what you want to convey is, "I get annoyed when you leave on the kitchen light." You are taking ownership of your feelings rather than determining the reality of what is and is not annoying. You are appealing to your partner's concern for how you feel – their love for you – not to an objective standard you are implying they should live up to (and are not), which will only motivate them to run and hide (emotionally and/or physically). It will not motivate them to change their behavior and certainly not to feel closer to you.

Note that the injunction to stick to subjective material applies to the exploration phase, not necessarily the resolution phase. If you're trying to decide which car to buy, you will first have to get through the discussion of "I don't want to be a guy who drives a minivan because it makes me feel old;" once we understand the feelings that drive us,[4] we can absolutely then discuss the objective things like relative fuel mileages and safety ratings. You're not going to buy a junk car just because you had a dog named Pinto as a kid, but you may well choose to buy a Ford in part

---

[3] Answer: no.
[4] No pun intended.

because of how you feel about buying American (alongside considerations of cost and safety and such).

Pitfall Alert!

The English language is funny in a lot of ways. We park in a driveway and drive on a parkway. The word "one" seems to be missing a W, but "two" has got an extra. And talking about feelings... well, that's its own fine kettle of fish. (Speaking of which, figures of speech can be a real minefield.) It can often be hard to find a word to explain what we're experiencing. But even the word "feel" is a bit troublesome.

Take, for example, "I feel like everyone's out to get me." That's not really a *feeling*, an emotion. The feeling you're having is maybe nervous, anxious, angry, bitter. You *believe* that everyone's out to get you. You *assess* that as being the case. But you don't *feel* it in the sense of feeling an emotion, which is really what we're trying to get at here, because our assessments don't actually motivate us to act; our emotions do. (See sidebar "Recognizing Your Feelings" in chapter 1.) Remember that the goal is to invite your spouse into your world and avoid pushing them into defensiveness.

Let's say you think your spouse is being selfish. You may think you can get away with something like, "I feel like you don't really care about me." That may not sound so problematic, but consider if you were to phrase it like this: "I feel like you are a big fat jerk." Not a winner, right? (Note also that "big fat jerk" isn't on the feelings wheel.)

Notice what happened here. Those statements start off sounding a lot like an I-statement, but quickly veer into You territory. No go. That doesn't count as an I-statement; it's not really about you, and it's not really a feeling, despite the fact that you say "I feel." (The same thing happened to Alex at the beginning of this chapter with the comment, "I feel like your family has been coming over a whole lot lately.")

Here's a pro tip on how to tell the difference between a real I-statement and a counterfeit: generally speaking, if you can replace the word "feel" with the word "am"

> If you can replace the word "feel" with the word "am" and the sentence still makes sense, you're good to go. If you can replace the word "feel" with the word "think," you're not on target.

and the sentence still makes sense, you're good to go. If you can replace the word "feel" with the word "think," you're not on target. So:

- "I feel angry about what happened today." → "I *am* angry about what happened today." This one checks out.
- "I feel that this is a big problem in our marriage." → "I *am* that this is a big problem in our marriage." No dice. "I *think* that this is a big problem in our marriage." This is a thought, an assessment, but not a feeling.

"I feel like" is also a bit fraught as an opener, unless you're trying to use a simile: "I feel like a butterfly in the wind." This is a good description of your emotional state. "I feel like all you ever do is criticize me" – nope. A little closer to a description of emotions might be something like, "I feel like slapping someone in the face!" Really this means "I want to slap someone in the face." But it's a little closer to the feeling – you can probably accurately deduce that someone is feeling angry if they say something like this; still, you're better off going directly with the feeling if you can. Something like, "I'm so mad I want to slap someone in the face!" Follow up the "I feel" with one word, maybe two, to describe how you're feeling. You can use more than that if there's no good word and you need to paint a picture, but be very careful not to fall back into a You statement.

Another challenge here is trying to convert your sense of what you're going through into I-language. For example, the experience you're having in your marriage is that your spouse never really listens to you. But you can't say, "I feel like you never listen," because that is neither a feeling nor a real I-statement (and you are inviting an argument). But if you just say "angry," it doesn't really cover it, does it?

So how would you say this from an "I" perspective? I would suggest something like, "I feel unheard." You keep the focus on you. Does your spouse listen to you? I don't know. *You* don't know. Maybe they do and maybe they don't, but *you feel* unheard. If we're not debating facts, then we don't have to argue about whether your spouse is or is not listening; the only thing that matters here is that you feel unheard. If we accept the premise that this is deliberately one half of the conversation, then your spouse can accept that you feel this way without taking it as an accusation that they aren't listening.

(I will concede that "unheard" is debatable as an emotion word. I think this wording does the trick, though. It allows you to convey your experience without requiring the other party to take a stand for their position or their honor. It's much harder to pull that off with "I feel like you don't listen." Another example which might be iffy but I think is useful nonetheless is "I feel attacked." This is a common experience people have in their relationships, and it doesn't have to mean "You are attacking me" – it can just mean "That's how I feel and I'm not trying to get you to own up to anything." But your intention really must be to be heard and understood, not to actually get them to own up to some transgression you believe they have committed – whether or not they did in fact commit that transgression.)

Like I've said already, this isn't about perfection – saying exactly the right word in exactly the right way. You do the best you can.

STICK TO I

When you are speaking about yourself and trying to invite your partner into your experience, it's important not to fall into one of these unhelpful modes, which are not I-centric:

1. Accusing/Blaming

Stay away from accusation and blame. Far away. This is *guaranteed* to kill your communication. The flip side of "accuse" is "defend," which we know is a dead end. You are absolutely not going to get contrition and openness in response to accusing your partner or blaming them for something.

"You never help out around here! The only thing you care about is your career!"

"You're right – I really don't care that much about you or the kids. Has that been bothering you?"

> Stay away from accusation and blame. Far away.

I would not expect this response from anybody ever. Even if they don't open their mouths to argue with you and shift the blame, they are certainly hardening up inside and becoming less receptive to anything else you have to say. You know this, because it's true for you as well. Consider how you feel if your partner says this to you (in a tone that indicates they are not asking an informational question): *"Why are you always on your phone?!"* Now consider how you feel if instead they say this: "You know, I have been feeling unseen lately, and kind of lonely in the marriage." Which version puts you on the defensive, and which version makes you feel empathetic and maybe even a little sad?[5]

Note that accusing and blaming yield defensiveness *even if you are totally, 100% right* (and arguably *especially* if you are right). Your partner may well have ruined the whole party because they got too drunk. But if you dig into them with "you ruined the whole party because you got fall-down drunk and acted like an idiot!" – once again, you are inviting an argument, not a resolution.

(Think now for a moment how you would address this in "I" language. Go ahead, I'll wait.

Okay, here's one way to do it: "Last night you got drunk and you made some comments about Angie [objective, nonjudgmental observation], and I was super super embarrassed [back to my feelings]. And I'm angry at you for putting me in that position [more feelings]."

How about Alex's line from the opening of this chapter, "You don't really make it so pleasant when my parents are here" – what could we do with that one? One possible approach: "When my parents are here you often don't say much to them, and I usually end up feeling pretty awkward and uncomfortable.")

Note that you can accuse somebody not just with your words but with your tone. It's impossible to convey this well in writing, but I think you probably know what I'm talking about. An easy example: "It looks like somebody ate the last cookie" might be a neutral observation, but it certainly sounds like an accusation if you position your eyebrows just so and inflect it harshly: "It looks like SOMEBODY ate the last cookie..." Nonverbal communication is powerful; you can make any words sound (and feel) accusatory with the right tone of voice and body language.

I want to point out something important here: I am not telling you to avoid accusation and blame because it's the nice thing to do, or because you'll hurt your partner's feelings, or because it's "not fair." Those may or may not be the case; but I am telling you to do it this way because *this is the way to get what you want.* Remember I said I am all about what works and not about who's right and who's wrong?

---

[5] If you feel yourself getting a little defensive at the second version too, you're not wrong. We all tend to hear implied judgments in anything that is said about us; this is a major impediment to the kind of communication you want to have because you find yourself arguing back on what you heard. We'll address this problem in the chapter on being the listener.

Blaming doesn't work. If you want results, if you want change, if you want connection and relationship, don't go there. Go with empathic dialogue.

2. Judging/Labeling

"You're so insensitive!" "You're a slob!" Once again, these are You-statements. They are judgments of the other party, and they won't go over well. Think about how you react when someone throws something like this at you. Do you say, "Heh, you got me there"? No, that is not how you go. Instead, you tighten up, defend, probably counterattack – and all the more so if you know the judgment to be true!

Remember that "I feel like you're insensitive" or "I feel like you don't care about our family" are also nonstarters. So are judgments and labels that come across indirectly: "Only a moron would believe that..." means "you're a moron" (even if you say "I *feel like* only a moron would believe that..."), "Can't you think about anyone besides yourself?!" means "you're selfish." If you want effective communication, you've got to get in the mindset of talking about yourself and not about someone else.

Thus, "you're so insensitive" becomes "I was really hurt by that comment you made earlier." "Can't you think about anyone besides yourself?" becomes "I feel angry and left out that you didn't pick up food for me when you got some for yourself." You are not commenting on what this says about the person who did it. You are simply sharing where you're at.

If you are using your words to deliver a commentary on your spouse instead of to share your own feelings – and here you must be honest with yourself, because it's really easy to get sucked into delivering a small, backhanded jab just under the radar – you will encounter resistance and, as noted above, you will not get what *you* need out of this process.

3. Assuming/Ascribing

It is so easy to make assumptions about others, or to *ascribe* intentions to them, because we all experience the world the way we experience it, and it is often very difficult to even conceive that someone experiences it differently.[6] Recognize, however, that without someone telling you what their inner experience is, you cannot

---

[6] Regrettably, most people think exactly this – that everyone sees and experiences things the same way they do. This is another reason why the world of politics is so dysfunctional

know. You can guess. You can deduce. You may even get it right. But *you cannot KNOW.*

Have you ever been in a situation where someone did something really offensive to you, and you tell your friend, and they don't seem bothered by it? Or even something as trivial as you liked a movie and your buddy thought it was terrible? Other people experience the world in different ways, about events and interactions and situations and all kinds of things large and small, and this is true *even about things you would never think could be this way.*

Here's another common example: many people can relate to appreciating, wanting, or needing a hug from a loved one after a hard day at work, or after a pet dies, or after any number of difficult experiences. I have not seen any formal studies, but I would guess this

> Other people experience the world in different ways, even about things you would never think could be this way.

applies to the majority of people (in our culture), and likely you are one of them. Consider that *some people don't like hugs – at all.*[7]

> *As a teenager I was once at a youth group event where we ended the evening singing a song together, swaying in a big circle with our arms around each other. Except for Josh. Josh was swaying along but had a gap on either side between him and the next person in the circle. I was relatively new to the group and hadn't witnessed this before; as an egocentric and judgmental teenager, I thought he was being weird and obnoxious. Later, in an eye-opening moment, Josh shared aloud how much he appreciated the group for providing a space where he was not expected to engage in physical contact. He just doesn't like it.*

People are so different, in so many ways. In fact, it is this reality that empathic dialogue is coming to address head-on. You and your spouse will learn to share your experiences with each other and to be open to hearing each other's. You will

---

and why so many people from political party X are dead sure that people from political party Y are all idiots. "Given the same input data, how could any reasonable person come to a different conclusion from my own?"

[7] If you are a non-hugger, consider that other people may like hugs very much, may not find them icky or invasive, and may simply not resonate with your experience the same way you don't resonate with theirs.

learn to stop assuming they feel a certain way and ascribing thoughts or intentions to them. You will really be able to *communicate*. It's going to be awesome.

Let's illustrate further with some clear examples. Here are some ways to assume what your spouse is thinking or to ascribe intent to them:

- "You're just trying to hurt my feelings."
- "You only ever think about yourself!"
- "When you forget to call to tell me you're running late, it shows that you don't consider my needs."
- "You want to have your cake and eat it too!"
- "I feel like you just don't care." (Whoopsie! Not a true I-statement!)

See how these are not only talking about your spouse but are also addressing things inside their brain that you cannot possibly know for sure?

Ah, but let's say you really do think these things are true and they're hurting you. How do you convey that? As we explained, you can refer to your spouse's behavior – not their thoughts or intentions – and then come back to you. Like so:

- "When you text with other women, *I wonder if* you're doing it just to hurt my feelings."
- "When you leave the sink full of dishes, *the message I hear from that is* that my needs really aren't that important to you."
- "When you forget to call me to tell me you're running late, *the impression I get is* that I'm just not that important."
- "If you promise that you'll be home by a certain time but aren't, *what I think to myself is* that you want to have your cake and eat it too."
- "Sometimes I text you and don't hear back all day, and *I get the feeling that* you're too busy to care about me."

You would want to follow up any of these phrases with a good old "I feel" statement to convey your internal experience of what's happening. Other good phrases to use include:

- "It seems to me that..."

- "I start to worry that..."
- "I interpret it to mean that..."[8]

In all these cases, it's great to tack on something like "...and then I start to feel..." See how these examples *refer* to your spouse but fundamentally are talking about you and your feelings? That's what we're aiming for.

Note that you have to be genuine when saying things like "The impression I get is..." or "It seems to me that..." These statements are deliberately tentative, as you should be – like we said, you just don't know. If you in your head are convinced that really your spouse *is* deliberately ignoring you but you are couching it in tentative language like "it seems" just so they can't argue back, or to appear open-minded, you are unlikely to succeed at having open communication, of which genuineness is a pretty important feature.

I once worked with a couple who simply could not stop assuming things about each other. Livia and James were experts at this. It was a constant theme of their arguments; it would have been funny if it weren't so tragic. Livia complained that when James was setting up the grill on their camping trip and "had a look on his face," he was angry at her for making a comment about how late it was getting. James had no idea what Livia was talking about; he didn't even remember the comment she'd made. (This is so common – one person assumes their spouse is reacting to some deliberate provocation and it turns out their spouse didn't even notice it, let alone intend it.) He remembered being tense about getting the food on the fire, but he wasn't at all angry at her. Livia dismissed his response, insisting he was angry at her for that comment. James was perplexed.

---

[8] One suggestion I've seen is "The story I tell myself is..." I am not a big fan of this one (but if you are, feel free to use it!). To me this sounds like you're selling yourself out from the get-go – like you're saying, "I know this is just a made-up issue that isn't real, but..." You know what? Maybe it's all in your head, and maybe it isn't, but the point here is that your partner has to accept your issue as your issue and take it seriously. When you hedge your comments like this, I think you're a little bit giving them license to dismiss it. Not the best approach, in my opinion. What *can* be helpful is to acknowledge that "This is just how I'm seeing things and I'm sure you have a different view on this." That gives space for both your perspective and your partner's to have realness and validity.

But then later in the very same session, James did exactly the same thing! He ascribed to Livia an attitude of detachment from him, asserting that she no longer really liked being around him; he thought she might even hate him. Livia was utterly confused; she was here in marriage counseling because she loved him, not because she hated him. Sure, things were a bit distant at home now – that's what they were coming to work on; yet to say that she didn't want to be around him at all – she couldn't fathom it. But he wouldn't let go of that position.

So they both kept going round and round, ascribing mindsets and emotional states to each other, despite my repeated attempts to get them to recognize what they were both doing.

4. Timelining

This one is less insidious than the above categories, but still not so productive. Timelining is when you run down the chronology of events that have happened. This may not be overly focused on your partner, but it's also not really focused on how you're feeling. Perhaps you want to convey that you are annoyed by a certain situation, but rather than centering on that point, you give a whole history of the problem, or every example of when it's happened in the past.

It's not necessary. Recall that it simply doesn't matter if your version of events is correct or not. You are not trying to get your partner to agree with you. You're trying to elicit their understanding and empathy for you. You don't need to establish the veracity of your claim, and in fact, listing a whole bunch of data points just provides more opportunities for your partner to get hooked into arguing about one of them, or more incentive for them to tune you out.

Timelining sounds like this:

"Yesterday was a total disaster, because you forgot to walk the dogs again, and then I called you and told you about it and you said you did but really you didn't, and I wasn't sure so I ended up doing it myself, and that made me late to my dentist appointment and I ended up having to wait there even longer, and I appreciate that you called back to apologize but it still messed up the whole day, and last time you forgot

to walk the dogs the same thing happened, and..."

I understand the feeling of pressure to get it all out, believe me I do. But this approach will confound and misdirect your partner. What you need from them is not to memorize the itinerary of your day but to understand how hard it is for you to go through this kind of thing. (Notice also how the above timeline didn't mention a feeling. Even if the speaker gets to it at the end, it's buried under all those details.) This would suffice: "You forgot to walk the dogs again this morning, and that made my day really hard, and I'm feeling really frustrated."

It's totally legitimate to need validation for the various different parts of the badness of the day. You can accomplish that if you remember to chunk it down into separate statements: "I get so annoyed when you forget to walk the dogs, because it means one more thing for me to do." [You let them reflect back this part (see the following chapter).] "And also today I ended up late for my dentist appointment because I had to walk them myself, and that cost me more time, which was really stressful for me." [They reflect.] And so on. This way, you are not just laying out a series of events; rather, you are seeking understanding and validation regarding various aspects of your experience.

Note that even if you start every sentence with "I," if you're just running through a timeline of events without sharing how you felt about them, you're still not going to get very far. (And even if you do include feelings, you still need to do it in small chunks if you want to have a successful dialogue.)

ONE MORE LOOK AT I-STATEMENTS

Although the principle sounds straightforward, it can sometimes be challenging to figure out how to convey the important points using I-statements. Don't worry – practice makes progress![9] Let's check out a few more examples of how to frame what you need to say in terms of your own experience:

---

9   I like this expression a lot more than "Practice makes perfect." No, it doesn't. I'm not expecting perfection from you, and you should not expect it from yourself or your partner either. If you put in the effort and see improvement, that's fantastic. Nobody ever gets to perfect.

About Your Spouse		About You
You never listen!	→	I feel unheard.
I feel like you don't care about me.	→	I feel unloved.
Don't blame me for your mistakes!	→	It seems to me that you're holding me responsible for what happened. I find that frustrating because I really don't see it that way. And in fact, I'm kind of angry that you would think such a thing.
You're not supposed to say it like that! You need to read that book again!	→	I feel myself getting defensive when you talk about me that way.
How can you possibly accuse me of lying to you about this???	→	I feel sad and also angry to hear that you think I would lie to you about something like this.
Why are you always so busy?	→	I wish we had more time together. I've been feeling lonely lately. And when I see you on your phone so much I start feeling resentful.

One more point about I-statements: I encourage you to stick to "When you [action], I feel [feeling]" rather than "When you [action] *it makes me* [feeling]." Colloquially this makes sense, but the problem is that it subtly reinforces the idea that you are the source of how I feel, and that's not really true. You cannot *make* me feel any way. How I feel about something is a choice I can make. Just because you insult me doesn't mean I have to get upset about it. The reality is that events don't make us feel any which way; rather, it's our *thoughts* about those events that affect our feelings.[10] You might be able to get away with "It makes me feel..." without your spouse feeling accused, but I think it helps to avoid the kind of language that implies that one of you is responsible for the feelings of the other.

MAKING REQUESTS

In the previous chapter, we pointed out that trying to solve a problem on the spot is usually ineffective, because you need to fully understand it from both parties' perspectives before a good solution can really be reached. That said, if there's a change you're looking for, there's nothing wrong with asking for it. This is most viable for relatively small issues that don't come with a lot of baggage, like "Please turn off the computer when you head to bed" or "Could we go to a different restaurant tonight?" (You can probably understand why it's not so simple with bigger relationship issues: "Hey, I've been feeling a bit claustrophobic lately. Could we separate for a month or two so I can get some space? Great, thanks.") The catch is that you often don't know what is a small issue and what is not. But that's okay – you're not meant to know everything that's inside your partner's head at all times; you're meant to get in there as needed, with their help.

Making a request would look like this: "When X happens, I feel Y because the message I get from that is Z. I would really appreciate if..." For example, "When you call me 'Babe' I feel angry because in my mind it's kind of a demeaning term. I would really appreciate if you would use some other word when you speak to me." In this case, it's unlikely that your partner has a strong emotional reason for calling you "Babe"; probably they'll be able to understand and empathize with what you're saying and agree to your request.

> You're not meant to know everything that's inside your partner's head at all times; you're meant to get in there as needed, with their help.

But you still have to hold out for the possibility that there *is* an emotional reason behind

---

[10] This is a fundamental principle of cognitive behavioral therapy, but it's also not a strikingly new idea: Shakespeare famously wrote, "There is nothing either good or bad, but thinking makes it so;" Marcus Aurelius said, "People are not disturbed by things, but by the views they take of them." There have been many variations of this concept throughout the ages.

it – e.g., their late father used to call their mother "Babe" and they always saw their father as a role model, etc. This doesn't mean you have to accept being called a name you don't like; it just means you have to go through some exploration to understand the meaning of this for them as well before trying to find a mutually acceptable solution. If that were the case here, your partner could validate your perspective – "Yeah, I hear how that makes you feel put down" – without agreeing to your request. Then you would head into exploring further both of your perspectives on what pet names you both like or dislike and why you feel that way before circling back to work on a solution.

A request that you make should be small and specific. "I would like you to stop calling me 'Babe'" is on target. "I feel angry about the way you speak to me and I need you to stop being nasty to me" is not very helpful. What does it mean to be nasty to you? What is your partner doing wrong? What should they do instead? You haven't given them a clear indication of what it is they should actually *do*. And regardless of how obvious you think it is, they may genuinely not know! What is obvious to you is not necessarily obvious to others.[11] A small and specific request might instead sound like, "When you don't let me finish what I'm saying, I get very frustrated. I need you to stop cutting me off when I'm speaking, please." This is a statement about your feelings and needs, and mentions a specific step you'd like your partner to take.[12]

Remember to keep it subjective. It doesn't matter how "other women" or "all men" feel about being called "Babe"; it matters how *you* feel. Don't lecture on the history of the word and why it's objectively a denigrating term; just talk about your own experience. Likewise, instead of explaining why it's more hygienic to hang the toilet paper over the front rather than back towards the wall, go with "I prefer it" or "It makes me more comfortable to imagine this is more hygienic" or just "It would make me happy if you would hang the toilet paper over this way and not

---

[11] Note also that this statement is kind of judgy – you've labeled your partner as being mean and have probably provoked a good bit of defensiveness.

[12] Point of clarification: You do *not* have to be small and specific when it comes to your feelings. In the exploration phase you are entitled to feel how you feel, whether or not you can come up with specific examples or reasons (although those will certainly help your partner better understand why you're feeling the way you do). "I feel unloved in this marriage." It's just how you feel; it is not a statement about reality, and it does not require you to prove your case. It also does not require your partner to agree that they don't love you (or to insist or prove that they do), only to care that you feel this way.

that way." Your partner can argue about a bacteria count, but not about what you like and don't like.[13] Your ability to influence your partner depends less upon how thoroughly you convince them or how much pressure you put on them and more on the overall strength of the relationship.

If you *know* your partner has their own feelings about the issue you want to bring up, your best bet is to request an exploration conversation rather than going right to a request for the outcome you want. You know you're going to have to go there anyway. It probably would not be a winning approach to come out with "I've really been missing my family lately. I'd appreciate if we could move back to rural Morocco to be near them." Rather, you

> Your ability to influence your partner depends less upon how thoroughly you convince them or how much pressure you put on them and more on the overall strength of the relationship.

could share how you're feeling and ask to explore together: "I've really been missing my family lately. I've been thinking about what it would mean for us to move back closer to them. Could we have a feelings talk sometime this week and just explore this together?"

You are certainly allowed to want things and seek changes in your marriage; you just need to come at it with an understanding that your partner likely has their own views on the same issue, and with a readiness to hear that out before you stake your flag on a particular solution.

A FEW MORE DON'TS

I want to bring up some other hazards of communication that people often trip up on. These are not specific to empathic dialogue and really are pretty universal points for good communication, but I thought it important to make mention of them to be clear that these are no-nos. The truth is, if you're sticking to the process – timeouts, I-statements, focus on you, small chunks at a time – you are unlikely to fall into one of these anyway. But since we all slip up in attempts at good communication[14], it's good to be aware of some of these danger zones.

---

13 FYI, this example is a real dispute from the early days of my marriage. Now we just hang it the way my wife likes it.

14 I include myself in this statement.

Always and Never

Like Justin Bieber and that French pigeon in *An American Tail* sang, "Never say never." Always and never are the kind of adverbs that usually pop up out of frustration rather than statistical analysis. "You *always* leave your socks on the floor!" "We *never* get to spend any time together anymore." (In Alex and Randy's story above, it's "We never get to hang out with my family.") Statements like these are almost certainly not literally true, and the answer you're inevitably going to get back is something like, "Well, I don't see any socks on the floor right *now*!" or "What are you talking about? We just went out for a picnic last week!" This does nothing to address the fact that you've been feeling alone and unseen, which is what you ought to be focusing on anyway.

Kitchen Sinking

We mentioned earlier that you need to keep your remarks to segments of a few sentences at a time when sharing everything you've got going on inside, so that your spouse can take it in without getting overloaded. Likewise, it's important to keep your discussion focused on a single issue or area. If you're discussing your desire for more physical affection, you can talk about various times when this came up for you, or different ways in which it's affecting you; but don't go into every other lack you're feeling in the marriage (i.e., "everything but the kitchen sink"). Your wish for physical affection and your frustration at the lack of financial accountability in the marriage are two separate issues, needing two separate conversations. (It's possible to have those conversations back-to-back if both of you are game, but it should be clear that it's a separate conversation, not rolling from one thing into the other.) If they are the same issue, however – both of these experiences are contributing to your feelings of distance and mistrust – then that can be one conversation.

Kitchen sinking throws everything in all at once and is overwhelming to your spouse. How are they supposed to productively respond to 11 different complaints? What could they even say that would feel better to you after you've laid out such a range of issues? You may feel a little relief by getting everything off your chest, but when you put it all out there at once, it's got nowhere to go. You'll find it comfortably nestled back on your chest pretty quickly. Not to mention the fact that your spouse certainly feels much worse. So again, whether you are right or wrong about your 11 issues, you will not get what you want out of a discussion if you dump them all out on your spouse in one go.

Putdowns/Name Calling

Look, we can all get a little nasty sometimes. Usually this is when we've gotten angry and aren't making good decisions anymore, which means it is past the point where someone should have called a timeout. Then we say something mean in the heat of the moment and feel bad. It's normal to find ourselves in this place when we're emotionally overloaded, which again is why it's so important to take a break before you get there. If the conversation has gotten to the point where one of you is putting the other down it's time to get out, rather than letting it escalate further.

Note that it's possible for your partner to say something to you that you find hurtful, and they honestly didn't realize it. "You can be so nutty sometimes!" can be meant as an insult or an expression of endearment. (This is just another thing you can dialogue about later on, using the same strategies we're discussing.) Remember that people see the world differently!

On the other hand, if you believe that putting down your partner is a good way to maintain the upper hand in a marriage, then you need a different book. You do not need this book. The book you are reading right now assumes that marriage is a collaborative, respectful enterprise, not a competitive, power-oriented one. If you are trying to "win" in your marriage, I recommend you think through that before trying to improve your communication.

Likewise, if you see that your partner views putting you down as a valid relationship strategy – if they deliberately put you down and call you names (picking out the most spiteful ones) in order to hurt you – you probably need to consider whether this marriage is viable. We all make mistakes, but an ongoing pattern of emotional abuse is a strategy, not a mistake (see sidebar "Domestic Abuse" below). Getting called a nasty name in the heat of the moment is obviously a hurtful experience; but if your partner can recognize when they are not angry that that's not how they want to behave and express remorse, you don't necessarily need to question the whole marriage. (This is not an easy decision to make; consulting with a professional is a good idea.)

Mocking/Teasing

Mocking your spouse, like putting them down, is a fundamental lack of respect and has no place in a loving relationship. You can and should be respectful towards your spouse even when you disagree, even when you are hurt, even when you are angry. It is possible to mock and tease each other in a good-natured way, which is a loving feature of some relationships, as long as it's not taken too far. You have to be honest with yourself. If you're trying to cut your spouse down a notch, consider whether that is going to get you the marriage you want. If you're just being playful, *and your spouse appreciates the joking nature of it*, then you're okay. *The person on the receiving end is the one who gets to decide!* Saying "I'm just kidding around, geez," does not make it okay to say things that are hurtful, even if you don't mean them to be.

> You can and should be respectful towards your spouse even when you disagree, even when you are hurt, even when you are angry.

Also, recognize that teasing has a time and a place. If you are in an argument with your spouse, that is not a time to employ "good-natured" teasing. Nor is it a good time when you're in the middle of empathic dialogue, in which you are trying to convey deep empathy. This is hard to do if you're being goofy or perhaps even a bit edgy.

Threats and Getting Physical

This is probably extraordinarily obvious, but I just wanted to go on record as saying that physical violence is never acceptable in your marriage. Getting physical doesn't just mean punching and slapping, though: punching the wall, throwing objects (even not directly at someone), and threatening physical violence are also forms of abuse. They create fear in the marriage, even if no physical harm actually occurs.

Less severely (perhaps), but also very damaging to a marriage, are threats of any kind – of divorce/breakup, of emotional withdrawal, of unspecified "consequences." Threats are aggressive and frightening. They push the receiver into fight-or-flight mode and they destroy trust in a marriage. If threats and violence are a part of your marriage, please seek professional help (see sidebar "Domestic Abuse").

Domestic Abuse

Although I described physical violence as abuse, it's important to be aware that domestic abuse is far more than just physical. Abuse can be emotional, mental, financial, sexual, and spiritual; in fact, these other forms of abuse are almost always experienced by the victim as far worse than the physical violence that's going on in the marriage.

Here is a short (not comprehensive) list of some relationship red flags (check out ncadv.org for more info). It is a form of abuse if your spouse:

- Throws objects, breaks your possessions, punches holes in the wall to frighten you.
- Tries to control who you see and talk to, where you go, or what you wear.
- Puts you down and humiliates you (especially in public).
- Is very jealous and repeatedly accuses you of cheating without any evidence.
- Blames you for every problem in the marriage, including their own behavior.
- Threatens to harm or kill you.
- Puts you on an allowance, scrutinizes your spending, prevents you from working or keeping money that you earn.
- Cuts you off from family and friends.
- Forces you to be sexual at times/in ways you do not want.

A full treatment of the issue of abuse is beyond the scope of this book. But I want to make it clear that if you are a victim of abuse, *better communication will not help you.* The abuse is not your fault and there is nothing you can do to make it stop. It is critical for you to get help and support from a victim services provider – not from a self-help book and not in couples counseling. Please find your local services for victims of domestic abuse, or call the National Domestic Violence Hotline at 1-800-799-7233.

HELP A PARTNER OUT

Thus far we've discussed at length the role of the speaker in this conversation-cut-in-two. Next we'll dig into what the listener has to do, which is equally, if not more, important. But the truth is that both of you are responsible for making this dialogue go well. And since you're a team, you are expected to help your teammate do their job too. You set them up for success. If they mess up, you don't start dumping on them for killing the dialogue process and ruining the marriage. That's not how a team works. In a team, when one person falls short, their teammate steps in to pick up the slack. People mess up. You are called upon to be understanding and supportive in those moments. You'd want the same done for you.

This starts with giving them a leg up from the get-go. Remember to cue your partner in that you're looking for a listening ear and that you'd like them to go into listener mode. If you run headlong into an exploration conversation or even just into a quick share and you're expecting your partner to be ready to hear you in a skillful way, you may find yourself disappointed and irritated. If you really need them to be there to listen, let them know up front. This is certainly true when you have a significant

> In a team, when one person falls short, their teammate steps in to pick up the slack.

and/or sensitive issue to bring up; but as we noted, this tool is not only useful for major conversations. Even when it's a relatively small matter – you just want to share an annoying comment your coworker made today or you're excited about the new shoes you got – sharing your experience from an "I" perspective and being heard and validated is a pretty sweet feeling. And it can help to cue your partner in when that's what you're looking for.

Another important way you support your partner is by remembering to chunk it down. The listener's job will be (duh) to listen, and to reflect back what they're hearing (see the next chapter). If you speak on and on about everything on your mind, there's no way they can meaningfully capture what you're trying to convey. Share one or two thoughts at a time, a few sentences, then give them space to chew on that and *get* it.

Perhaps the most important way you'll help your partner with their part is to redirect them when they aren't on point. What if they aren't doing a great job as listener and are jumping in with their own perspectives, arguing about what you're saying, getting defensive? Those are definitely not within the scope of their half of the conversation while you are the speaker and they are the listener.

First off, remember to assume good will. It is likely (although not impossible) that your partner isn't just trying to derail the process to hurt or control you, and does in fact care about what you have to say. If they are escalating, getting emotional, refusing to follow the process – probably they are being overtaken by their own emotional reaction to the situation. This is human. You too have surely experienced the feeling of being triggered into a not-so-good state by something your partner says. It's also certainly possible that they've just forgotten the process for a moment – like offering solutions when you're still in the exploration phase.

We've spoken about defensiveness a number of times; it is a natural reaction to emotional pressure. That doesn't mean it's a *good* thing; it just means it's natural. It's bound to happen sometimes. Hopefully you will both learn to be mindful of it and work to manage it in yourselves. In the meantime, be prepared to face it coming from your partner sometimes. It's frustrating, but don't let that throw you off course; think about how hard it is to remain non-defensive when you're on the listening end!

It can help to pepper the conversation with reminders that this is about you and what things look like in your world, not about the ultimate reality, and that you are taking ownership of your reactions. That sounds like this:

- "I just want to reiterate that I'm just telling you how I saw it; I'm not assuming this is 100% the reality."
- "I may be wrong about what happened, but here is the experience I had..."
- "I don't know what's in your head, but in my head, the message I got in that moment was..."
- "I'm not saying it's your fault that I'm angry; it's just my reaction to what I perceived in that moment."

Reminding both of you that this is purely a subjective telling can help keep things on track. Of course, it's still possible for your partner to fall into a defensive position. The solution is to deal with it as just part of the process and redirect your partner back onto a more helpful path. Don't go into a whole tirade about it. A short intervention will often do:

- "I think we're getting off track."
- "Whoa whoa... we're in my world right now, remember?"
- "Hey, hang on – can we go back to me speaking and you listening, and then we'll switch soon?"
- "I'm feeling a bit frustrated because I don't get the sense you are taking in what I'm saying."

Even just holding up one hand in a "stop" gesture can be effective (although I recommend agreeing on this as a signal ahead of time if you want to use that). You know what doesn't help? Calling them out. *"Stop being so defensive!"* You know what that gets you? More defensiveness.

Another approach that can be very helpful is viewing the process itself with a healthy dose of empathy. Look, it's hard to hear things that you don't agree with, that put you in a bad light, that are screaming for a response. It makes sense to struggle with feelings of defensiveness! Empathizing with that experience can go a long way:

- "I can understand this is hard for you to hear. Are we okay to keep going, or do you need a break?"
- "It looks like this is stressful for you. I really appreciate how hard you're working to get through this."

> When a person feels heard, they are generally much more prepared to hear someone else.

If your partner has really gotten very emotional or defensive, and you are calm enough to switch roles and let them get some of their stuff out first, that can help too: when a person feels heard, they are generally much more prepared to hear someone else.

THE SPEAKER'S ROLE: IN SUM

You're going to go out there and share with your mate what they need to know about your experience, your feelings, what it's like to be you in the situation at hand. You have a job to do. You cannot just dump out everything in your head and heart in an unrestrained manner and expect that to produce good communication or a good marriage. You have responsibilities in this role, just as the listener has responsibilities, which we will discuss going forward. Your responsibilities include:

- Attending to your emotional state – not broaching a topic when you're too wound up, and taking a timeout as needed. (Remember, strike when the iron is cold!)
- Managing your mindset – assume good will, not ill intent.
- Not eliciting defensiveness – choose words that invite them to join you in your experience rather than to defend their own position; speak about your subjective experience (I statements, feelings over facts).
- Setting your partner up for success – cueing them in that you want to be heard/use the empathic dialogue process; getting things back on track if your partner flubs it – reminding them that you are just trying to explore if they start to resolve; politely and kindly jogging their memory that you are the speaker if they begin to share their own perspective; not getting drawn into an argument about the facts.

If you can commit to doing your part here, we are already in a much better position to get the communication in your marriage back on track. Let's see the do-over with Alex and Randy:

Alex: *Is this a good time to have a conversation about something?*

Randy: *Good enough – the kids are all playing nicely! What's going on?*

Alex: *Well, I just want to cue you in that I'd like to say what's going on for me and be heard a little bit before we work on fixing anything, 'kay?*

Randy: *Absolutely. Shoot.*

Alex: *Okay, so, the issue is... I think I'm feeling kind of jealous because your family comes over so much more often than mine does. It seems a little unbalanced and unfair to me, and I'm actually a bit angry too.*

Randy: *But your parents were just here for Zack's graduation two weeks ago!*

Alex: *I know I know I know, but hang on – we're in my world right now please. Stay with me here.*

Randy: *Right, sorry. So... you're feeling jealous and upset about how often my family and your family come to visit?*

Alex: *Yeah. Thanks. That's what I want to talk about.*

Randy: *Okay, help me understand that...*

Chapter 4

LOVE Your Partner

Blake: *Ugh. I totally messed up this mulligatawny soup. I spent so much time on it and now it's just a mess!*

Tyler: *Oh, honey, I'm sorry. Look, it's no big deal, let's just go out for dinner tonight.*

Blake: *I don't WANT to go out for dinner! I want my mulligatawny soup!!!*

Tyler: *So... let's go out and get mulligatawny soup?*

Blake: *Tyler, STOP IT already.*

Tyler: *Why are you getting so upset? I'm not minimizing your efforts. I'm just trying to help!*

Blake: *You're not helping! You're just avoiding like you always do.*

Tyler: *What are you talking about? You said you want mulligatawny soup and I said, 'Let's go get some!' And now you're mad at me! Why does it always have to go this way?*

We are about to enter what is probably the most critical, and most difficult, element of empathic dialogue, namely, the role of the listener. Let's tread carefully. Effective listening is not always easy. No doubt you can think of many times where you said something and the sound waves entered another person's ears, but you knew full well they didn't actually *hear* you. (If you own any teenagers, you can probably think of several times this past week alone.)

Good communication requires more than just allowing sound waves to enter your ears. It requires more than just "paying attention" too.

Matt and Amanda had been married for two years when they came in to see me. Communication problems, they explained. As they introduced themselves and their situation, it sounded pretty typical. They didn't talk about anything anymore beyond the practical day-to-day stuff. They had issues they couldn't resolve. She wanted to communicate more and felt like it was pulling teeth with him; he didn't disagree with that assessment but wasn't sure how to move forward.

I asked what typically happens when an issue comes up. Amanda explained that she would get emotional and try to explain to him what the problem was, and he wouldn't respond. A classic presentation, I thought – the woman getting emotional and the man, uncomfortable with emotions, would scarcely listen before pushing back, or shutting her down, or blowing her off – anything to end the conversation as quickly as possible.

It turned out that wasn't quite it.

Amanda was not accusing him of not listening. Both of them agreed that he'd listen to what she had to say. But when she said he wouldn't respond, she meant that literally. He would stare at her and say nothing. Just nothing. He wouldn't nod, or go "mmm," or otherwise react in any way. When she was done speaking, he would just get up and leave.

Paying attention? Yes. Listening? Hard to call it that.

If your spouse as the speaker is sharing their experience with you, inviting you into their world, then what they need from you is a response that indicates you're getting in there with them. They need to know that you *understand* them and *care* about them. They need your *empathy*. That is what you're going to try to accomplish as the listener.

Let's be clear: *it is totally normal not to understand what is in your partner's head right off the bat.* You need to hear it explicitly, otherwise you are assuming (see unhelpful mode #3, assuming/ascribing, in the previous chapter).

Humans are not so consistent that the signs we give off can be relied upon to communicate what we're trying to communicate, nor is it a given that we can dependably understand what we're trying to understand. Please let go of your assumptions that you know what your partner is thinking and feeling or where they're coming from with a certain comment or behavior. You might be right – but you might not. Assuming you *don't* know is generally the safer path! Remember, you are going to be called to let go of your own perspectives, your own template of how the world is, and enter your partner's world as fully as possible. As we said in the previous chapter, you need to try to put aside your own brain and try to adopt theirs for the time being.

The other upshot here is that since you can't know from the outset what your partner is thinking and feeling, and since it can actually be quite difficult to put your own stuff out of the way entirely, it is likely that you will not fully understand your partner right away. You will try (this is good) and you will fail (this is not bad). It is normal to not instantly understand someone else's different way of looking at things. It is also normal to mess up your job as the listener sometimes. Like any new skill, it will take time to practice and integrate. Don't despair that this doesn't go perfectly smoothly at first. If you have one positive moment in one upcoming conversation, that's progress. If you are capable of taking one small step forward, then you are capable of taking more. That's how change happens.

> **If you are capable of taking one small step forward, then you are capable of taking more.**

CATEGORY A AND CATEGORY B

When you are in the position of listener and your spouse is sharing something they want you to understand, there are only four things you can do in that moment that will get you anywhere good. *Only four!* These comprise what I call "Category A" responses. But before we get into Category A, I want to go over and knock out the Category B responses so we know clearly where *not* to go as we walk down this listening path. Category B is full of responses that (a) seem like they ought to work but do not, and (b) may have a time and a place to employ later on. These can be very tempting to use when listening to your spouse, but I promise you they will take you in the wrong direction. Let's go through the list of Category B responses:

1. Explaining

This is probably the most common and most tempting trap people fall into when trying to deal with a difficult marital issue. Your spouse is unhappy with something that happened or something you did or said, so you try to *explain* what really happened or what you really meant (you see Tyler doing this in the mulligatawny vignette above).

"That comment wasn't meant to be insulting, I was just pointing out that your reaction was a very emotional one!"

"No, I only got upset after you turned off the TV."

"I didn't yell, I just raised my voice slightly. There's a difference."

The reason to avoid this strategy is not because you must allow your spouse to think they are right and you must accept being wrong. The reason to avoid this strategy is because *explaining does not work.* I will prove it to you. You have tried this strategy many times, and it has never made things better. Am I right?

I know it seems very logical. "My spouse is upset at me, and if I could just *explain* to them what actually happened, it would fix the problem!" Right? I get it. But since it doesn't work, it behooves you to give up that fantasy. An angry spouse does not hear an explanation of why they should not be angry about this issue and then all of a sudden feel instantly better.[1]

> Until I know you're listening to me, I'm not listening to you.

Why doesn't explaining work? Because *until I know you're listening to me, I'm not listening to you.* Feeling heard allows us to be open to hearing others. You want very much for

---

[1] There are limited exceptions to this, such as when there is a very clear and significant factual confusion that is *located in the present*, i.e., where you can point to the fact in front of you and do not have to call on anyone's memory or credibility:
"Who is this number that texted you saying 'Hi sweetie' WITH A KISSY-WINKY EMOJI?!?!"
"Honey, honey – that's my mom – she got a new number. Here, let's call her right now."
But even then, there are times when it might be helpful to avoid trying to explain away the problem.

your explanation to go in and affect how your spouse is dealing with the situation. It is unlikely to do so until they feel heard.

Additionally, explaining your perspective to get them to shift theirs is essentially an attempt – however well-meaning – to get them to change how they feel, to let go of their emotions. People do not want to have their feelings taken away from them. When you're angry, you want to be angry. You want to be allowed to experience your anger, not to be told to "Calm down already!" When you're sad about something, you don't want someone to come tell you jokes and cheer you up. (Remember when you were a kid and you were pouting and someone would be funny or tickle you and make you smile? I remember this. It was a horrible feeling. You just wanted to be mad and you were coerced into laughing. So not cool.)

Trying to push out negative feelings is not a winning strategy. The more you push on them, the more they push back. (Worse, if you succeed at pushing them aside, they go underground and just cause more trouble under the surface.) This is true even though your intention may well be to help your spouse feel better! But, if we're going to be honest, more often than not a person who is trying to explain away their spouse's bad feelings is doing it not as much to reduce their spouse's distress as to spare *themselves* the experience of being the subject of the anger or the cause of the hurt of someone they care about. Trying to manage your spouse's emotions for *your* sake is *definitely* not going to go over well.

Rest assured, you will have a chance to share your perspective on the matter at hand. If you are in the role of the listener, now is not the time.

2.   Solving

Remember, we are still in the exploration phase and we are deliberately *not* trying to solve the problem here. Jumping in with a solution short-circuits the whole process and usually leaves deeper problems in place. As we said earlier, you cannot solve a problem you don't understand. I cannot tell you how many times in my professional experience and in my own life I have seen people (often me) who believe they understand the problem only to find out it's substantially different from what they thought it was.

One of the many stressors in Carlos and Isabel's life was the new business. Isabel was in the early stages of launching her own beauty salon and – big surprise! – it was a lot of work. With Carlos also working full-time, three kids at home, and a handful of standard marital issues thrown into the mix, they were well on their way to falling apart.

One of the repeated arguments they would get into involved Carlos objecting to Isabel's staying late at the salon again and missing dinner, followed by Isabel's defensiveness and anger. The fight would usually end with Isabel throwing up her hands and declaring that she would solve the whole issue by just shutting down the salon; it was too much for them. And then she would bitterly complain that Carlos had hated the salon idea from the beginning and that she didn't know if she could be happy just being a stay-at-home mom.

But Carlos did not want Isabel to be a stay-at-home mom, nor did he want her to abandon her dreams of entrepreneurship. He just missed having her at home, and he also wanted a little recognition for how hard it was to manage the evening routine without her. He swore up and down that he did not want her to have to give up the salon, but somehow it never sunk in. It took her a while, but through the process of empathic dialogue, she came around to seeing what he was really getting at. She had been totally convinced that Carlos would have been happier if she just dropped the whole thing; it turned out that was simply not the case.

Let's briefly recap some ideas from chapter 3 about the problem of solving. We had brought up the common situation of women wanting to share something and men trying to fix it (like with Tyler and Blake above). I'm going to take a moment to speak to both sides of the conversation here.

SOLVERS: when your spouse shares a problem with you, *it does not mean they want your solution.* They want to be heard. They want you to be a listener, the components of which we will detail below. Do not fall for the trap of trying to solve a problem, even if it really, really sounds like that's what's needed. Until they directly ask you for a solution, that is not what they're looking for; what they're looking for is your *empathy* (which is what Category A is going to be all about). Remember, "Nobody cares how much you know until they know how

> **You can have the best solution in the world, but it matters little if your spouse doesn't feel your love and care.**

much you care." You can have the best solution in the world, but it matters little if your spouse doesn't feel your love and care! (This is why Tyler's attempt at addressing the situation via the going-out-for-dinner route doesn't lead anywhere good.)

SHARERS: please recognize that this is how some folks (especially men) think. They want to solve your problem. They want to be your hero. Assuming you are in a meaningful relationship where your spouse does truly care about you, this is probably an attempt on their part, even if misguided, to show that. So when they slip into problem-solving mode, your best bet is not to get angry or offended; just redirect them into listening and empathizing rather than solving. (Better yet, remember to cue them in at the outset!) This is just how many people (especially men) are wired. If you can accept that and take steps to address it, everyone wins.

3. Apologizing

Surprise! Bet you didn't expect to find this one on the list. Apologizing?! Is apologizing bad now? Was your grandfather/clergyperson/coach wrong when they told you to deal with any marital problem by just apologizing and telling your spouse they're right? (Well, I don't think that's great advice anyway, but that's a different story.)

Apologizing is not bad. It's just not Category A. Just like you can't solve a problem you don't understand, you can't apologize for an offense you don't understand. What exactly was the impact of that comment you made? Did it hurt your spouse's feelings, or offend their sense of values? Were they angry, or humiliated? An apology lands much better when you know what you're apologizing for.

> Just like you can't solve a problem you don't understand, you can't apologize for an offense you don't understand.

Abiola and Kenneth were a curious pair – not the kind of people one would have imagined getting together. She was a high-end fashion executive and showed up to our sessions outfitted as if to prove it. He talked more about his surfing hobby than his work and often came dressed as if he was ready to head out to the beach soon. (This was in Baltimore, Maryland. Not a hotbed of surfing activity.) And yet they got along quite well and had a thriving marriage, which was being slowly worn away by increasing fighting about the usual stresses and frictions in a marriage.

Abiola gave an example of one of their usual fights: on their last vacation they arrived at her cousin's beach house, where they were staying, and Kenneth asked Abiola for the keys. Surprised, Abiola shot back, "You don't have the keys? You had them when you were driving!"

"What are you talking about?" he spat. "It's YOUR cousin's house!" Then they fell right into their usual pattern, with Abiola really laying into him and Kenneth shutting down and being sullen for the rest of the day. To her credit, Abiola took the initiative that evening to admit she was wrong for losing her temper and she apologized to Kenneth for yelling at him. She was stunned when he responded with, "That's a fake apology." Abiola knew she meant it sincerely and she took great offense at his rejection. What went wrong?

The problem is that Kenneth was not upset about being yelled at nearly as much as he was upset about her calling him an idiot in her very first response to him. Of course, you can see in her words above that she didn't SAY that. But it was clear to Kenneth from her tone that that's exactly what she meant. Abiola didn't disagree; she recognized that her tone had been very condescending. She had hurt him by contemptuously putting him down, but her apology didn't address that part at all. It's no wonder that it didn't hit the mark.

Moreover, an apology can sometimes be another way of making bad feelings go away (similar to the goal of explaining), especially if it's used too soon. I don't want you to be angry, and I definitely don't want you to be angry *at me* (that makes me feel guilty), so I'll apologize to make this all go away. It seems like a decent strategy, but in truth, it's not fully genuine. Imagine you go up to your spouse and when you say, "Honey, I'm really angry because—" they interrupt with "I'M SORRY!" Do you feel restitution has been made? Do you feel satisfied that your spouse cares about your problem? Even if you genuinely feel sorry for causing an issue, unless you hear out your spouse and make an effort to understand their particular experience, you're still not connecting in the way you can if you take the time to listen properly first and only then apologize.

But guess what? Just as with solutions, often an apology isn't even needed once you've gone through a good empathic dialogue. It might be – apologizing when you are wrong or when you've hurt someone, even unintentionally, is indeed a good thing! But it also might not, because everyone's perspectives have become clearer and perhaps there really hasn't been any grievous wrong. The truth is, your empathy is a lot more valuable to your spouse than your words of confession and apology. And if it

> Your empathy is a lot more valuable to your spouse than your words of confession and apology.

turns out an apology is still in order, you will likely find it much easier to deliver, because you are now more connected to your spouse and to the feelings you've caused intentionally or unintentionally; you are more in tune with their pain that needs comforting. When that is the case, your apology will also resonate more deeply with your spouse.

4. Reassuring

Reassuring seems like a really caring thing to do. "Don't worry, everything's going to work out!" (In Tyler and Blake's case, it sounded like "it's no big deal.") It sounds loving, and it may well be coming from a loving place (although it can also be used defensively, as in, "You forgot ALL the food for the camping trip???" "Don't worry, everything's going to work out fine [and therefore there's no need to blame or get mad at me]!"). But reassuring is, even more plainly than the above strategies, a way of avoiding difficult feelings. I want to take away your stress, anxiety, anger, etc., so I try to

> There's no way through the difficult feelings except *through the difficult feelings.*

comfort you with promises of a positive outcome. Sorry, Buster. I'm gonna say it again: there's no way through the difficult feelings except *through the difficult feelings.*

Harvey and Madison could not figure out why they felt so disconnected from each other. When the pandemic hit, they both transitioned to working from home full-time, and though the initial adjustment was a bit tricky, they'd gotten into a groove they really liked. They rarely fought, and when they did, they made up quickly afterwards. They were nice people. But they still felt like they were drifting apart.

The major stress in their lives came from Madison's parents, who were pushy and difficult in a number of ways. Harvey and Madison were good at managing their boundaries, but they could never have a straight conversation about the situation. I once watched one unfold in the therapy office. Madison was irritated at her mom regarding the usual train wreck that was Thanksgiving planning. Harvey was attentive and totally agreed with all of Madison's points. And he responded with, "Look, Madison, you don't have to worry about it. It's like this every year. We are going to be just fine in the end!" And he gave her a big hug.

Madison was, to Harvey's surprise and consternation, nonplussed. I helped them to explore the moment. And indeed, here was Madison's reaction: "He just doesn't get it. We're not on the same wavelength." Madison didn't want Harvey to tell her it would be fine in the end. She knew it would be fine in the end! She just wanted to be heard. She wanted Harvey to be a part of her experience – a part of her life. When Harvey came to understand this, it was a game-changer. Of course they survived Thanksgiving, as they always did. But now they did it with a deeper understanding of the other person's internal experience throughout. And that is where the relationship lives.

Remember, until your spouse feels heard, they are not hearing you anyway. If you move to reassuring before you go through the Category A activities, your reassurance will probably not hit the mark.

5.   Advocating

Let's say your partner comes home from grad school one day visibly upset. "What's wrong?" you sensitively ask. "My idiot professor gave me a lousy grade on this paper I worked my tail off on. And it was a great paper! I told you from the beginning that rotten [expletive] didn't like me." Now you, being the sensitive type, recognize that the professor is a human being like any other human being with flaws and foibles, and probably doesn't deserve such harsh criticism. You choose to advocate for them, hoping to give your mate some perspective that will help them see the situation more clearly and calm down a bit. This is because you really care about your partner, and because you are a fool.

"Oh, come on now, honey," you cluck. "She probably just had a bad day and took it out on you. Don't take it personally!" You think you are being helpful, which is why you are surprised when this turns into a Big Giant Fight. What you are in fact doing is Not Taking Your Partner's Side, and they feel that strongly. Isn't one of the coolest features of a good marriage having someone who's got your back – even when you're not at your best? I think it is.

Advocating is when you defend someone else from your partner's judgment, or try to give someone else the benefit of the doubt (as above), or play devil's advocate ("Let's consider the other side here"). None of these are helpful when your partner is just looking for some empathy. Ah, but what if your partner is truly in the wrong on this one? Good question. The answer is that in that moment it is entirely irrelevant whether they are right or wrong. Remember that we are not in the resolution phase right now, and no action is going to be taken based on this conversation. If your partner clamors they are going to file a lawsuit against the professor for discrimination, then right now, you hear them out (and proceed with Category A); a little later on, you can try to bring some perspective to the situation. But not when you are acting as a listener to your partner's ardent feelings. Even if you are totally correct about the situation, it won't work.

Advocating in the above example might also sound like this:

- "I imagine she's just as harsh on all the other students."
- "Look, she's been a professor for a long time. I'm pretty sure she knows what she's doing."
- "Is it possible you didn't follow the guidelines like the assignment said?"
- "Well, maybe you just didn't do that great a job this time..."
- "There's probably some reason she did that."

You know what a better answer would be? "That rotten [expletive]!" Empathy is about being *with* your partner, about having their back, even when they mess things up. You are not agreeing or disagreeing with what they did. You're just loving them all the same.

> **Empathy is about being *with* your partner, about having their back, even when they mess things up.**

6. Comparing

When someone tells a tale of woe, the reaction of some listeners is to respond with, "You think *your* interview was bad? Listen to what happened to *me* [or so-

and-so]!" This is definitely not empathy. This is pretty much the opposite – "My experience is more significant than yours."

It's possible for comparing to be done in an empathic way: let's say your spouse shares with you something nasty their friend said or did. Perhaps you can relate. Perhaps something similar happened to you. Perhaps you are inclined to say so: "Oh, I totally get it, one time my friend Susie said..." This is *possibly* a positive contribution to the conversation – but there's a "but."

First of all, it has to be coming from a place of empathy, not one-upmanship (as in the interview example just cited) or egocentrism, meaning you just want to talk about you and you're not really trying to connect with your spouse over *their* experience. You have to be honest with yourself. Why are you sharing this story? Is it to provide empathy to your spouse, or is it to get *yourself* heard? If you cannot genuinely say your intention is to benefit them by letting them know they're not alone, not crazy, not weird, etc., then you probably shouldn't share it.

Even if you do truly mean to join with your spouse in their feelings and not turn the focus to yours, you still need to check with your spouse to see if what you're doing is actually helping. For some people, in some situations, hearing that others have been through the same thing can be super supportive. Other people, or in other situations, might experience it as self-centered and disconnecting. The good news is, you don't need to know what's in your spouse's head without them (you know it!) *communicating* that to you! You can just ask them if it would be helpful to hear about a similar situation that happened to you. I would recommend that, in the absence of a clear green light, you do not assume that a that-happened-to-me-too story is welcome.

7. Correcting

Correcting something your spouse said is generally not a helpful part of the listening process. Sometimes it works well, as in the fact-in-front-of-you situations we touched on before. So if it clearly averts an argument, that's a good thing:

"I can't believe you threw out my favorite T-shirt!!!"

"I didn't, it's right here."

But this doesn't work at all if it's a "historical" correction:

"I can't believe you threw out my favorite T-shirt!!!"

"But you told me to get rid of it!"

If you are certain about this fact, you can try to jog their memory; but if the response is something to the effect of, "What are you *talking* about???" – get off that train immediately and pivot to Category A. And if the disagreement is one of a longstanding nature – who does more of the housework, or how much time you spend with each other – definitely don't go for a correction; it will only magnify the argument.

If you believe that communicating with your spouse is about getting the facts right, you are likely to get stuck in this mode. Even if you have come to recognize that it's *not* about fact-finding, it's pretty easy to fall into this trap – you're listening to your spouse, then all of a sudden you pick up a detail that isn't accurate and you feel compelled to make a correction. It can be a pretty powerful urge, particularly if they are upset at you for something that happened and you believe their account of it is erroneous.

But, as with explaining, this tends not to defuse the argument (especially if you've argued about this point or similar ones before). In the first T-shirt example above, a correction is likely to stop a charging spouse in their tracks as a result of the sudden reality check. Short of something that stark, your attempts to correct your spouse's recollection of events are unlikely to succeed. (Again, you can back me up here yourself: has it ever happened that your spouse was mad at you, then you pointed out that they had the facts wrong, and instantly everything was better? I didn't think so.) Remember, this doesn't mean that you have to accept their version as correct; it just means you aren't focused on what is correct right now and instead you are focused on caring about how your spouse feels in the moment.

So how do you deal with it when they say something you really believe is incorrect? What you do is you fulfill your role as the listener (keep reading). Then, when it's your turn to be the speaker, you do not rebut what they said; you simply share your reaction to what you heard: "It really bothers me to hear that you're angry at me for leaving my shoes out. I am pretty certain I put my shoes away, and I think you might have tripped on the kids' shoes actually." Your spouse's job here is not to accept or refute your recollection but rather to *empathize with how frustrated you feel (or hurt or whatever your feeling is) to be accused of something you didn't do.* Remember, we may never agree on what actually happened in that incident, but if you care how I feel about it and I care how you feel about it, we have a pretty darn good relationship even if we don't have agreement on the facts.

Also, let's be honest here: can we admit that our memory simply isn't perfect? Sure, maybe you have a *pretty good* memory; maybe your spouse will even agree that generally speaking your memory is better. But it's not *perfect.* You at least *sometimes* misremember events. Everyone does. If it has never happened to you that you were 100% dead sure you were remembering something correctly and then you turned out to be wrong, then you are probably not from planet Earth and there are many people who would like to do a television interview with you.

> We may never agree on what actually happened in that incident, but if you care how I feel about it and I care how you feel about it, we have a pretty darn good relationship.

Research has demonstrated many times over that memory is famously unreliable. So let's have some humility anyway about insisting that our narrative is the correct one, mmkay? (This is another good reason we don't argue about the facts. It is super likely that both of you will be absolutely certain of your version, and at least one of you – possibly both of you – will just be wrong.)

Instead of trying to correct your spouse, accept that although you are fairly certain you are right, you will never really know for sure what happened, and move on to caring about your spouse instead of trying to prove it. Of course, this is easier if both of you are on board with the process. If one person keeps trying to prove their story, it's hard for the other to resist pushing back – hard, but not impossible. You can refuse to get sucked in to that dynamic and sidestep the facts in favor of feelings: "Look, we disagree on what happened there, but let's not get stuck on that. It seems like you're upset at me for _____. Tell me more about that."

8.   Arguing/Debating

Sometimes this is just a heightened form of correcting – you're going back and forth about what happened or what should happen. Again, stay away from trying

to ascertain what "really" happened in the past; you're not a character on *Law &
Order*. It also applies to the future, though: debating the merits of a certain course
of action in your childrearing policy is not relevant until you've gone through the
listening and exploration that's needed. Maybe your preschooler should be expected
to do certain chores at home and maybe not but the arguments in favor or against
are a waste of breath until you both understand where the other person is coming
from emotionally ("I'm worried he'll grow up to be entitled;" "I feel guilty taking
away his playtime"). During the resolution conversation, debating the merits –
within the context of your understanding of each other's feelings – may have a useful place.

That said, it's important to remember that in some marriages a friendly back-
and-forth is comfortable, appreciated, even expected, and in others it is not. Don't
assume that what's normal for you is also normal for your spouse. Ask!

9. Convincing

Here's another flavor of some of the previous Category B activities. Maybe you
respond to something your spouse says by trying to convince them that's not how
it happened (correcting), or that's not what you meant (explaining), or that they
should do something different (solving). Or you're just trying to convince them to
think or feel differently: "Do you really think it makes sense to get angry at your
supervisor over this mistake?" If you're trying to convince them, you are not taking
in their perspective and feelings; you are trying to put yours into them. That's the
opposite of what we're trying to accomplish here. This is especially true if it comes
with a hint of pressure: "Here's why we need to be getting a new car right now..."

10. Rationalizing/Justifying

Again, these are closely related to explaining
and arguing. When your spouse shares how they feel
about something you did and you respond not by
denying that it happened (correcting) but by ration-
alizing or justifying your actions, what you are doing

> Sorry to sound
> like a broken
> record – this is
> not about right
> or wrong.

is you're trying to make yourself be not wrong. The critical point here, again, is
that you don't have to do that. Because – sorry to sound like a broken record – this

is not about right or wrong. Even if you had good reason to do what you did, you will get much farther if you stop to understand the impact it had on them before considering for yourself whether whatever you said or did was in fact acceptable or not.

Remember that none of the content of the exploration phase "goes to court" – meaning, you are not held in future discussions to opinions and feelings you express now – and make sure you are both in agreement on this. (It's helpful to repeat that before or even during the conversation so everyone remembers what the goal is.) That way, if your spouse is hurt by something you did, you don't feel compelled to justify your actions so as not to have a black mark on your record forever and ever.

Let's say your spouse tells you they were uncomfortable that you lost your temper with the kids last night. You may fear that if you don't clear your name – you were right to be angry because of such-and-such reasons; you didn't "lose your temper," you chose to raise your voice to make a point; etc. – your spouse will think you're out of control, a bad parent, untrustworthy, etc. The point is that holding back from justifying/explaining/correcting is *not* an admission that you think it was wrong to raise your voice, or even that you did so! It is simply accepting that this is their reality and trying to understand how they felt. If you can both hold onto that perspective – and it can definitely help to explicitly put it back out there from time to time – you can make it through the listening without getting suckered into justifying.

(Note that the way *not* to do this well is to hear your spouse out and say, "Well, I think you're wrong, but I hear you think that." That is obviously not empathic communication. Rather, you might at times during the conversation say, "Just checking – we're living in your world right now, right?" Or if you hear something you feel an urge to justify, you can say, "I'm going to really try to see how you see this; but I'll have a chance to share my point of view later, right?" This can help you relieve the pressure to set the record straight right away. We'll discuss this more below.)

People Are Different and That's Okay

Another common dynamic that you may experience is that the more one party tries to reassure or explain or convince, the more the other insists that the problem is a problem. This is very frustrating for both parties! Mom might be nervous about Junior going for his first sleepover, while Dad thinks he'll be just fine. So he reassures Mom that Junior can handle it. What's Mom's response? She brings up more reasons why they should be worried; Dad has an answer for each one, or else he just dismisses her concerns as overprotectiveness. Which leads to Mom ratcheting up the anxiety, and so on. What's happening here?

Mom is trying to convince Dad that there is a real concern here and that she's right to be apprehensive. Dad is trying to establish that there really aren't any valid concerns and get Mom to calm down. *This is unnecessary and unproductive.* This brings us to another key principle worth keeping in your pocket: **you and your spouse do not need to feel the same way about things**. It is totally allowed for Mom to be nervous and Dad to be confident. Nobody has to convince the other person that their own perspective is the correct one or get their spouse to feel more like they do. You can have different feelings and different experiences of the situation and *that's just fine.*

Instead of going back and forth over who is "correct," the way out of this is (surprise!) empathic dialogue, in which you explore and seek to understand the feelings each of you is having about the situation. If you approach this as a debate, it will become one. If you approach this from a "help me understand" mindset, you will get much further.

What do we do about Junior? Whatever the answer is, it will not be arrived at by convincing Mom to calm down or Dad to tense up. First, both of them need to have their feelings heard. Mom is anxious about Junior having a miserable time and feeling bad about himself, which leads her to question herself as a parent. Dad is more worried that he'll never be able to face challenges if Mom keeps coddling him (and in fact is quite angry in general that she's been doing so for so long). There's a lot under the surface here. And once they go through it all, *nobody has to change how they feel.* You feel nervous. I feel confident. *No problem.*

The truth is, it's likely Mom's anxiety will go down a little bit just by getting Dad's understanding, and Dad's annoyance at her will be lessened by her validating how he feels, but not because they actively tried to get the other person to let go of their feelings. Now that there is mutual understanding and empathy, they can move to the resolution phase even as they continue to feel disparately about the situation and work on solutions that might meet both of their needs. It's not a zero-sum game where either Junior goes or he doesn't. Once they know what the concerns are, they can come up with ideas to address them. For example, maybe Junior takes a cell phone with him to ease Mom's safety concerns, and at the same time they work on messaging that communicates to Junior they have confidence he can do this. But the solution is secondary and the dialogue is primary – not just in terms of communication success, but even for Junior's benefit: *far more than Junior needs to go to this sleepover, he needs parents who have a loving, secure marriage.*

CATEGORY C

Category C responses include all the things you should *never* do when you are the listener. This certainly includes all the don'ts we mentioned in the speaker section, such as mocking, name-calling, shouting, threatening, etc. Let's add a few more important ones to keep in mind as the listener:

1.   Invalidating

We are going to talk a lot about validation soon. So *in*validating your spouse is definitely going in the wrong direction. Invalidating says, "Your feelings don't matter." That is very much not the message you want to convey in your marriage. Generally people don't say that outright (though you'd be surprised by the things I hear in the therapy room...). Instead, they respond to their spouse complaining, "This house is such a mess!" with comments like, "What's the big deal?" Which really means, "It's *not* a big deal." Which really means, "Maybe you think this is a big deal, but you're wrong." Which ultimately means, "Your feelings don't matter." [Cue wrong-answer buzzer sound.]

Invalidating also conveys the message that what your spouse is feeling isn't *valid,* meaning that they *shouldn't* feel that way. It positions you as the judge of what is right and what is wrong. Unless perhaps you are the Pope, you probably are not in that position. And I don't know about you, but I would not much like to be married to the Pope anyway.

Apart from people who have a genuine psychotic disorder, everyone's feelings and reactions to a given situation make sense on some level.[2] You may not like what you're hearing, you may not agree with it, but you should not invalidate it.

2. Counterattacking

If you believe you are being attacked (whether or not that is actually the case), you are likely to get defensive. If you get defensive, you are likely to get angry. If you get angry, you are likely to lash out, blame, and attack. It may be true that the best defense is a good offense, but you are not playing football and you should not be aiming to take down your spouse.

A counterattack is when you throw the hot potato back at your spouse. "I am so frustrated that you didn't clean up the kitchen like you said you would," they say to you. "Well if you hadn't left all your dishes out maybe it wouldn't look like such a disaster!!!" You try to take the blame off of you and put it on them. But if you're kicking around blame, you're already off track. You probably recognize that this is not a great way to approach communication in your marriage, but maybe you find yourself there anyway when you are worked up. Understandable! Don't

> It may be true that the best defense is a good offense, but you are not playing football and you should not be aiming to take down your spouse.

---

[2] To be clear, just because someone has a mental illness doesn't mean their feelings *don't* make sense. I just mean to say that only if they have a mental disorder that affects their thinking, such as paranoid schizophrenia, is it legitimate to suppose this.

forget to take a break when you start feeling things ramping up. Come back later and do it well instead. (Note that if you are using this strategy in a calculated fashion to avoid having to admit wrongdoing or change your behavior, you are most certainly heading for marital failure.)

Tit for Tat

One of the tactics people sometimes use in dealing with marital conflict is to return fire on their spouse, behaving in the same way they are accusing their spouse of doing. When confronted with this, they explain that they want their spouse to "see what it feels like." This always and only makes things worse. It is a documented fact that not once in the history of the universe has someone said, "Wow, I didn't realize what I was doing was so hurtful, but now that you're hurting me in the same way, I have so much more empathy for you and I will definitely not do that again!" This does not happen. What happens is that the spouse gets angrier, nastier, and more defensive.

If the goal is to get your spouse to change what they're doing, this is not a good strategy. (If your goal is really just to hurt them so you can feel some sense of satisfaction, please check in with yourself to see if that course of action aligns with your personal values.) Trying to get people to change by causing pain has been shown not to work very well (check out the research on spanking children if you'd like to verify that). Sure, you're hurt. Sure, you want to make that clear. It is a natural human response to want to pay it back. It is also an unhelpful one. If you are looking for good communication and a good marriage, you are called upon to rise above that inclination and do it differently. This means taking a timeout as needed, then pushing yourself to use the communication strategies in this book to achieve real dialogue and real growth.

3. Whatabouting

Instead of pushing the blame for a particular situation back onto your spouse, you can always find something else to blame them for! This is another great strategy for prolonging a fight and increasing feelings of bitterness and resentment all around.

"I'm upset that you forgot to put the laundry in the dryer again."

"Well I'M upset that you let your friends use the car without asking me!"

Now you have *two* fights, not just one. Similar to the injunction against kitchen sinking, stick to one issue at a time. If you're mad that your spouse forgot to walk the dogs, that's perfectly legitimate; the time to deal with that is *not* when they're upset about the kitchen. Nor is it legitimate to throw that complaint out there simply as a way of avoiding your spouse's anger. Nothing about empathic dialogue absolves you of taking responsibility for mistakes you've made.

You may also be incensed at the hypocrisy of your spouse for getting upset at you for something they themselves do/did! Again, totally legitimate. Deal with it later. In that moment, you hear out their feelings about this situation. Later, when it's your turn as speaker, you'll share how infuriating it is to hear them get angry at you over something they themselves are guilty of.[3] Stick to the issue at hand; don't "whatabout" a different (even if related) one.

CATEGORY A

Finally, and well out of order, we arrive at Category A. Category A comprises the only four things you want to do when you are the listener. *Four things, and nothing else.* Ready? They are:

1. Listen
2. Reflect in your Own Words
3. Validate
4. Empathize

Don't worry, you actually won't have trouble remembering this, because the acronym is LOVE.[4] And these are so important, I'm going to repeat them here:

---

[3] See how I didn't say "...over them being a hypocrite"? That would be labeling or even name-calling. Accurate? Perhaps. Productive? No.

[4] Okay, I had to massage it a bit with the Own Words part – but that part isn't trivial, I promise. Read on.

1. **L**isten

2. Reflect in your **O**wn Words

3. **V**alidate

4. **E**mpathize

Time for the deep dive. Let's go.

* * *

Blake: *Ugh. I totally messed up this mulligatawny soup. I spent so much time on it and now it's just a mess!*

Tyler: *Oh, honey, I'm sorry. You sound totally frustrated.*

Blake: *Seriously. My whole afternoon for nothing.*

Tyler: *Yeah, no wonder you're all upset. I'm sorry that happened to you.*

[They hug. And nobody gets yelled at.]

Chapter 5

Listening

Mel: GAAAH. I just had the most crazymaking call with the site supervisor.

Terrence: What happened?

Mel: Well, first he brought up the cybersecurity issue again and then— Hey, are you listening?

Terrence: Yeah, I'm listening.

Mel: Okay, well, maybe stop looking at your phone when I'm talking.

Terrence: I'm not looking at my phone. Don't worry, I'm listening.

Mel: Okay, so, he brings up the same old issues again and then he says he's going to have to find a contractor to deal with it and—

[DING! There's a notification on Terrence's phone. Terrence reaches for it instinctively but then puts it back down.]

Mel: How is this listening?

Terrence: I'm listening! You just said the supervisor's being a jerk again and he wants to find a contractor.

Mel: Whatever. What's for dinner?

Let's talk about what goes into the listening part of communication. As we noted, proper listening requires more than just hearing what is said. It is much more active than that. Recall that the job of the speaker is to help the listener see what the world looks like through their eyes – ergo, the job of the listener is to try to see exactly that. You're going to try to go live in their universe for a little bit and get a feel for what it's like over there. You are leaving your own universe. You are leaving your own perspective. Your opinions – just for the time being – are not relevant. As we suggested previously, it's as if you're taking out your brain and leaving it on the table beside you while you try to temporarily adopt your spouse's brain.

So listening is actually going to be a very active process as you try to understand what your spouse is saying as fully as possible while at the same time being mindful of your own biases creeping in. If your spouse is sharing their experience of getting pulled over by the cops, perhaps they'll talk about how scary it was. You might feel more angry than scared, or embarrassed, or whatever your own personal experience would be. It is very easy to filter what your spouse is sharing through your own lens. It is critical to try to understand what *their* lens is and to not allow yourself to interpret what they're saying through *your* lens. What does this situation mean in your spouse's world? It is almost certainly different, if only a little bit, from what it means in your world. Don't settle for assumptions and preconceptions. Really clear your mind of preconceived notions and listen closely to how your spouse describes their feelings around the subject matter at hand. Don't think about how *you* would handle the situation if it were you. *Certainly* don't sit there thinking about what you're going to say in response. Just try to understand as you listen.

Being an active participant in the listening process also requires you to engage in some basic listening etiquette. To wit:

GIVE YOUR FULL ATTENTION

I wish this were obvious enough that I didn't need to say it, but just in case: *turn off your phone*. This means actually off, or on silent (not vibrate), or in a different room where you can't hear it. Even if you don't pick it up, when you get that deliciously enticing notification sound or buzz, your focus is pulled away from your spouse. It adds to your cognitive load, and you will need all your mental and emotional faculties on board to knock this out of the park.

Not always will you be sitting down to a planned empathic dialogue session; sometimes you find yourselves moving into one more organically. No problem! That's life. When your phone rings in the middle, just say, "Hey, one sec, let me turn this off" instead of ignoring it and allowing the dings to keep coming (or worse, checking them briefly to make sure you don't miss an important celebrity meme). It's an easy way to convey respect for your spouse and for the process.

Full attention also means making eye contact if you're facing each other (and if this is a cultural norm for you – in America it certainly is, but if you and/or your spouse are from another culture, possibly not). You do not *have* to face each other – meaningful talks on a long drive can be wonderful, as can pillow talk at night. But if you *are* facing each other, looking around the room at your watch, or at your phone (*Turn. Off. Your. Phone.*) are good ways to totally blow your attempt at connecting.

> It's not enough just to pay attention to your spouse; you want to *demonstrate* that you're paying attention as well.

But it's not enough just to pay attention to your spouse; you want to *demonstrate* that you're paying attention as well. There are many ways we accomplish this, in addition to eye contact:

- Your posture: Leaning back, slouching, resting your arms behind your head – all these "relaxed" positions convey nonchalance and a dash of apathy. You would not sit like that if your boss were speaking with you about an important project or a raise. When you are talking about something that is truly important to you, you are likely sitting up, maybe leaning a bit forward, with your body turned towards the other person. These are good practices in an important marital conversation as well.

- Your arms: Likewise, your hands and arms convey a lot of information. An excellent way to communicate to your spouse that you don't think much of what they're saying is to cross your arms as you're listening. (Combine that with leaning back and you'll nail the arrogant and skeptical look.) If your hands are constantly moving around, fixing your hair, or fiddling with your phone (*NO!*), it can be distracting and again send the message that you are not fully present. (If keeping your hands static is challenging for you, a fidget toy – one that doesn't make noise! – can be helpful, so long as it doesn't require you to look at it or focus on it beyond keeping your hands busy.)

- Your face: Wipe that scowl off your face. You may not like what you're hearing, especially if your spouse is mad at you (and *especially* if you're sure they're wrong), but showing all kinds of reactions on your face, shaking your head as you listen, or employing other prickly nonverbal communications isn't any less provocative than coming out and saying what you're thinking anyway (arguably it's more so). So the grimace, the eye-roll, the snort, the huff, the deep sigh, the temple rub – drop it. You will have the opportunity to share your feelings about what you're hearing, but that opportunity is not now. By contrast, nodding, cocking your head, raising your eyebrows at appropriate times – these convey attention and interest. (Minimal verbal responses – what they call "encouragers" – such as "Mm-hmm," "Yeah," "I see," and so on are also valuable to this end.[1])

PAY ATTENTION TO YOURSELF, TOO

This point in the process can actually be the hardest part of the whole thing: you hear your spouse saying something about the marriage, about you, about something (they think) you said, and in an instant you can feel yourself stretched to the limit, seething, highly defensive. *This is normal.* But it doesn't mean you just let it all out. Managing your own reaction is a key part of getting communication to work. This can be tough. Trust me, I know it can. I am human. I find myself in the same position at times.

> Managing your own reaction is a key part of getting communication to work. This can be tough.

One time Chana was furious with me for not laying down the line with the kids after a particularly egregious incident of their disrespecting her authority. She heatedly shared (well after the incident) that she felt disrespected by me for my choice, as well as unsupported and undercut. I felt strongly that what had been needed in that situation was a softer approach – not because she was wrong that they had been totally out of line (they had), but because, in my view, hardlining it with them would just have

---

[1] Note that these can all be culture-specific. In the US, encouragers are a normal part of conversation. When my wife and I visited South Korea to meet her birth family, we learned that they are a *critical* part of conversation there, especially from someone of lower social or familial status to someone of higher status.

elicited pushback and zero self-reflection, growth, or forward movement on their part. It was very difficult for me to hear her feelings about the situation and how she saw my role in it, but I gritted my teeth (if only because I tend to report these things back to my clients and I wanted to look good) and did my best to accept her view as simply her view of things, not necessarily the reality.

And this is an example of the speaker doing it well! It's 16 times harder when your spouse *isn't* doing a great job speaking about themselves and is instead accusing you, blaming you, judging you, or otherwise drawing freely from the list of don'ts. Pay attention to your emotional state as you do your listening job so you don't lose your cool when it's too much for you.

Another common reaction you might have to hearing your spouse's anger about a certain situation is to feel guilty. You may recognize (consciously or unconsciously) that they're actually right, at least in part, and again you begin to defend yourself, or try to spin the situation to make yourself look less bad, or perhaps even run right into apologizing to rid yourself of that most uncomfortable guilty feeling. But this too is a result of focusing on your own feelings in the moment rather than putting yourself aside and getting into your spouse's world.

So yes, this is a pivotal and challenging moment. But it's doable. You can get through this without losing your commitment to being a listener. Here are some strategies for getting through those situations:

- Restate at the beginning of the conversation that both of you recognize that the speaker is simply sharing their perspective and not demanding that it be accepted as the gospel truth. (It is more effective to do this at the get-go than on the fly, because responding to their perspective with "Okay but this is just your perspective, right?" tends to be heard as "I'm listening but I don't agree," which is dismissive and even inflammatory.[2])

- Acknowledge in your head, or even out loud to your spouse, that you're feeling defensive and take a minute to reset yourself in a position of being in their world.

- Just take a few deep breaths to calm down the ol' autonomic nervous system.

---

[2] On the other hand, it can be darn helpful for the speaker to remind the listener that they know what they're saying just represents their own perspective and not objective reality.

- Say, "Hang on, this is hard for me, but I really want to listen." Proceed slowly so you don't get overwhelmed.

- Take a break! If you are getting too emotionally reactive, remember to call a timeout for the sake of the marriage. Interrupt if you have to. Interrupting may not be an optimal communication device, but it's better than waiting too long and blowing up. Don't try to white-knuckle it through only to lose your cool a few minutes later!

If it feels like you have been swallowing a lot of hard-to-hear comments and you can't listen to any more of it, it's also fair to ask for a role reversal so that you can relieve some of that emotional pressure: "Honey, hold on a sec, I think I'm a little overloaded and there's some things you're saying that are really bothering me. Would we be able to switch so I can say some of my stuff for a bit?" Then you can – with appropriate speaker practices – unload some of the feelings that are building up. *But this must be done with your spouse's permission.* If they are still wound up in their own emotions and are not in a place to listen to you, it is futile to try to get them to do so in order for you to be able to lower your own reactivity, and the best approach in that case would again be to take a break.

If you find that none of these strategies is working for you and/or you are simply unable to control your reactions in these situations, that despite your best efforts you can't seem to move the needle towards more self-restraint – consider seeking out a therapist who can help you learn the skills of emotion regulation. You will gain an awful lot not just in managing these conversations with your spouse but in many areas of your life.[3]

HELP A PARTNER OUT AGAIN

Just as the speaker has a responsibility to support the listener in doing their job by helping them stay on track, so it is incumbent upon the listener to save the speaker when the speaker isn't on point. One way this might be necessary is to stop them every few sentences so you can take in what they're saying. If they aren't putting in

---

[3]   I am not in any way implying here that you are a bad or defective person if you get really emotional; many people, through no fault of their own, never picked up the skills of self-regulation and can gain a lot from learning them. For some, issues like trauma, attachment disturbances, or neurodivergence can increase the difficulty and can be markedly improved with therapy and mental health care.

appropriate pauses, jump in as needed so you can make sure you're absorbing their message. You won't come out with much if you sit and listen for 20 minutes straight.

Another common pitfall of the speaker is the tendency to fall back into speaking about you instead of themselves. If you notice this happening, gently redirect them: "Wait wait wait – I'm feeling a little defensive here – I think you're talking about me again. Could you help me understand *you?*" Be constructive; don't just scold them with "THAT'S NOT HOW YOU'RE SUPPOSED TO DO THIS." That is just another step in the wrong direction.

Similarly, if your partner has gotten stuck in facts, timelines, or he-said-she-said, move the conversation back towards feelings. You can do this nonconfrontationally:

- "...and so when that happened, how did you feel?"
- "What is/was that like for you?"
- "What about that bothers you?"
- "How did that make you feel?"
- What was it like to be you in that moment?
- Help me understand your experience there.
- What's the message to you when I do that?
- Why is it important for me to know this?

> You can't control your partner or make them talk to you the way you would like, but you *can* support them in staying on track.

You can't control your partner or make them talk to you the way you would like, but you *can* support them in staying on track.

ASKING QUESTIONS

Again, listening isn't meant to be a silent process. You can ask questions to clarify and deepen your understanding. BUT – you must be vigilant about staying in your partner's world. If you are truly trying to understand them, your question is probably okay. If you are even in part trying to get *them* to understand *you* – to make a point of your own – such a question is not okay, meaning, it will not take you in the right direction. So, when you are the listener:

DO ask questions:

- To keep up with your partner: "Can you repeat that? I don't think I understood that part."
- To make sure you got the right information: "Wait, so your *mother* said that, or it was your sister?"
- To clarify: "So you're saying what happened made you feel jealous? Or more just angry?"
- To deepen your understanding: "When you say you felt insecure, what is it about spending the weekend apart that makes you feel that way?"
- To connect to other things they've shared: "Is that feeling similar to what you told me happened with your cousin last Thanksgiving?"

But DON'T ask questions:

- To elicit facts: "How many text messages did that creepy guy send you?"
- To correct/challenge something that was said: "Are you sure that's what I was doing when you walked in?"
- To pivot the conversation in a different direction: "So if you feel overloaded with all the housework, why are you always going out with your friends at night?"
- To produce a particular answer (i.e., leading questions): "And so then you felt better about the situation, right?"
- To promote your own position: "But don't you see why I made that decision?"
- To corner your partner into a particular position: "Do you really think the mainstream media is objective, or do you just not care about the truth?"
- To analyze your partner: "Is it possible that you feel that way because of how your father treated you when you were a child?"
- To judge your partner: "Why would you keep talking to him at that point?!?"

Basically, anything that sounds like a Category B activity could go on this list.

Some unhelpful questions can be recognized by whether they could equally be communicated as a statement. Check out some of the examples above. The intent of "Are you sure that's what I was doing when you walked in?" is really, "That's not what I was doing when you walked in." "Don't you see why I made that decision?" is really, "I had a good reason to make that decision."

Tone also makes a big difference. "Why did you get into the car with her?" might be a genuine exploratory question if your partner was sharing how they felt nervous about their rideshare, or it might be very judgmental if it's said more like "Why [the heck] did you get into the car with her???" The bottom line is that you need to make sure you are trying to get into their world, without bringing your own stuff in there with you. Listening is about mentally and emotionally following your partner wherever they go as they show you around their internal terrain. If they lead you forward, you walk with them forward. If they turn to the right, you follow them to the right. If you lose them among some trees, you say, "Hey, where did you go? I didn't follow you there." You don't say, "Do you think maybe you should be turning left here?" This backseat driver kind of attitude is the opposite of real listening.

> Listening is about mentally and emotionally following your partner wherever they go as they show you around their internal terrain.

Even a well-meaning question can be poorly received if you're bringing your own assumptions and opinions into the mix. For example, let's say one of the points of friction in your marriage is that your partner is always late to things, and you are the punctual type.[4] So your partner is talking about this frustrating experience they had trying to get to their conference on time, and the directions were off, and there was no parking, etc., and you're following along, and you ask, "was part of the frustration that you were supposed to be there already 10 minutes earlier?" This is you bringing in your own stuff. You already know that your partner doesn't much mind being late the same way you do. They hadn't mentioned the lateness as a problem or a contributor to their stress. This would likely not be received as a true listening question, because it's coming from your own perspective and not the one they are sharing with you now.

---

[4] If this is an issue in your marriage, you are in the company of many other couples.

Look, it's really, really hard to get *totally* out of your own head and into someone else's; if you're genuinely trying to do so, an off-target question probably won't sink the process. But if you're not really putting the effort into neutrally listening to them and instead are just filtering everything they say through your own lens, such a question will likely convey exactly that.

GIVE ME EXAMPLES

Sometimes people share a feeling about their partner or marriage and their partner responds with, "Give me an example of when I did that." This is usually not coming from an empathic place. If you are saying this in an angry, annoyed, or skeptical tone – and your partner is going to pick that up, make no mistake – you are back to arguing about facts. The implication of this "question" is that if they can't come up with an example, it means their perception is invalid, their version of the situation is made up, and they shouldn't feel the way they do. It means you are right and they are wrong. Of course, if this is where you're coming from, then even if they do provide an example, you will likely argue that that's not what happened, or that's not what you meant, or you employ some other Category B tactic, and things will not end well.

On the other hand, if you are genuinely confused as to why they are feeling the way they're feeling, maybe an example *would* help. If you come from a "help me understand" place (remember that one?), the tone will be markedly different: "I'm not really clear what you mean when you feel tension between us sometimes. Can you give me an example of that?"

> Even if your partner cannot come up with an example, they are still entitled to their feelings.

Note, however, that even if your partner cannot come up with an example, *they are still entitled to their feelings*, and you should listen, reflect in your own words, validate, and empathize nonetheless. If it is frustrating to you that they seem to be having a negative reaction to something you don't think you did and you don't have any examples of, you are absolutely encouraged to share this when it's your turn to be the speaker. But right now, you are in your partner's world, and even if there is a hole in the map, it won't help much to patch it up with something that doesn't reflect the terrain; better to leave it an unknown for now, and perhaps on another exploration journey you'll try again to map it out.

You may be wondering how on earth you're going to fix the problem if you don't think you're actually doing it and you're not allowed to ask for examples. Ah, but recall, we are not trying to fix the problem! At this point we are just exploring it to the best of our ability and conveying our empathy. Solutions later.

A LITTLE LISTENING IS A LOT

Not only does listening take more effort than you might have thought, it can also, all on its own, be more powerful than you imagined. Sometimes when I'm too angry to respond well (but not so angry that I'm going to lose my cool), I just shut up, listen, and nod – and that can be enough (provided I'm able to keep stupid comments from getting out of my mouth.) Just my willingness to listen to how you feel without having to argue – that says a lot.

* * *

Mel: *GAAAH. I just had the most crazymaking call with the site supervisor.*

Terrence: *What happened?*

Mel: *Well, –*

Terrence: *Hang on, let me silence my phone.*

[Terrence turns the phone to silent and faces Mel.]

Terrence: *Okay, shoot, I'm listening now.*

Chapter 6

Reflecting in Your Own Words

Shira: *I'm worried that Kayla isn't going to like her new teacher.*

Levi: *Mm-hmm.*

Shira: *And she's so anxious in school already, I'm just nervous it's going to make things even worse.*

Levi: *Mm-hmm.*

Shira: *And then we'll have a situation like we did two years ago, which I am not going through again.*

Levi: *Mm-hmm.*

Shira: *Are you even listening?*

Levi: *Mm-hmm.*

In the last chapter, we pointed out that it's not enough to listen to your spouse; you have to *show* them that you're listening too. If you're scrolling on your phone while they talk to you, they are not going to feel heard, even if you can repeat everything they said verbatim. (In fact, this is a great way to prove you're right AND upset your spouse – just respond to "You're not listening to me!" with "Sure I am!" and then proceed to accurately rattle off everything they just said. Add a subtle smirk for extra effect.)

Likewise, it is not enough to understand what your spouse is saying either. You have to *show* them you understand. That's what Reflecting in Your Own Words does. When you reflect back what you've heard from them, they can be confident that you got the message they're trying to convey. The marriage benefits *somewhat* from you getting the message and a *whole lot* from your spouse *knowing* that you got the message. So it won't cut it to just say, "I understand" or "I get it" or "mm-hmm."[1]

> It is not enough to understand what your spouse is saying either. You have to *show* them you understand.

Because maybe you do and maybe you don't. But until your spouse hears you reflect it back to them, they simply can't be sure. (Recall our previous remarks on the human inability to know what's in someone else's head.) You want them to be sure.

And this of course assumes that you *do* get it! The other objective that Reflecting in Your Own Words accomplishes is to confirm that this is in fact the case. Because no matter how obvious it seems, you will sometimes find that you just aren't on the same page. The whole point of communicating with each other is to get on the same page.[2] To do that, you need to compare pages! It's true that some couples are so in tune that they can finish each other's sentences. This usually takes a lot of time and a lot of good communication to get there. Rare – *very* rare – is the couple that sees the world so similarly to each other that they're always on the same page to begin with. Don't assume you are that couple.

Reflecting in Your Own Words ensures that you understand what's being shared. If you don't understand, you aren't going to be able to make any change in the situation (if the situation calls for a change). Remember, you can't solve a problem you don't understand!

---

[1] We did note in the last chapter that using encouragers like these along the way is indeed a good way to show you're engaged and paying attention; they just don't replace the need for a fuller reflection. Encouragers may demonstrate that you are listening, but they don't demonstrate that you are understanding.

[2] Remember that being on the same page doesn't mean agreeing on your perspectives or adopting the same feelings as your partner. Ultimately, you and your partner are reading from different books as you go through life. But stepping into their world means taking a look at their book and reading along with them for a bit. You can't do that if you're not looking at the same page.

WHAT'S THE POINT?

When you are Reflecting in Your Own Words you are trying to make your spouse feel heard. To do so, you are going to recap what you heard them say. Since, as we know well by now, this is not about facts, you do not need to capture every detail they mentioned. This is not a test, and you are not trying to prove the excellence of your memory by demonstrating that you can remember everything they tell you. You are trying to show you get what they're going through. More important than remembering the details is capturing the experience they're having.

An analogy: Imagine your friend pours their heart and soul into a painting. They really unleash their creativity, articulating themselves through this expressive medium, investing the canvas with a piece of themselves. They bring you before this piece of art that is hugely significant to them and show it to you, hoping it will convey to you some of the profound meaning about themselves they put into it. They want you to understand the depth, the meaning, the feelings that went into it. You take it in slowly, considering the various elements in the painting, the colors, the focus, the techniques used. You close your eyes and share your impression: "There is a large horse in the middle of the painting... a bit right of center. He has a red saddle. He seems to be sniffing at a tree that appears to be, oh, maybe a Japanese maple? Looks like it's springtime." Is your friend feeling understood, appreciated, connected? I doubt it. This is not what we might call "getting it." Getting it looks like this: "There's a horse there – he is full of energy and vitality, and the whole painting seems like it's coming to life around him. He's beneath a tree – but not overshadowed. He's still front and center. There's a lot of joy here." See? The artist is nodding along with you. It doesn't matter if you noticed the red saddle or not. You got the message. (If the red saddle is in fact part of the message, the artist will let you know that as you try to grasp the greater message being conveyed here.)

> More important than remembering the details is capturing the experience they're having.

The truth is, reflecting may not be the best term for what we're doing here. I went with that word because it's familiar and commonly used in therapy circles, but I don't like it as a metaphor for our process. A reflection is when a beam of light hits a surface and that same beam of light bounces back (in Imago Therapy, this kind of listening process is actually called "mirroring"). But that's not a great approach. Reflecting in Your Own Words is not just bouncing back the same words you just heard. You can't just respond to "I am angry and hurt that you forgot my birthday" with "You are angry and hurt that I forgot your birthday." Merely repeating back what you heard is in fact quite irritating (have someone try it out on you and see for yourself!). This is why, as we noted earlier, the "in Your Own Words" part is crucial.

Really, this process is more like a video camera than a mirror: the beam of light is captured by the camera, stored, and then faithfully reproduced for the viewer. You are the camera. You take in what your spouse says, integrate it into yourself, and then share it back again so that they know it's inside you now. It's like in English class when you were asked to explain in your own words the theme of whatever classic work of literature they were trying to force you to appreciate. It was not supposed to be a test of whether you memorized the book; it was a question of whether you now understand the concepts, have made them a part of you, and can carry them around with you. You are trying to make your spouse a part of you.

> You take in what your spouse says, integrate it into yourself, and then share it back again so that they know it's inside you now.

Rod and Li had been together for a number of years in varying configurations of their marriage. Rod was often abroad, tackling complicated engineering projects, and they were generally content with their loosely defined partnership. Over time, however, Li began feeling increasingly dissatisfied with their communication. Nothing she said seemed to get across to him – in her view. Rod was baffled and frustrated; he didn't know what wasn't working and was perfectly ready to do whatever was needed to improve things, if he could figure out what that was.

I watched them in action. Often when Li would try to share something with Rod he would repeat it back matter-of-factly, as if he were being tested on the material he had heard. It wasn't a word-for-word recap, but sometimes it was close. "I'm saying what she said, aren't I? Why isn't that good enough?"

I explained it to him in the following way to appeal to his mathematical persona: "If you teach me how to solve a certain geometry problem and I can repeat back to you *what you said, that doesn't mean I understand the mathematical concepts. It just means I have good recall. How do you know if I actually grasped the principles? If I can then teach it to someone else. That doesn't require me to remember what you said at all; if I understood what you taught me, then I've integrated the knowledge into my own mind. I can pass on the concepts to someone else, even if I forget we ever had this conversation — and when I do so, it will come from a deeper part of me than just my working memory."*

HOW TO DO IT

So how is reflecting done? In some ways, it's pretty simple. You just say back what you heard – not the words, but the ideas. Start your sentence with "you."

"You feel unsupported when I don't have time to discuss your project with you."

"You're uncomfortable with the way I was talking to your friends at the bar yesterday."

> How is reflecting done? Start your sentence with "you."

I recommend staying away from some catch-phrases that you may have seen in other books or on a website somewhere, such as "What I hear you saying..." or "I understand that you feel..." See how these sentences started with "I"? You are ever so slightly keeping the focus on you, when your role at this point is to leave your own experience as much as possible and get into your partner's world. That's why I encourage people to go right into "you."

If you're not 100% clear on what your partner is trying to convey, you can be a little more tentative with your reflection:

"Are you saying that you felt kind of ignored at the party?"

"So you were totally excited at first but then it kind of got boring?"

Asking questions for clarification is also totally fine (as we mentioned in the listening section):

"Okay, so you weren't sure what you were supposed to do in that situation, so you felt... actually, I'm not quite sure. How did you feel then?"

It's also okay to guess a little bit, to extrapolate, to infer, to conjecture. Maybe your partner is telling you about the job interview that went poorly today. You might reflect, "You feel really bad about how you showed up in the interview." They nod their head. "I wonder if maybe you're saying you're also embarrassed about not looking professional enough?" Your partner didn't say this, but you know them pretty well; this kind of issue has been mentioned before. And maybe you get a sense of shame as they speak, you hear a wavering in their voice. So you conjecture that this is a piece of it too. Don't worry if you're not certain – if you're being sincere in trying to understand your partner, they'll let you know if you're off target. Your effort counts for a lot – and not only that, but by offering a reasonable perspective to consider, you are also opening the door for them to chew on something perhaps they hadn't thought of. It's funny, but the fact is that often we learn more about how we feel when someone else helps us discover it in ourselves. (Indeed, it's because of this fact that I have a job as a therapist!)

> *Chana and I were having a "feelings talk." We often do this at length on Friday nights after the kids have gone to bed (or after we've determined that it's the time they should be in bed and we lock ourselves in our room). We were discussing a training program I had enrolled in that was so far sub-awesome. Chana talked about how she was feeling skeptical about the whole thing. I reflected back what I understood her to be saying (despite feeling an internal pressure from the notes of judgment I was sensing). She did not seem satisfied. I checked myself to make sure I was genuinely understanding her and not dragging my own feelings into it, and I tried again. Still not quite. I thought for a moment and said, "I wonder if there's something else you're feeling that maybe you haven't said here? I think I got everything you said already, can't think of anything you said I missed there."*
>
> *She thought for a moment, then replied, "Well, I guess I just don't know how it's going to turn out."*
>
> *"Oh," I mused, "So maybe it's a feeling of... uncertainty?"*
>
> *That nailed it – and opened up an entirely new vista of what she was going through that deepened not only my understanding of her experience but her own understanding as well.*

It's important that your guesses be just that – guesses, not assertions. If you *declare* that really your partner is not just angry at her sister but she's in fact angry with her whole family for letting her down as a child – if you have an "I know how you're *really* feeling" attitude – then you aren't really hearing your partner, you are constructing your own image of what you believe them to be experiencing (or worse, what you think they *should* be experiencing). This is the very antithesis of what we're trying to achieve, which is to get a clear picture of where your partner is actually at. Remember that you are putting yourself into their world right now. It is normal, even expected, that you perceive things differently than they do; as the listener, your job is to detach from your own interpretations (put your brain on the table beside you) and try your best to understand theirs. You want to eliminate your own filters from interfering in the communication. The "I know how you're *really* feeling" attitude is the very opposite of the "help me understand" mindset, and if that's where you're at, it means their communication is hardly getting across. You're telling them what it's like to be a citizen of their planet while sitting firmly on your own. This will not go over well.

> **Remember that you are putting yourself into their world right now.**

In addition, if you are "guessing" at something your partner didn't say as a clever way to defend yourself or to sneak in your own point, that will not serve you at all either; it will move you in quite the opposite direction.

Lesley: *"I can't believe you didn't lock the car last night! I'm so angry at you!"*

Robin: *"You're mad that I forgot to lock the car. Do you think you might also be a little angry at yourself because you so often forget important things too?"*

[Large fight ensues.]

Your sincerity in trying to understand your partner doesn't come through only in the content of your reflections but also in the tone. You're trying to match where they're at. Empathy means you're sharing their experience. If they're annoyed, your tone should have a little of that in there too. If they're sad, your voice should echo that; you don't want to sound chipper if they're talking about their dying pet. You also don't want to just be rehashing what they're saying in a monotone. If you want to convey that you care, you gotta get in there with them. If they're happy, you're happy *with* them. If they're angry, you're angry *with* them.

But you should not be angry *at* them. If you don't like what your partner is saying – you disagree with it, you resent it, you're insulted by it – those are all legitimate reactions, but remember, you're in *their* world right now. Your anger has no place here – just for the moment. As noted, this may well be the hardest part of the empathic dialogue process. You are having a strong emotional reaction to what you're hearing, but you're called upon to put it off for now. It's doable. You can pull it off. It's not easy, but I have faith that you can make this happen. Hang on to that anger for now. We're not sweeping it under the rug; we're just postponing dealing with it for a short while. We'll circle back when it's your turn to speak and we're back in your world again: "You know, I am really angry that you seem to see me as a lazy person. I work really hard to make ends meet for us, and to hear that you think I'm lazy – that really burns."

Here's the thing: it is possible, and normal, to be angry at your partner for what they're saying and at the same time to care that they're hurting in what they're experiencing. When you feel that anger and pushback rising inside you, take a deep breath; pause for a moment; and look inside yourself for the part of you that truly does feel bad that the person you love most in the world is in pain. Speak from there. Speak from the part that loves and cares, the part that absolutely hates that your soulmate is suffering. It's in there. The other part of you – the hurt part, the mad part, all those parts – will get a chance to air their feelings when you're the speaker if you can just hang on for a bit. You can do this.

> **Take a deep breath; pause for a moment; and look inside yourself for the part of you that truly does feel bad that the person you love most in the world is in pain.**

HOW NOT TO DO IT

Let's go over some of the don'ts for Reflecting in Your Own Words:

Don't argue about the facts.

I know we've been over this. But people do it so often that I have to hammer it home. When your spouse says that when X happened, they felt Y, *do not argue about X*. Just stick to reflecting how *they* remember the experience in *their* head. Because that's where we are right now, in *their* head. If it helps you take some of the pressure off, you can say it like this: "You remember me coming home half an hour late, and you were really disappointed." Please don't overemphasize the word YOU or otherwise inflect your words so as to make it clear that you personally disagree with this, *BUT*... That will come across loud and clear and will put you back into the conflict mode you are reading this book to avoid. If you really can't swallow what you're hearing, you're best off being open about that without losing your empathy:

> *"When you tried to stab me with your spork, I felt really scared."*

> *"Wow. I can't say I remember it like that, but I can totally understand why you'd feel scared in that situation."*

Or, if necessary:

> *"Wow. I'm having a real hard time hearing that's how you remember what happened. Actually, I'm pretty angry about this. I need a break and I'll hear you out more a little later."*

Don't make your own points.

Remember that you're in your spouse's world, and your brain is on the table beside you. This is not the time to bring in your own thoughts and feelings – not explicitly and also not passive-aggressively. Explicit comments are easier to spot, of course. They often start with "but":

> *"I hear that you are angry that I came late, but really I was there on time, I just couldn't find parking."*

> *"You feel hurt when I make fun of your mother. But I wasn't actually making fun of her, I was just trying to point out that..."*

These are actually examples of the cardinal sin of Explaining. What you're saying may well be true. But it won't help. Any time you follow up your reflection with the word "but" (or "however" or "nevertheless" – don't be a wise guy) you are heading in the wrong direction. Usually the stuff that comes before the "but" is the good stuff. Just stop there.

The passive-aggressive responses are harder to name and call out, and therefore usually even more frustrating and more damaging to the marriage.

Donna: *"I really feel disrespected when I ask you to take out the garbage and you say it will get done, and then you fall asleep and I have to do it myself."*

Diego: *"Got it, so, you feel disrespected when you command me to do something and I don't jump up, salute, and obey your wishes that very second."* [*It's hard to convey condescending sarcasm in text, but I think you get the idea.*]

Donna did not say anything about commanding or saluting. Diego introduced those words himself, and it's not because he misheard her. He's making a point (in a rather obnoxious fashion, no less). It's as if he came out and said, "You are an unreasonable tyrant." Actually, Diego would be better off saying that outright than pretending to reflect but doing so disingenuously. Donna is *definitely* feeling even more irritated now, and they are much further from making this problem any better.

Communication Styles

You may have already read or heard about passive vs. assertive vs. aggressive communication styles. We won't be delving too much into these concepts, useful as they are, but I wanted to speak to them briefly since they provide helpful context for what we're trying to do. Let's start by defining them:

Passive communication is when you don't speak clearly for your wants, needs, and experience. You give up control to others to avoid conflict. You allow other people's needs to take precedence and you let them trample your own rights. This is surrender.

Aggressive communication is the opposite: you allow space only for your own wants, needs, and experience and deny or block out anyone else's. You insist on and seize control; you trample other people's rights in order to get your way. This is an attack.

Passive-aggressive communication is where you superficially appear to be pleasant and compliant but in fact are trying to make a point or get your way surreptitiously. You don't respect others' rights but refuse to take a stand for yours. This is sabotage.

Assertive communication is when you stand up for your own rights without trampling the rights of others. You acknowledge both your own needs and those of the people you interact with. You share control over the situation with others rather than seizing or relinquishing it entirely. This is diplomacy.

Here's how each of these might look in an example situation. Let's say it's important to you that your spouse come to your friend's birthday party with you – but they tell you they've already got plans to see a movie with a different friend:

Passive: "Okay, that's fine." (You're not fine with it, but you don't say so and just go along with it.)

Aggressive: "Why are *your* friends always more important than *my* friends? Can't you for once be a little supportive?!" (You attack your spouse for their choice.)

Passive-aggressive: "Well, that's fine, I guess you know who's important in your life." (You're not fine with it, but you're pretending you are while subtly criticizing your spouse.)

Assertive: "Hm. This is a really important event to me. Is there a way we could figure something out so that you can be there?" (You state your position while still respecting that your spouse has their own and acknowledging the need for cooperation.)

You may already have guessed that empathic dialogue is unapologetically assertive. You cannot have a meaningful relationship if you are walking all over your spouse (aggressive), but neither can you have a relationship if you allow your spouse to walk all over you (passive). (You do see a lot of relationships where there is passive-aggressive communication going on, because this communication style is much more insidious and harder to spot, and it wears away at a relationship over the long term rather than causing rapid collapse.) There are two people in this relationship, and its long-term success depends on both of you showing up in it equally. Our entire discussion of effective communication is situated firmly within the framework of assertiveness.

Don't psychoanalyze.

Even if you're going to do some conjecturing, your goal is not to explain the roots of why your spouse feels the way they do.

"So you're unhappy with the new shoes you bought... is that perhaps because you've got a deep, gaping hole inside that you've been trying to fill with material things but can never quite succeed?"

This does not make a person feel heard. If it is too far afield from where they are, it simply won't hit the mark. It comes across to them like you're listening to someone else entirely. (And this is true even if you're such a brilliant psychologist that you totally nail the problem on the head – if it's so far from their awareness that it doesn't resonate with their experience, they won't feel heard.)

Your spouse needs you to help carry the heavy bags they've got with them, not open them up and sift through them. There's a reason therapists do not take their spouses on as clients. This is such a bad idea it would make a good rom-com movie.

Psychoanalyzing is also a great way for people to deflect blame:

"Is it possible that the real reason you thought I was yelling is because your father was emotionally abusive to your mother and you, and so you interpreted my slight change in volume as aggression?"

Please don't.

Don't judge.

"Of course you're angry at yourself for getting sassy with your coworker! That was totally not the way to handle that situation."

We mentioned the interdiction on judging earlier when discussing the role of the speaker, and it goes for the listener too. Empathy and judgment are incompatible. You want your spouse to feel heard, loved, cared about. You cannot feel those things at the same time as you are feeling judged. Feeling heard brings you closer to your spouse. Feeling judged pushes you away.

> Empathy and judgment are incompatible.

Really, all the Category B activities we mentioned in chapter 5 could go on this list of don'ts. It's very easy to start with a reflection and then twist it into one of these other things. Caution is warranted. Stick to trying to understand your spouse's experience. *Do not* insert your own experience, thoughts, opinions, feelings, wishes, wants, or needs back into your reflections.

WHEN YOU TRY TO REFLECT AND YOU GET IT WRONG

What happens when you are really truly trying to understand your partner, you reflect back what you're hearing, and they shake their head and go, "No, that's not it" – then what?

Important point #1: This is normal, remember? You do not live inside your partner's head. You do not experience the world in the same way they do. How could you possibly know what's in there until they communicate it to you clearly? You cannot. If you don't correctly understand your partner on the first (or second, or third) go, *do not panic*. This is okay.

Even more important point #2: *You lose no points for getting it wrong.* Really! You may not get the big payoff of a deep connection through mutual understanding if you swing and miss, but you don't strain the marriage either, and you don't end up in the doghouse. There is one caveat to this, and that is that you must be *genuinely trying* to understand your partner. If you're not listening, if you're scrolling through Instagram while they speak, if you're trying to sneak in your own agenda in your reflection, then yeah, you'll probably make things worse. But if you are really really truly putting in an effort to understand what's going on for your partner, then even if you don't hit the mark, you are still contributing to the marriage. Effort counts for a lot in relationships. Your genuine attempts to understand your partner say a whole lot about your love and care for them.

> If you are really truly putting in an effort to understand what's going on for your partner, then even if you don't hit the mark, you are still contributing to the marriage.

There are a lot of reasons you might get it wrong when you try to reflect:

1. **You weren't really listening as well as you could have.** Hey, this happens to the best of us – you might be tired, stressed, preoccupied, etc. You might discover at this point that you really aren't in shape to do any good listening right now after all.

2. **You were listening, but really you were still focused on how YOU felt about the situation.** You were listening, but really you were still focused on how YOU felt about the situation. It's possible you are human and were sidetracked by your own biases; you're still stuck on your own planet. Check in with yourself and give it another go.

3. **You have different understandings of the same words.** What counts as shouting? What does it mean if two people "hooked up"? If I say I'm angry, does that mean I'm about to lose my temper?

Marlon and Monica were both intelligent, articulate professionals who had been in an on-again, off-again relationship for over a decade. Both were very frustrated with the state of their communications. Marlon was eager to make whatever changes he could to improve things, but he couldn't figure out why his sincere efforts seemed to bear no fruit. Monica felt unheard despite Marlon's attempts to be there for her, but she had trouble expressing the nature of the problem to him.

With empathic dialogue, we were able to start breaking through the impasse. They were different in many ways, and there was a lot of work to do to help them see each other's point of view. One telling moment came when Marlon described his feeling of frustration in the relationship and Monica reflected that he seemed to be feeling "stuck." Marlon rejected this reflection and seemed almost offended. "It's not stuck," he protested. "Stuck means you can't go anywhere." As he tried to explain himself further, I suggested that "Maybe you mean that the relationship is 'stalled' instead of 'stuck'?" "Yeah, stalled." He sounded much more satisfied with that word. "Fine!" huffed Monica, rolling her eyes. "Stalled!" She was exasperated. But this was actually a great teaching moment. I stepped in to explain.

To Marlon, the word "stuck" meant that they could not move forward. That very much rubbed him the wrong way; he did not want to throw in the towel and accept that things could not get better. To Monica, "stuck" just sounded like a temporary description: we're stuck now, but we can get UNstuck! Nobody was right or wrong. But this is exactly the kind of work we're trying to do here – to understand each other and leave our own templates behind. We don't need to argue over the "real" meaning of a word. Instead, we need to understand what it means to each other. A word is just a word, after all. It's your experience I really want to grasp; the word describing it is just the door handle.

4. **Your spouse didn't say what they think they said.** Sometimes it's hard to put an experience into words. Have you ever described a real mountaintop moment and had others fail to appreciate the magnitude of it? You can talk all about your vacation to Iceland, but if your spouse nods and says, "Yeah, it sounds great!" – that probably doesn't fully capture what you intended to convey. It can also be really hard to share painful experiences, and so we sometimes soft-pedal those and don't give the full oomph in the retelling – and then when we hear how it landed on someone else, it's just not the same.

5. **Your spouse didn't say everything they needed to say.** Big experiences are... big. It's normal to have to expand, to rehash, to describe it from different angles before the true picture becomes clear. Moreover, we often fail to state specific points explicitly because we so completely take them for granted; it's incredibly obvious to us that such-and-such is true, so we don't even think to mention it.

6. **You are two different people and see the world differently.** This is the reality. It's hard to grasp how someone else experiences the world. It's hard to take off your glasses and put on someone else's. *That's why we're doing this.*

> It's hard to grasp how someone else experiences the world. It's hard to take off your glasses and put on someone else's. *That's why we're doing this.*

The solution isn't so novel: try again. If your reflection doesn't hit the mark, there's no need to get agitated: just ask them to tell you again so you can give it another shot. If you're not clear on how they're feeling, ask for clarification! (You can do this even before you try to reflect, if you don't think you got it.) You can also reflect what you did understand and leave out the rest for now. Remember, this is a process. If you get a little bit today and a little bit more tomorrow, that's great progress.

You're not stupid if you struggle to understand your spouse. People are different. People communicate differently. *This takes work.* It is a sign of respect and love to put that work into understanding someone else's point of view. As we noted, the exploration of your feelings is not meant to be a one-shot deal; it's more likely a series of conversations over the course of your marriage. If you need to, take a break and try again tomorrow. (Of course, if you can't seem to understand each other at all despite repeated attempts, it might be wise to seek professional help in figuring out where the disconnect is.)

How Is Couples Counseling Going to Help?

Once you have a grasp of how empathic dialogue works, do you really need a couples counselor to give you the same information?

Good question! If communication was just about knowing what to do, you probably wouldn't. But it's unfortunately not that easy. You can't just read what to do and then you're good to go. This is true for any skill you want to learn. You do not become a good kickboxer by reading about how to extend your foot into your opponent's solar plexus. You need a coach to help you be your best. So too with empathic dialogue. It is a skill that, like any other skill, requires practice and feedback in order to master. Here are some ways a couples counselor can help you do that:

- **By ensuring you stick to your roles.** It's easy to forget you're just supposed to be listening and reflecting right now. A counselor can catch you when you start talking about yourself again and redirect you appropriately.
- **By helping you articulate the feelings you're trying to convey.** People are complex. Trying to understand ourselves is a lifetime of work. Having someone around who is a professional at understand-

ing people's inner workings could be useful in helping you express something you're having trouble communicating clearly.

- **By noticing where the listener isn't getting it.** Sometimes you get stuck in this frustrating cycle where the speaker is trying to convey something and the listener just isn't getting it. A counselor can help the listener get over that hump, or possibly identify what blockage might exist that's keeping them from letting it in.

- **By keeping you focused on the issues.** It's easy to veer off into a discussion on other topics that get brought up, or just less-important aspects of the main issue at hand. Having a professional there to help keep things focused is an invaluable aid.

- **By helping keep the emotional temperature down.** As we've noted, keeping calm as both the speaker and the listener can prove to be challenging at times. A counselor can help manage those moments and guide you back to emotional safety when things get a bit hairy.

These are by no means the only functions a couples counselor can serve. Don't knock it till you've tried it! (And if you've tried it and are now knocking it, please consider giving it another try – there are, unfortunately, some less-than-excellent counselors out there.) The goal, of course, is for you to learn how to manage all these functions on your own. That will take time and practice. In the meantime, if you need help getting these conversations to work for you, a couples counselor can be a great support.

A NOTE FOR THE SPEAKER

I made the claim above that not getting it right when trying to reflect to your spouse does not result in more conflict. In my experience, this is the natural outcome of an incorrect reflection: people generally do not get angry at someone who is sincere but mistaken. However, if you, as the speaker, *do* find yourself getting angry at your spouse in this situation, it behooves you to remind yourself that they really are trying, for your benefit. Appreciate that they are putting effort into understanding you

> **Appreciate that they are putting effort into understanding you because they love you.**

because they love you. It may be frustrating, but it's not an offense against you. Rather than heaving a giant sigh, rolling your eyes, etc., remember that this is normal and try again to say your piece. Politely respond something like, "Well, that's not exactly it. It's more like..."

Even if your spouse pulls out one of the don'ts – they argue, judge, psychoanalyze, etc. – do your best to keep your cool and recenter the conversation: "Hey, I want to listen to your perspective too, but I can't do it right now. Can we stay in my world right now and we'll get to you in a bit?" It does not help to point a finger and call them out, "YOU'RE NOT DOING THIS RIGHT!" This is a collaborative effort, not a competition to see who can win the relationship contest.

Another good way to handle this is to come up with a signal ahead of time that you will use to help each other stay on track – a hand up in a stop signal, a timeout T, a tug on your ear – whatever works for you to help the listener remember to stay in the speaker's world.

BRINGING IT HOME

Once you've heard what your partner shared and you accurately captured and reflected it – then what? Then you keep going. My favorite question for the listener to ask here is, "Is there anything else I should know about this?" This usually prompts some thinking on the speaker's end, followed by more information for the listener to take in and reflect, or else a "No, I think you got it."

Actually, when you're really in the zone, you will find that the conversation keeps going on its own. You'll reflect what you heard, and your partner, unprompted, will go, "Yeah, and..." This is a good sign. Having been properly heard and *gotten*, they are naturally propelled forward. Recall the metaphor of your following behind your partner as they lead you around their world. I imagine this dynamic as the speaker reaching a gate: they walk ahead, stop at the gate; you walk along to meet them. If you're on track, the gate opens and they walk a few more strides ahead to the next gate.[3] It feels very natural if you're in sync.

---

[3] Remember, we said that the speaker has to chunk things down and pause every few sentences to let the listener catch up. You don't run all the way down a path that your partner isn't familiar with and hope they can keep up!

If you find that your attempts at reflecting aren't hitting the mark, or if you feel like you haven't quite understood your partner deeply enough, here is a method of stepping things up to try to make that connection. Instead of reflecting to your partner what you think they are saying, try to put yourself fully in their shoes and *speak as if you are them*. This means that instead of saying, "You feel kind of nervous and kind of excited in situation X," you say, "Okay, I'm you now. I'm in situation X. I feel kind of nervous and kind of excited..." *Be* your partner for a little bit. Try to really think of how they're feeling and seeing things, and speak that truth. When I have clients do this in a therapy session, I'll act as an interviewer and ask questions of the listener, who is pretending to be their partner. "What did you feel then? What was it like when that happened?" This approach can help deepen both the listener's understanding and the speaker's feeling of being heard and understood. Careful – this is not the time for sarcasm or wit. Don't poke fun at your partner's idiosyncrasies – exaggerating a cute lisp, imitating their signature awkward smile. Not the time for it.

Capturing the speaker's experience in this way can be powerful. If I see you really expressing what I'm going through in a genuine way like that, it compellingly hits home. I know you are carrying me with you in your heart. And that's the only place I want to be.

* * *

Shira: *I'm worried that Kayla isn't going to like her new teacher.*

Levi: *Mm-hmm.*

Shira: *And she's so anxious in school already, I'm just nervous it's going to make things even worse.*

Levi: *You're concerned about how Kayla's going to get along with her teacher and whether it's going to cause her more stress and anxiety about school.*

Shira: *Yeah, and then we'll have a situation like we did two years ago, which I am NOT going through again.*

Levi: *You really don't want to deal with a difficult time like that again.*

Shira: *Exactly! And...*

Chapter 7

Validating and Empathizing

Carl: I guess I find Mr. Dickens a bit scary. He kind of reminds me of my principal in middle school. I know I should just get over it and say something, but he's my boss, and he's just intimidating.

Lana: You feel kind of scared of Mr. Dickens and you wish you could say something to him.

Carl: Right. Even though I know there's really no reason to be. I feel like an idiot.

Lana: Yeah, you're afraid, but like you said, there's no reason to be. He's not going to bite your head off or anything. And we know he can't fire you. You're going to be fine! I think you should just give it a shot and talk to him about it.

Carl: Yeah, but... yeah. I guess you're right. [Shuts down, slinks to his man cave, drinks a beer.]

We're going to combine the last two components of empathic dialogue together because by the time you've made it this far, you can almost coast to the finish line; these parts are a lot less taxing than the first two. Additionally, as you get more practiced at this process, you may find yourself blending the two of them together in your responses anyway. Here we go:

VALIDATING

The third component of empathic dialogue is *validating*. There are many definitions and approaches to what this actually means. The way I want to use it is pretty straightforward, as follows: validating what your spouse says to you simply means conveying to them that their feelings about this matter are valid. They make sense. You are saying to them, "You are not crazy for feeling the way you do." (You can actually say that.)

One of the reasons people don't communicate very well, or at all, is because we're afraid to be vulnerable. We're afraid to put our real feelings out there. We wonder if our spouse will be there for us, will support us, will love us despite the secrets we keep inside – the fears, the dreams, the hurts. Perhaps somewhere deep down, maybe even out of our conscious minds, we think maybe they won't. If I tell you I'm afraid of spiders, will you make fun of me? If I tell you I've always wanted to be a pro wrestler, will you laugh at me?[1] If I share with you what excites me, will you reject me? Validation is about creating the safety for us to talk about these things with each other. If I have entered your world sufficiently, then I can learn what it is about spiders or pro wrestling or high-heel shoes or anything else that affects you the way it does. And I can get to the point where I can go, *Yeah, that makes sense. You're not a baby, or a loser, or a pervert, or a bad person in any way – you're just a human being who's different from me.*[2]

What happens if I *don't* validate your feelings? Well, your experience is very real to you. If I insist that you shouldn't feel the way you do, that most people don't feel that way, that it doesn't make sense to feel that way – you are going to hold on to your experience even tighter. People do not easily let others take their reality away from them. This is the root of many, many arguments: one person tries to share their feelings, and their spouse sets right in on negating them:

---

[1] This is true about me, by the way.

[2] It is of course possible that your partner's inner world is *not* something that makes sense. I once worked with a client who saw a woman taking a photograph outside of her school, and she became terrified that the woman was a terrorist who was going to try to blow up the school. Something like this would be indicative of some serious trauma, or mental illness, or some other brokenness that needs attention. Another (rare) situation where you may not be able to understand your partner is if they are sociopathic and their moral poverty is such that they enjoy things like torturing animals for pleasure. In this case, I don't think improving communication is what's called for.

Layla: *I can't believe Amira said that to me!*

Brooks: *Well, it's really not as bad as you're making it out to be.*

Layla: *Not as bad?!? She literally trashed my whole family in front of everyone!*

Brooks: *Yeah but who cares what Amira says? Everyone knows she's crazy anyway.*

Layla: *OF COURSE SHE'S FRICKING CRAZY!!! THAT'S WHY THIS WHOLE EVENING BLEW UP!!!*

Brooks has good intentions – he wants to reassure Layla and make her feel better. He may be quite right that nobody gives a hoot what Amira says. But Layla keeps escalating, because he is in effect trying to take away her outrage. It won't work. Instead, he needs to let it be okay for her to be outraged. He needs to say, "Yeah, you're not crazy for being upset with her." Only once Layla feels validated will she be able to move on from her place of outrage. We all have this need. If you try to take away my feelings, I will hold on all the more strongly. This feeling is a part of me. If I let it go, will it disappear? Will this part of me just fall away into oblivion? Or will you keep it alive and hold it with me? Is my experience something that matters to you, or is it more important for you to bolster your own experience as the "real" one – in effect, for you to be right?

> If you try to take away my feelings, I will hold on all the more strongly.

When you try to argue your position, or even just share your own point of view before you validate, it provokes your spouse to dig in further to *make you understand.* People want to be understood. People want their experience to be recognized as real. That is what we call "validating." I can't just let you take my feelings away from me. But if you offer to help carry them *with* me, I'll be willing to let them go more easily. Validating is far more powerful than apologizing, solving, or any of the Category B activities we are all used to using. It is what allows us to move forward together from where each one of us currently stands.

Here are some more words you can use to validate your spouse's feelings:

- "It makes sense that you would feel disappointed."
- "I totally see how you could be angry about that."
- "I'd feel the same way!"

- "That seems like a reasonable reaction."
- "I think anyone might get their hopes up in a situation like that!"
- "I understand how that would make you feel upset."[3]

Remember not to add "but" at the end of this step either! If you say, "I get that you feel that way, but…," whatever you say next is guaranteed to be a move in the wrong direction, a step backward and not forward. You're bringing *you* into the mix again, and it's still premature.

WHAT IF YOU DON'T GET IT?

The essence of the validation step is communicating to your spouse that you recognize their feelings are valid. But what if you *don't*? What if you think they're nuts? Or just not making sense? What this means is that you need to do more listening and reflecting. For 97% of people reading this book, *there will be an explanation that makes your spouse's perspective make sense on some level.*[4] It is not the way you see things. It is not the reaction you would have. But they are different from you, and their reaction is understandable too. It is valid.

So, ask them to help you understand: "I get that you're angry at me; but I really don't understand why it's upsetting to you that I bought myself a new pair of shoes. Can you help me understand that?" Buying new shoes seems like the most normal thing in the world to you. Your old shoes were starting to come apart at the sole, and they were rubbing your heel in that annoying, intermittent way that leaves a blister.[5] What's the big deal if you buy a new pair? It's not like you can't afford it. The answer is that there is something in your spouse's world that makes this hurtful to them, and it is your job to try to understand what that is, within *their* framework. It is good to be clear where you personally stand as regards the purchase of new shoes. But it is a mistake to use that as the launching point to understand your spouse's perspective on it. Again, your spouse is probably not crazy. There is some

---

[3] Be careful with this one. I've seen people say this with a tone that makes it mean, "You should recognize that I am very smart and sensitive, and I have correctly understood you, so I have done my part here; I score the relationship points, and now it's time for my opinion, and you listen to me." Check your motives.

[4] But see Mindset #4 in chapter 11.

[5] You know, where you keep checking the inside of the shoe to see if there's something there and there isn't?

way this makes sense, and you want to get to the point of being able to say, "You know, given the way you see this, I can understand why you'd be so angry about it."

That's not the same thing as saying the way your spouse sees it is the "correct" way, or that it's the "normal" way to see things. Once again, we are not interested in who is *right*. You are not *agreeing* with their perspective; you are just validating it as one possible way to see and experience the situation. If you don't see the validity, it is almost certain you just haven't heard the details yet that would enable you to do so. (As we mentioned earlier, sometimes you just don't think to say something that seems patently obvious to you – and once you finally mention it, you are shocked to discover that your spouse didn't already think the same thing! Your spouse may be having exactly this experience with *you*.)

> You are not *agreeing* with their perspective; you are just validating it as one possible way to see and experience the situation.

People Are Different, Part 2 (and It's Still Okay)

We noted earlier that people can have different reactions to the same situation, and you don't have to convince each other to feel more like you do. No need for that at all. Likewise, people have different sensitivities, different preferences, different perspectives on even the smallest or most "obvious" things you would never have thought to question. You may be well aware that some people like spicy food and some don't. That's an easy one. It's not always that simple.

For me, it took a long time to recognize, and accept, that not everyone likes making jokes in class. Who wouldn't want to add some humor to a boring situation? The answer is: some people. And that's okay. We don't have to agree. We just have to be respectful of others in class. (I still make jokes when I'm in a classroom kind of situation, but fewer of them, and I moderate myself more.)

Staying totally serious and focused is a valid way to be. It's not how I choose to be, but other people can be that way. There's enough room at the table for everyone. Feeling sad when you fail a class is valid, and not caring too much is also valid. Doing things by the book is valid, and blazing your own path is also valid. I can't judge you by my standards, and you can't judge me by yours. What we all need from the people in our lives is to see us through the lens of *our own* standards, and to accept the rainbow of different ways to be. Your experience is your experience. I won't try to take that away from you or tell you it should be otherwise. That's not to say I won't try to help you grow, mature, and handle the strains and stresses of life more effectively (hey, I'm a therapist). But you can be sure I'm not going to even try that until I get fully into where you are right *now*.

You're not the same as me. And that's okay.

Interrupting is a great example of this. Some people don't mind being interrupted. Some people do. This often has to do with familial and cultural norms – in some families that's just how they talk. In some cultures it's normal and expected. It's not a massive moral right or wrong – it's just different ways of doing.[6] The point of empathic dialogue is not to agree on whether it is morally right or wrong. It's to understand how your spouse sees and feels about the world. (Maybe one of you *does* see it as an objective moral wrong. That's great food for empathic dialogue, and it's far better for your marriage than a debate.)

Bill and Mira were barreling towards middle age and both were already on their second marriage. They were desperately trying to avoid the mistakes that sank their previous marriages but were not succeeding all that well. Fights of increasing intensity were tearing away at their marriage, and they were doing their best to reverse the trend. One of the major topics of those fights was money. Money is inherently symbolic – those little pieces of paper (or numbers on a screen) don't have any intrinsic

---

6   Note that if you *do* believe it's rude to interrupt, but you feel okay about doing it to your partner and only call foul when they do it to you – that's not great relationshipping, is it?

value; they are only placeholders for what they can do for you.

For Bill, what those numbers represented was security. His parents were self-made successes who had both grown up in poverty, and their worldview naturally had a significant impact on him. At the heart of all his financial decisions was making sure he did not end up without the resources he needed (especially looking down the road to his retirement years). Simply put, he was stingy. The fact that he was extremely well-off made no difference. Before paying for an urgent lifesaving device for his mother-in-law, he hopped on Amazon to see if he could find a cheaper brand.

Mira, by contrast, saw money merely as a means to help others. She had spent her professional life first as a social worker, then as a nonprofit administrator, always striving to make the world a better place. She would gladly write out a check if it meant making a difference to someone in need.

You can see how these two perspectives might not have harmonized terribly well. Mira would call Bill cheap; Bill would malign Mira as irresponsible. Neither was an accurate charge. Bill was not a selfish miser; he simply had anxiety about the future baked into his being from a young age. Mira wasn't an impulsive spender; she just was willing to accept more risk in favor of a value that was of greater importance to her.

Nobody was right or wrong here. What was needed was not a verdict on their dispute but rather a dialogue and a serious dose of validation.

So let's say your partner tells you, "I was very insulted when you cut me off in mid-sentence." You may be inclined to say, "Well I don't make such a big deal of it when *you* do that to *me*." This may be true. But it is irrelevant. The point is that your *partner* doesn't like it. Loving someone means taking their needs and sensitivities into account even when they are not the same as yours.[7] You are trying to walk a mile in their shoes. Walking a

> Loving someone means taking their needs and sensitivities into account even when they are not the same as yours.

---

[7] An even worse way to handle that would be, "Oh, like *you* never interrupt *me*!" Sarcasm is entirely counterproductive when you're trying to communicate well, and it will only lead to escalation.

mile in someone's shoes doesn't mean shoving them aside, stepping into their place, and saying your feet feel just fine. It means you actually have to take *off* your shoes and then put theirs *on*!

AGREEMENT NOT REQUIRED

It is important to recognize that *validating* someone's feelings does not mean *agreeing* with them. You can understand and validate why someone reacted the way they did without agreeing that it was the right thing to do, or that you in fact said the thing they're upset about, or that things happened the way they remember it at all. It is precisely because there are different valid ways of being that your view can be valid and mine can too, and we don't have to agree on whose view is better or righter – even though sometimes the facts can only support one of them. Validating just means you accept that your partner, as a person distinct from you, had the emotional response that they did to their *perception* of the situation.

It can be helpful for the speaker to put this out there at the outset of the conversation (and sometimes in the middle too): "I am really looking just for some validation. I don't need you to agree with me." This can free up the listener to really be there in validating their partner without having the nagging concern in the back of their head that it will be taken as agreement to a position they are not comfortable with. It is *not* helpful for the *listener* to point this out: "Yeah, I get that you feel that way, but I don't agree." This lets the air right out of the balloon. Much better to have the principle established to begin with – meaning, when we engage in dialogue like this, we both have already resolved that we can validate each other and it doesn't indicate agreement – and/or for the *speaker* to acknowledge it again at the beginning of or during a dialogue.

> Validating also does not mean submitting, relinquishing your opinions, or giving up your right to speak.

Validating also does not mean submitting, relinquishing your opinions, or giving up your right to speak. None of that is supposed to happen here. All we are doing is exploring your partner's world and understanding it; we'll get back to your world soon enough. (You *do* have to wait your turn though.)

Since agreement is not required, you can take this validation thing pretty far.

To take an absurdly sensitive topic for an example, imagine your partner is sharing their feelings about abortion – and they are quite the opposite of yours. Perhaps you have strong feelings about this. You can still say, "I can understand why that's important to you" or "I see how you could be worried about that," even when their perspective is total anathema to you. (I'm not saying this is necessarily easy; I'm just saying it can absolutely be done.)

Even if your partner is expressing a reaction to something that *did not happen at all* – "I'm feeling too self-conscious to go to the party tonight – the last time we went, everyone stared at me the whole night" – you can validate their feelings without agreeing with the premise: "I can totally get why you'd feel self-conscious. That feeling of everyone looking at you is so uncomfortable." Does that mean that you concede that people were staring at your partner, or that you're not going to go to the party because of their possibly excessive self-consciousness? Not necessarily. Remember, we're not yet talking about solutions; we're just exploring.

EMPATHIZING

Recall my definition of empathy from way back in the introduction: *the ability to understand and share in the feelings of another.* It's not enough to have a detached, academic knowledge of their feelings. Empathy does not occur from a distance. Nor is it enough to mirror their demeanor. If you walk past a funeral, sure, you probably turn solemn for a moment; perhaps you feel *compassion* for a family in mourning. But *empathy* goes further. Empathy would mean spending a little bit of time to contemplate what it really means to lose someone close to you, and to share in that emotional reality. If you feel somber and reverent as you pass the funeral, but don't stop and feel a sinking feeling in your gut in this situation, you probably haven't hit empathy yet.

This is really the core of what we're doing here. Listening, Reflecting in Your Own Words, and Validating are really all there only to get us to this point. It doesn't really matter if you listen super well to your partner but you don't actually give a darn. Empathy is the ultimate expression of relationship. It says, "I care

> Empathy is the ultimate expression of relationship. It says, "I care about you. You are important to me. We are in this together."

about you. You are important to me. We are in this together." This is the bottom line that supports a relationship for the long term.

Empathy builds bridges of love. It also builds overpasses of compassion. By this I mean to say that all the crazy, bizarre, annoying, infuriating, and/or hurtful things your partner does in your marriage become far less painful to you when you have it; you can accept that your partner is imperfect (just as you are) and rise above the day-to-day provocations rather than let them eat away at your love and connection. Your partner does what they do for a reason – just like you. If you truly had complete understanding and empathy for what they've been through that made them who they are, your grievances against them would virtually disappear. That doesn't mean you'd agree with all their choices or condone all their behaviors, but there would be a lot more tolerance and a lot less heartache.

Lance and Jenna were young professionals who I had seen for a few months in the wake of a calamitous incident of infidelity. We worked through the crisis and repaired their marriage over the course of several months. They would return to see me at intervals over the years when life got tough – the birth of their first child, a relapse of substance abuse, and other times of need. Lance reminded me of the ideal husband from a century ago – a hard worker, motivated and competent to support his family, but not very emotionally in tune. To his credit, he learned a lot about being emotionally present and supportive through our work and he took it seriously.

One of Lance's recurring complaints was the way Jenna would totally lose her cool over seemingly mild provocations – she would break down crying in public, scream at him, threaten to humiliate him in front of his boss. In response, he would panic, get overloaded, and resort to calling her immature, overdramatic, crazy. As we delved into empathic dialogue, he and I both learned more about the terrible childhood Jenna had, her frightening and unstable parents, her miserable school days. As I explained to him more about the effects and manifestations of trauma, he slowly came around to seeing that his wife was truly not immature or a drama queen. She was just reacting to life from a place of deep hurt and distress. This understanding radically changed the way he was able to handle and respond to her emotional flare-ups.

I also helped Lance to express, and Jenna to understand, what it was like for him to be on the spot like that in the face of those flare-ups. She perceived him as being uncaring, distant, even cruel. She didn't realize the intense embarrassment and fear he experienced (coming from his own particular nature and history) when she launched into such an episode. Her recognition of and empathy for his position likewise made a huge difference in her feelings about their situation. It hurt a lot less to think of Lance as hurting emotionally himself rather than actually not caring.

SAYING IT AND SEEING IT

Empathy sounds like this:

- "I'm so sorry you are feeling ___."[8]
- "Wow. That's so tough."
- "Wow! That's so amazing!!!"
- "It pains me to hear that you are feeling ___."[9]
- "This must be so hard for you."
- "I'm so happy for you!"
- "That really stinks."

Arguably, however, even more important than the words you use are the nonverbal aspects of your communication. Much as we noted that your nonverbals say a lot about your listening, they say a lot about your empathy as well. You can say the words "I feel so sorry for you" with a tone of concern, detachment, or sarcasm, and it will convey very different messages in each case. I've had many sessions that go something like this:

DJ: I just feel so distant from you sometimes. When you spend the whole night playing video games, I feel... unwanted. I really don't know if you even love me anymore.

---

[8] This is another one of the English language's unhelpful linguistic quirks: sometimes we use "sorry" to mean "I feel bad" and not "I apologize." Remember, apologizing is Category B!

[9] Be careful with this one too: you have to remember that you are focusing on the pain you have *on behalf of your partner*, not your own pain. For example, if your partner says they feel unloved, you may empathically feel pain for them; you may also feel hurt/guilty/angry/etc. that your attempts to make them feel loved haven't been working. You need to keep those two parts of yourself separate: right now you're dealing with, and speaking from, the part that's feeling for your partner; later, when you are the speaker, you will have a chance to share the part that has feelings about you.

Scott (in the same tone as you would remark on the weather):
You feel distant and unwanted. You don't know if I love you.

He got the information down. But there's no empathy. He's not feeling DJ's feelings. You cannot possibly take information like this *into you* – to really be real with the fact that the person you love *actually questions if you love them* – and not be moved by that. Imagine going to the memorial service for the mother of a close friend. Would you be flippant, or chilled out, or even just neutral? "Gee, Dave, shame you lost your mom, huh?" Or would your voice be quieter than normal? Laden with emotion? Tentative? Think how you would need to express yourself to convey the message to your friend that you grieve for their loss, that their pain is your pain. Think how you need to express to your partner that you share their feelings with them, whatever they are. Do you need to lean in? Are you standing tall, for something positive and exciting? With your head a bit bent, for something sad?

The truth is, sometimes the nonverbal messages will carry the day. After hearing about a tough situation your mate went through, a heavy sigh, a slump of the shoulders, and a "yeah..." might be a total bullseye; a disapproving snort can convey shared outrage on their behalf. Or you might just do the validation part along with a nod and a squeeze of the hand: "You feel drained managing the kids all day. I would feel totally exhausted too if I had to do that." Nod. Squeeze. What you do is often more powerful than what you say in these situations. (That said, the wordless approach is likely to be more successful once you've got this system down enough that your partner recognizes that you are trying to be empathic and not, say, dismissive.)

When appropriate, you can cap it off with a meaningful hope for the future. What do you want for your partner? If they're sharing something positive, you can revel in that with them and wish for them that which you know they wish for themselves (because you have been listening empathically): "That's amazing that you got the promotion! I really hope this new position allows you the room for creativity you've been wanting." If it's something less than positive, you can let them know how you want it to be for them: "I'm sorry you feel so unheard in this marriage. Of course you're angry about that! I can totally understand that. I really hope we can work on things so that you feel heard, and important, and cared about."

You're showing you're with them not just in their now but in their future as well.

Offering empathy means you don't keep yourself at arm's length, separate from your partner's emotional world. You are *on* that world. You are *in* that world. If your partner is going through a dark time, you don't call to them from outside the cave they're in with an acknowledgment of how lame it is to be stuck in the dark. *You get in the cave with them.* You bear the darkness together. That's love.

* * *

Carl: I guess I find Mr. Dickens a bit scary. He kind of reminds me of my principal in middle school. I know I should just get over it and say something, but he's my boss, and he's just intimidating.

Lana: You feel kind of scared of Mr. Dickens and you wish you could say something to him.

Carl: Right. Even though I know there's really no reason to be. I feel like an idiot.

Lana: Yeah. Jeez. I get why you'd feel like an idiot. You really wish you could get over this feeling.

Carl: Right.

Lana: [Gives Carl a hug.] I'm sorry you have to deal with that guy. I hope this stressful situation is over soon.

[Lana doesn't say it, but Carl knows it: she's got his back. Always.]

Chapter 8

Beginnings, Middles, and Endings

Adam: *I feel frustrated when I'm trying to get the kids dressed for school and there's no socks in their drawer and it turns into a giant circus trying to get them out the door.*

Raina: *Yeah, I can understand that being a frustrating situation. I'm so overwhelmed managing all the household stuff that sometimes I don't even have a chance to put their socks away.*

Adam: *I know how overwhelming the housework can be. I think if the laundry was prioritized then I'd be able to spend more time helping you instead of hunting for clothes.*

Raina: *You know, you always say you want to help but I'm very angry because that never seems to happen!*

Adam: *Well maybe if you APPRECIATED ANYTHING I DID AROUND HERE I'd be more motivated to help!!!*

This conversation seems to start off well, but it turns into yet another verbal ping-pong match. Let's look into the mechanics of moving back and forth in empathic dialogue, as well as moving in and out of it.

MOVING IN

As we discussed in chapter 3, before you get into a dialogue you have to make sure it's the right time – not right before bed, not during the morning carpool rush, etc.

Once you know that you've got the right timing, don't forget to cue your spouse in. It is wise to not jump right into sharing your feelings – especially the big ones – without a heads-up first. Your spouse might well be dealing with their own emotional stuff at the time, or they may be preoccupied, tired, hungry, etc. It does nobody any good to try to have an important conversation when one or both of you are physically, emotionally, or mentally compromised at the time.

On Texting

Texting is convenient. You can message someone and respond to them on your own timetable instead of being a captive audience; you can get them needed information even if they're not reachable right this moment. So it's great for asking your significant other to get some cash at the ATM if they're passing by on the way home, or for letting them know you're running late for dinner. But it is *not* great for anything that has emotional content, and *certainly* not about your marriage. Relationships are not about convenience. A relationship is very much a you-get-out-what-you-put-in kind of proposal. If you don't work at it, it won't be awesome.

Dealing with conflict is not what you have to do to preserve a loving relationship. It is *part of* a loving relationship. Not only that, but it is a big contributor to the development of such a relationship. Communicating about such matters via text definitely feels easier and safer, but it also deprives you of the growthful experience of having difficult conversations and doing it well.

Granted, not everyone is ready at every moment to accept the challenge of excellent communication. Even so, there's a simpler reason to avoid dealing with your marital issues by text: it nearly always goes poorly. You simply cannot convey your tone, facial expressions, or body language in a text (no matter how many emojis or GIFs you use) – and when you're mad at each other, you tend to interpret those words on the screen in the worst possible way. This is a recipe for disaster. If you've tried having important conversations by text, you have probably had such an experience. And even when it doesn't go off the rails, the back-and-forth ends up taking much longer: texting is obviously slower than speaking, and the asynchronous exchange can stretch out over an entire day (or more), keeping you emotionally stuck in the issue at hand, taking your focus away from other important things in your life, and leaving you drained.

Yes, it's hard to sit face-to-face with someone and have a difficult discussion. When you get a handle on the skills we've been working on, it becomes much more achievable. You'll get there. In the meantime (and afterwards too), stay away from text conversations about the marriage if you want to see it flourish.

Even if your spouse is perfectly calm and relaxed, they still need to know what's coming so they can get in the right mindset. "That noise in the basement is still going on" could easily be taken to mean "Could you go check that out?" (especially to a man, who, as we've mentioned, is trained to see things as problems he's meant to solve) when the intent might just be to vent and be heard about how annoying and stressful homeownership is. Don't assume they're ready to be empathic just because that's what you're in need of at that moment.

> Don't assume they're ready to be empathic just because that's what you're in need of at that moment.

Here are some ways you can start that off:

- "I've got some things on my mind. Can we have a talk later tonight?"
- "Something's been bothering me lately – it's not about you. Are you in a place to listen a little bit?" (Pro tip: being explicit that your big feelings are not about your spouse when they are not can take a lot of pressure off the situation!)
- "Hey, can we do an empathic dialogue this weekend? I feel like we could use a chat about the school situation."

If what you want to talk about *is* about the marriage, this kind of preface can feel a little scary on both ends. Practicing and getting good at empathic dialogue makes it a lot less so. When you know that you can discuss even very difficult issues in a way that leaves everyone feeling heard and respected, then even if your spouse is mad at you, you can feel confident that the conversation and its aftermath won't be utter misery. But if you haven't worked on this process, then it's tough from the get-go because as soon as you bring up An Issue, your spouse is already stressing about how unpleasant this is going to be (and likely not wrongly so). Without the most basic elements in place – a team mindset, an understanding that this is not about who is right – you can reasonably expect a bad outcome to difficult conversations.

Part of this is also doing your own personal work: for example, if you can't tolerate being wrong, or you know you *are* wrong and can't tolerate the feelings of guilt, you will have a hard time hearing anything from your spouse that sounds negative. If you are so rigid that you can't handle when things don't go exactly the way you wanted or when people behave in ways you don't approve of, it will be difficult to allow for other perspectives. Good communication is the foundation of a good marriage, but a marriage is between two people, and if one or both of those people have personal shortcomings that are causing problems, no amount of communication will make things right.[1]

On the flip side, sometimes it's your spouse who has something on their mind to discuss and not you; you can tell something is up with them, but they're not talking. Maybe they're sulking, or sniping, or pouting, or stomping, or whatever indirect mode they use of letting you and the world know they're not happy about something. Or they may not even be trying to let anyone know anything, but they're clearly sad or mad or whatever they're feeling. This is such a common and generally unsuccessful scenario that it's its own cultural cliché:

She: *Is everything okay?*

He: *Yes. Fine.*

She: *Are you sure?*

---

[1] It's actually possible that communicating about how uncomfortable it is to be wrong or deal with change or what have you can help a person work through that and change, especially if their partner is understanding and supportive. It's just very hard to do because the challenges they'd need to address are themselves barriers to dialogue and to change. Working on humility, flexibility, etc. might be something they need to do their own work around.

He: *YES.*

She: *Because you look upset. Is everything really okay?*

He: *I SAID I'M FINE!!!*

She: *Why are you getting angry? I'm just trying to help.*

HE: I'M NOT ANGRY!!! *[Storms off and slams the door.]*

Right?

What's a better way to do this? How can you address it when something's up with your spouse without making things worse?

For starters, instead of being vague ("Is everything okay?") be a little more specific: "You seem upset/irritated/down/etc. Can you tell me what's bothering you?" But keep it tentative – "you *seem*," not "you *are*." Nobody likes being told how they feel. (Recall from the chapter on Reflecting in Your Own Words that conjecturing how your spouse might feel can be helpful, but declaring how they *do* feel is not.) "It looks like you might be feeling stressed out" is better than "You're obviously stressed today." Leave room for them to consider and disagree. You won't get anywhere by forcing them to accept your perspective. Remember that you aren't trying to resolve the problem at this point – you're not trying to figure out how to pay the bills they are worried about, nor are you trying to make them stop feeling stressed. You're just trying to hear and understand what's going on for them (which, of course, will itself help with the stress). Stick with that aim. "Help me understand."

Now, you may recall that I said you should not engage in empathic dialogue when one of you is too emotionally ramped up. This is generally true; but here you can make a choice. If you see that your spouse is struggling with some big feelings, and you are feeling calm enough to help hold them, it is reasonable to try to open up the conversation. (There's a limit, of course – if your spouse is stomping around, raging, slamming doors, etc., please don't try talking at that point. Timeout is the only way to go.) Ask them if they can share with you. Come from a "help me understand" perspective. Again, if you've been working on these skills, it will be a less threatening proposition for your spouse. Let them unload their emotional burden. Do still hold them to respectful and constructive speech – you should not just sit there while they tear into you about what a rotten person you are for such and such reasons. You can keep turning it back to them with comments like "Tell me what that's like for *you*" and "I want to know how you feel, not what you think of me" (see "Help a Partner Out Again" in chapter 5).

You can offer your spouse a lot just by being there in the cave with them. That said, we've already recognized that listening to your spouse's feelings can be the most difficult part of the process, especially when those feelings are about you and you don't like what you're hearing. So if you feel yourself being pulled off your center and you hear yourself responding, or preparing to respond unhelpfully, it's still totally fair to reconsider and call a timeout: "You know, I thought I'd be able to handle this, but I'm not. Can we schedule a time to continue later?" Do that *before* you cross the line into Nastyville.

SWAPPING ROLES

The next skill we have to build in empathic dialogue is switching between speakers. So far we've been hammering down what the roles of each person are, and we've made it clear that the listener doesn't share their own feelings or opinions while they're the listener: one person speaks and one person listens. So how do you swap roles effectively?

Explicitly, that's how.

For starters, let's acknowledge that this cut-the-conversation-in-half thing is an artificial way of communicating with each other (intentionally so). As we noted earlier, you probably won't be using it for most of the things you need to say to each other.

"Honey, where's the butter?"

"You're feeling annoyed that you can't find the butter."

"I... I just need some butter for my sandwich."

It's actually a good thing that this feels unnatural at first. It helps us keep out of our more natural tendencies (which, for most of us, involves arguing that we're right and then getting angry). For now we're going to keep things pretty regimented with one person speaking and the other listening, and then a formal switch. As you get more practiced at this, the swap will happen more organically and more frequently as well – instead of one person sharing extensively and fully before hearing from the other, you might speak a bit then listen a bit, speak a bit then listen a bit. But even then, it's critical to be clear who's doing the speaking, because otherwise it quickly becomes a competition of two clashing perspectives between two people who think they're doing the speaking and the other person is supposed to be listening. An actual talking stick or other physical object can help you keep on track and remember who is doing the speaking and who is doing the LOVE.

So when you are in an empathic dialogue, and you are the listener and you would like to do some speaking, *it is critical for you to ask* if you can have a turn before you jump in and take one. This is not just politeness – it's vital for the success of your mission, because if your partner hasn't consciously made the switch to listening, to stepping out of their world and into yours, then inevitably they are not going to fully hear your perspective and will bring their own stuff into the listening process instead of really being where *you* are. Moreover, if they are still very emotional and are *not* ready to hand over the figurative microphone, if they have more they need to get out there before they can do some listening, then once again it won't do you any good to try to get them to hear you. It won't work. This is what went wrong in our opening vignette: both Adam and Raina seemed to be doing a good job talking about their feelings at first, but they kept trying to grab the mic back from each other and it turned into an argument.

> It is critical for you to ask if you can have a turn before you jump in and take one.

This means that you may have to hang on to your own feelings (or objections) and keep listening. This is hard. It's really hard. You really, really want to say something, but it's not your turn. I know how hard that is. But it is so effective, you will find it worth the effort. You may have to wait a few minutes until they finish going through their stuff. You may also have to wait hours or days to get your part in!

Chana was really angry with me. I can't even remember what it was about. (How many of your arguments does that apply to, right?) She was just mad about something, and tearing up at the same time, and this kills me because what that says to me is that I did something so bad that it made her cry, and of course I definitely did not believe I had done anything so atrocious. But I listened and reflected as best I could in that tense moment. And when she was satisfied that I had understood her, she calmed down a bit – but not all the way. (Emotions tend not to disappear instantly in the face of new experiences or information.) I asked if I could share my perspective at that point. And she said no. And I accepted it. Because she was being honest with herself and with me – she wasn't in a place to listen and be empathic. She was still worked up. There would have been no point in my trying to get my feelings heard. So I just shut up, and we both knew we'd circle back to my turn. It wasn't a super pleasant feeling. But there was a hidden confidence in it, because I knew it would happen eventually. I just had to be strong enough, and mature enough, to wait for the later payoff.

Waiting for your turn here is at least as hard as it was in kindergarten at the back of the line for the slide. It's even harder when you strongly take issue with what you're hearing. Sometimes you are so worked up by what you hear that you really can't continue. Still, you would be very wise to not get into an argument about it; you just need to be real with where you're at: "Hang on, I need a moment here – can I be speaker for a moment? I'm having a lot of trouble with what I'm hearing and the frustration is getting to me." If you can't say this calmly or your partner is too upset to listen, then the options are some silent listening or a good old timeout. You can do it! And the better you get at empathic dialogue, the more confidence you will have that your turn will come when the time is right.

When your turn comes, you get to share your own, different recollection of what happened (and, more importantly, how you feel about it). But you must be very careful not to turn this into a rebuttal. Do not go back through your partner's story and explain where they got it wrong. Once again, you need to get comfortable with the factlessness of these conversations. If you disagree with your partner's

> **The better you get at empathic dialogue, the more confidence you will have that your turn will come when the time is right.**

perspective of what happened, you can share your own perspective, which may be very different, and *nobody has to be right.* You can empathize with the feelings your partner experienced in their version of the story, and they can empathize with yours, and you just don't have to decide whose version is correct. What you have to do is *care.*

So if you are going to share a divergent narrative about the same incident, be sure it's an invitation to hear you and empathize, not an accusation that they're altering the story or an attempt to correct them. For example, your partner might share their annoyance that the drive home last night took twice as long as normal, and they were stressed out for the rest of the evening because of it. You can hear that and validate it, and then when it's your turn, you can share your own experience of the night: in your recollection, the drive really only took five minutes longer than normal, and your partner was actually kind of snippy well before you started driving home, and maybe you're feeling angry about that.

You are not trying to dispute your partner's account of last night here. *You are not going to argue over how long the drive actually took.* You will both go to the grave believing your own story about the length of that drive. At the same time, you will remain empathetic to how hard it was for your partner to arrive home so late. And they will offer empathy to you for how unpleasant the night must have been for you to have them snipping at you, fairly or unfairly. You will care about each other, and feel cared about, and it will be a giant success.

The other really productive way to use your turn is to share what you are experiencing *now* hearing them say their part. For example, after you talk about how unhappy you were that your partner was irritable last night, when your partner gets to be the speaker they may want to share what it's like for them to hear you say that: "I have to tell you, I'm feeling pretty hurt that this is the way you see it. I was trying to get you to leave the party for an hour and you basically ignored me, which was hurtful then. But now you're saying you don't even recognize at all why I was in a bad mood last night, and I just feel more hurt and more invisible." You now get to reflect and validate how crummy it must feel to be misunderstood and unseen like that (even though you are *dead sure* this is not how things happened). Get it? Empathy yes. Argument no.

This may also be a good place to pull out some Category B stuff. Maybe you want to apologize. "I'm sorry I didn't even notice you trying to get my attention to leave. I feel bad you had to stay there so long." Maybe you want to reassure: "I really think the babysitter is not going to ditch us because we came home late one time. I know you're worried about it. I think it's going to be okay." (Do *not* do these things if you have not fully gone through Category A, i.e., LOVE.) And it's a good idea to keep going with the same format – your partner can reflect, "You feel bad that you didn't notice my signals to try to get us out of there last night," then validate and empathize with that.

Another way you may want or need to switch roles is when you as the speaker notice that your partner isn't cutting it as the listener. The edginess is creeping into their voice, or they're bringing their own stuff into their reflections. Assuming they are genuinely invested in the process, they may simply be struggling too much with their own emotions to do a good job of stepping into your world right now. Hey, they're human. If you're in a calm enough place to be able to hand over the talking stick, go for it. (If you're not, it's probably time for a timeout.) You might ask them if they'd like the first shot at speaking. Or you can comment on the reaction you're seeing: "You seem angry right now. Is something bothering you?" (It's quite possible they didn't even realize this was the case, and your bringing it up and handing them the floor will allow them to explore that – with constructive results for all.)

> You can comment on the reaction you're seeing: "You seem angry right now. Is something bothering you?"

You can keep the cycle going back and forth as much as you need. If both of you are being genuine in trying to understand and validate your partner, and you keep away from arguing and butting heads, then this will take you to a good place. (That doesn't mean it will be all giggles and candy canes; as we noted, it can get pretty difficult at times. But you will come out feeling connected and confident about the marriage.) Remember that you don't have to have the whole conversation at once. In fact, you may not be able to! It can be emotionally draining to focus on these difficult feelings and interactions; it's normal to need a break. It can also just be a matter of time – maybe you set aside a half hour to dialogue, but there's more you need to discuss and no more time before you have to leave for your yoga class. If you have to dialogue in chunks, that's okay. (These should be decently large chunks. You will not have success with empathic dialogue in four-minute chunklets.) Again, it might be hard to hold on to what you want to get out, but if you don't have the time tonight, you may just have to put a pause on it and continue over the weekend.

ENDINGS

As we've noted, it's not uncommon for a round of empathic dialogue to end in a timeout or a To Be Continued. But of course there will also be times when you do get to wrap up an issue. And hopefully that is a warm and fuzzy feeling for you. (If it's not, that probably means there is more to talk about.) It's good to end with an acknowledgment of what's been accomplished:

- "I feel really heard. Thanks."

- "I feel so much better about this."

- "I'm really glad we're able to have these talks and deal with our issues in a helpful way."

- "I really appreciate your listening to me."

And, of course, a hug at the end is a nice way to tie a bow around it!

But the end is never really the end. Like we said earlier, empathic dialogue is not a one-and-done but a series of conversations over the course of your life. There are challenges you will face that will extend over your lifetime (childrearing comes immediately to mind). There are differences between you and your partner that may always be there, and you will be called upon to work together despite them rather than eliminate them. Much as exercise is not something you can do for a month to lose weight and then move on, good communication is a lifestyle and not a discrete action.

> Empathic dialogue is not a one-and-done but a series of conversations over the course of your life.

And, much as exercise requires repetition, empathic dialogue thrives on repetition too. Not only do you repeatedly engage in the process, but you may actually repeat the *same conversations* more than once. This might seem pointless, or at least indicative of an ineffective process, but that is only if you are stuck in the perspective of "Get Facts – Solve Problem." In such a context, it's true that repeating known information is of little value. But not so in empathic dialogue. Running in circles is meaningless if your goal is to get to a destination. But if your goal is simply to tune your body into shape, then running a few times around the track is quite constructive.[2]

---

[2] I am referring here to revisiting the same topic of conversation, not to repeating the same line over and over again in a single conversation. If your partner is sharing their feelings and you're trying to reflect them, but they just keep coming back to the same point and not moving forward, there is something stuck in the process that needs to be considered or brought to a professional for further help.

Having the same conversation over again is constructive, even if no new information is shared, because there is power in communicating to each other the messages of validation and empathy repeatedly. Trust, security, faith, love – these are not created in the flash of a brilliant monologue (despite cinematic depictions of exactly that). They are fortresses you build in your marriage, one brick at a time. Every conversation, every act of genuine reflection, every statement of empathy is a brick in that fortress. And you don't need each brick to be different. Having the same conversation you had last week and reaffirming your commitment to the process, your understanding of each other, your validation of your different perspectives, your empathy for the feelings they experienced in that one situation – you're building like a boss.

And then there will certainly be times when you *do* unearth new information when you rehash a conversation. Sometimes new details come out, or subtle nuances, whether because they were only remembered later on or because there may have been a hesitance to share vulnerable aspects before. Or, as you chew on the experience more and more, you come to a deeper understanding not only of each other but of yourself. This is an experience of intimacy and relationship that is hard to put into words. There is little that bonds you to each other quite like the simultaneous journey of mutual and self-discovery.

Savor it.

PRACTICE MAKES PROGRESS

Look, having these conversations can be hard. I'm not gonna sugarcoat it. But I don't take that to be a bad thing. Things that come easy to us are generally not the things we most value. Relationships take work. Communication takes work. It's worth the work.

But like anything you have to work for, starting at the highest level is probably not realistic. You don't work on your tennis skills by jumping into a match with [insert name of current tennis superstar here]. You start small and you work your way up. So in line with that, here is a ladder of exercises you can climb together to practice the skill of empathic dialogue. Block off regular practice sessions if you can – at breakfast on Sundays, or for 20 minutes over coffee one night a week. (Don't try to run through all of these in one sit-down! They're meant to be done one conversation at a time.) The more practice you get, the more you'll be able to draw on the skill when you need it.

At each rung on the ladder you're going to have an empathic dialogue (cut in halves, of course – taking turns being the speaker). You'll spend a little time sharing your own experience and being LOVEd by your partner, then you'll switch.

Exercise #1: a story from before you and your partner knew each other.

Think of an event in your life that had an emotional impact on you, whether positive or negative – the time you got lost at the fair, your high school graduation, the day your pet died, getting your first car – anything that was a big deal in your life. And just share that with your partner. Remember that as the speaker, the goal is to invite them into your experience, not drill them with information. And as the listener, you're not trying to memorize the details of your partner's story. You're trying to inhabit it. Ideally, after you're done with the exercise you would be able to repeat the story to someone else and convey exactly what it was like for your partner to go through that experience, and if your partner were listening, they'd be nodding their head and going, "Yeah, exactly."

> You're not trying to memorize the details of your partner's story. You're trying to inhabit it.

This exercise is the easiest to pull off because you have none of your own perspectives or biases on the story to color your reception; you weren't involved at all, even tangentially. (For those of you who have known each other since elementary school, you may have a bit more trouble coming up with a story that is totally disconnected from your partner, but you should be able to find something!) There is still always the possibility of more general biases or judgments coming out – why did you do that? How could your parents have said such a thing? Etc. You may find yourself somewhat triggered by things you hear in your partner's story, and your job is to leave those behind and totally enter into your partner's world.

Exercise #2: a story that happened to both of you that is *not* related to your relationship.

Pick a story from when you were already together (or, if you knew each other for a while before being in a relationship, that works too) – something that is not related to your relationship, just a mutual experience. You went to a friend's wedding and it was totally fantastic/terrible, or a meaningful class you attended, or you both spent time at the International Space Station together (I am being creative here). What was it like for you? This step is a little more of a challenge because you have your own experience of the event, and it is by definition not identical to your spouse's (even if it is similar). So really letting go of your own feelings about it and letting in your spouse's is a bit tougher than it was when you had no direct experience of the event at all; but since it is focused on an external person or event, the idea is that there is little potential for defensiveness to arise. Be mindful that you are understanding your spouse and not imposing your own experience onto their story.

Exercise #3: something you wish were different in your life, *not* related to your relationship.

This is still somewhat safe in that you're not discussing changes in the marriage directly, but it nonetheless presents a little added challenge because it almost certainly impacts your spouse as well. And these topics do tend to be of a sensitive nature. If you're wishing you could lose a little weight, your spouse likely has some investment in this issue, with their own feelings and perspectives about it – both in terms of what they think about your issue ("You really do need to take better care of yourself") and how it impacts them ("I can't say that extra weight isn't a bit of a turnoff"). But again, the listener is leaving their stuff out of it right now and just getting into the speaker's world, and this can be something of a challenge!

Exercise #4: a topic that is going *well* in your relationship.

Now it's getting personal. We want to bring the discussion around to something that is directly between the two of you. We are still hopefully going to avoid any defensiveness or opposition since this is something that is going *well* in the relationship, but we are circling closer to the really tough stuff where you will have not just *different* opinions but *conflicting* ones.

Exercise #5: a mutual problem you *both* wish was better in your relationship.

The heat goes up even more! The idea is to pick something that is not-so-positive to discuss together – how you both want to spend more time with the kids, or you wish you could go on a vacation abroad, or you both feel like your intimate life is flagging. Do not pick something that you believe is your partner's fault! If you can't go on vacation because expenses are so high, that's a shared problem. If *you* believe the reason for your financial situation is because your partner isn't working enough and *they* believe it's because you spend way too much money, *this is not a mutual problem*. This is a big giant honker of a conversation.

When neither of you views the problem as something caused by the other, the experience is shared, at least in part. But it can still be challenging because your partner's frustration with the situation can feel like blame, which of course elicits some defensiveness in you. And if you disagree on the source of the problem (even if you agree it's not each other), that can lead to an argument also (if you're not sticking with empathic dialogue).

Remember, you're just sharing how you feel about the situation – no accusations, no solutions – and inviting your partner to share in your wishfulness/regret/longing/etc.

Exercise #6: an issue that is a *small* disagreement in your relationship.

Don't go for the gold yet. In any marriage there are a myriad of small areas where there's friction, from the classic debates over toothpaste tube squeezing, toilet paper roll hanging, and dishwasher loading to points that may be idiosyncratic to your individual relationship, like your brother's annoying habit of leaving a mess whenever he comes over, or your partner's unusual way of cutting up everything on their plate into small pieces before eating a single bite. Here's where the rubber hits the road, so that's why we pick a small issue first. Can you share your feelings without being accusatory? Can you listen to your partner's experience without succumbing to the urge to defend yourself?

Exercise #7: an issue that is a *large* disagreement in your relationship.

This is not really even practice anymore. This is the core of what you need empathic dialogue for. There is a significant conflict in the marriage (which does not necessarily involve yelling and screaming, but perhaps it does), and you guys need to be able to live and to love as you sort through it. You want to move across the country, but your partner doesn't. Your partner's parents are toxic and they are causing both of you tremendous stress, but your partner refuses to set boundaries. There are all kinds of big ones out there. Recall that this process is not about making the problem go away; it's about maintaining and enjoying your marriage even as you continue

Recall that this process is not about making the problem go away; it's about maintaining and enjoying your marriage even as you continue to work on the problem.

to work on the problem. This will not be a short conversation or a one-timer. This is what your marriage is about. Take your time. Take it slow. Practice. You'll get there.

Molly and Grant were a middle-aged couple that had struggled to have their first and only child, who was the apple of their mutual eye. Molly wanted another one. Grant did not. Their marriage was on the line — not just from the seemingly hopeless difference of opinions at hand, but from many months of increasingly laborious arguments around it. Neither one was optimistic that there was a way out of this. Grant was as adamant as Molly was passionate. Couples counseling was a "last resort" (as it all too frequently is), but at any rate, they were skeptical as to what solution I could possibly provide to the impasse.[3]

Grant laid out his arguments. He had a physical disability, and he was often weak and tired. He barely managed to keep up with the responsibilities of having a single child. He was certain that he could not handle parenting a second one. Meanwhile, Molly advocated fiercely for the need to give their daughter a sibling. She argued, cajoled, pleaded, yearned. But the disagreement remained firmly in place.

Enter empathic dialogue. If ever there was a time it would seem this wouldn't work, this was it. Empathy or not, there's no way to have half a kid. And it didn't seem likely either one was going to be moved from their position. Ah, but recall, empathic dialogue is neither about resolving nor about convincing. I simply helped them share what was going on inside and empathize with each other.

Unsurprisingly, there was quite a lot under the surface. Over the course of a few sessions, Molly was able to share how her wish for a second child related to her worth as a woman, to her fraught family history, to the untimely death of her own sister years earlier, and perhaps most strongly, to her profound wish to give their daughter someone to rely on through thick and thin. Grant revealed – or discovered – his feelings of

---

[3] They were, of course, right to be skeptical about that; the job of a good couples counselor is not to propose a solution to the couple's problem; it's to help the couple find their own solutions.

self-doubt, his insecurity in the paternal role given his own father's absence from his life, his worries about the limitations of his physical abilities.

A lot came out over just five sessions. And after that, they walked away, grateful that their marriage had been saved.

I have no idea what they decided to do about having another baby.

* * *

Adam: I feel frustrated when I'm trying to get the kids dressed for school and there's no socks in their drawer and it turns into a giant circus trying to get them out the door.

Raina: Yeah, I can understand that being a frustrating situation.

Adam: It really is. I wish you'd make the laundry a priority so that this doesn't keep happening.

Raina: You keep finding yourself in a difficult situation when the laundry isn't done and you're kind of annoyed at me about it.

Adam: Yeah.

Raina: Yeah, that stinks. I don't want the mornings to be any crazier for you than they have to be.

Adam: Right... thanks.

Raina: Would it be okay if I shared my view of things a little bit?

Adam: Sure, go ahead.

Raina: Well, sometimes I'm so overwhelmed managing all the household stuff that I don't even have a chance to put the kids' socks away. I feel like I'm drowning in chores. And at the same time, I feel really bad when I can't pull off the things that are needed for you to do your part as well.

Adam: You're overwhelmed with housework and you can't always get the socks done on time... and you feel bad that it ends up affecting me.

Raina: Right. And also...

Chapter 9

Resolving Problems

Kai: *I was thinking maybe this year we could go to the beach again over summer vacation since it was such a hit last year.*

Tanya: *I don't know, maybe let's try something a little different this year.*

Kai: *Different? Like what? It's so hard to find something everyone will enjoy.*

Tanya: *Yeah, but I think the kids got a little bored at the end last year and it got a little crazy.*

Kai: *Well, that's going to happen no matter where we go!*

Tanya: *What about a road trip somewhere?*

Kai: *Cooped up in an RV all summer???*

Okay folks, here is it – the moment you've all been waiting for. Here's where we talk about how to actually resolve the problems you're dialoguing about. I want to emphasize again that resolution is not actually the objective of communication in your marriage. It is not the ultimate destination you need to reach in order to achieve marital happiness. If you throw on some sneakers and go for a jog down the block, more often than not it isn't because you have a goal of arriving at the end of the block. Probably the jog *is* the goal. You want to get your body to a certain level of fitness so that you feel good instead of tired and achy, have a healthy body instead of an ailing one, and ultimately enjoy your life more. The same thing is often true with communication: the communication *is* the destination. It's the process by which you get your *marriage* to a certain level of fitness so that it becomes a source of pleasure and growth for you, instead of something that makes you, well, tired and achy.

That said, yes, there are problems in life that need resolving. But, as we noted before, you didn't get married to solve problems. Problems are just part of the Great Road Trip of Life that you have to attend to while driving along in the vehicle of your relationship. So let's talk about how to do that.

The truth is, once you've gone through a good empathic dialogue, often there isn't even a problem to solve anymore. You may need to apologize for something, but you may not. You may need to change something, but you may not. The power of being heard and validated is such that you may discover that you feel happy and fulfilled despite not having gotten rid of the problem that your spouse wears ugly sweaters or that your in-laws are too nosy. A meaningful and intimate connection with a life partner can do that for you.

Another possibility is that you'll discover there isn't even a problem to solve but rather a simple miscommunication.

Michael was not the kind of person you typically picture as the stereotypical thera-pygoer. He was a truck driver, large in all dimensions, and sported a long beard and a significant number of aggressive-looking tattoos. His wife, Elena, was petite but vocal, and although it was she that made the call for the appointment for couples counseling, apparently it was Michael that insisted it happen. He felt invisible in the marriage, he said, like his thoughts and opinions didn't matter. He believed that Elena was not interested in listening to him. When she protested this, he cited an example of when he was trying to share his feelings with Elena, and her response was along the lines of "go talk to a therapist." Michael felt unwanted and blocked out.

In our second session we began learning the process of empathic dialogue. Elena took the role of listener and understood how her comment had hurt Michael. When he felt she got it and they switched roles, Elena spoke about how much she cared about Michael and felt overwhelmed by the deep and difficult emotions he was sharing with her; she didn't feel competent to help him deal with them and she meant genuinely that he should find a therapist to help him through these things. She didn't at all mean that she didn't want to hear them.

Michael was stunned to hear this. "Oh," he gulped. "I had no idea."

It is incredibly common for people to misunderstand what their spouse says or means. Then both parties get angry at each other and have a Big Giant Fight when the whole thing was a mistake. Sound familiar? It does to a lot of people (myself included). Of course, the wrong way to go about fixing this is to start explaining what you actually meant (Category B!). The only way out of this is with LOVE; and once you go through that, you may well discover that there is in fact no problem here! (Not only that, but the process of empathic dialogue will also have you feeling closer and more successful as a couple.)

But sometimes there is a problem you want to solve. What extracurriculars do we sign the kids up for? Should we buy a new car? Who should follow up with the contractor? There is a practical answer needed. Once you go through LOVE, the process of coming up with a solution is much, much easier. That's because before empathic dialogue, you don't really get what the argument is actually about. Remember, you can't solve a problem you don't fully understand! But once you do fully understand it, solving it is so much simpler.

> Once you go through LOVE, the process of coming up with a solution is much, much easier.

In the conversation at the beginning of the chapter, Kai and Tanya are having a typical argument about an apparently practical matter. And it seems like they're just at odds over personal preference. But it's rarely so simple. Actually, Tanya is dreading the beach because Kai's difficult sister tends to show up unannounced and pour stress into the beach house. In addition, getting the kids dressed and undressed for the beach several times a day usually falls on her, which is exhausting. For his part, Kai tends to have difficulty trying new things – better the devil you know than the devil you don't – and he can't tolerate the kids complaining they're bored or uncomfortable or what have you; at the beach they run around all day and are generally content, and that's much easier on him. Empathic dialogue will go a long way here. Kai can certainly understand that Tanya can't stand his sister (he can barely stand his sister, for Pete's sake), but he didn't even realize how hard it is for her to manage the dressing and undressing. Tanya is generally aware that Kai likes his routine and recognizes how hard it is for him to be thrown into a new situation. Once all the issues are on the table, and everyone is clear that their spouse gets their concerns and cares about them, it's really a short distance to a workable solution.

Moreover, the process of finding it is much more pleasant, because now that both spouses have felt each other's empathy, they feel like they're on the same team again. Now they are both searching for a solution that minimizes time with Kai's sister but doesn't require a massive change in the way things have been done. It's not a zero-sum game anymore; it's a collaborative riddle to solve.

Now, this doesn't mean that you can never take a stab at coming up with solutions until you 100% understand everything your spouse thinks and feels about the situation (as if 100% perfect understanding were even achievable). After all, new feelings will come up; situations will change over time. So total comprehension is a moving target, and you will likely need to start working on solutions before you get there. But if *here and now* you feel like there's an important point you haven't shared yet or your spouse hasn't understood yet, you are not ready to work on solutions. You may never hit 100%, but the more fully you explore together, the more likely you'll have a good conversation about solutions.

> The more fully you explore together, the more likely you'll have a good conversation about solutions.

COMING UP WITH SOLUTIONS

Finding solutions that fit is definitely easier after the exploration conversation. But that doesn't necessarily mean it's going to be *easy*. Real life comes with sticky problems. A helpful way to produce potential solutions is by starting with brainstorming. Brainstorming doesn't just mean proposing ideas; it means *just* proposing ideas. That is, when you are proposing ideas, you do not evaluate them at all. There is no weighing in on whether the idea that has been suggested is good or bad, realistic or unrealistic, sensible or crazy. You just toss them out there (ideally writing them down on a paper or tablet or something). Evaluating the ideas is a separate stage of the process and (stop me if you've heard this before) it's important to keep the different parts of the conversation separate.

The ideas you suggest are, by design, allowed to be wild and crazy. They don't have to fit your preconceived criteria yet. The fact that you don't have enough money or time or manpower isn't relevant for right now. Ignoring potential limitations is a tried-and-true way of spurring creativity and opening the door to re-sourceful, out-of-the-box ideas. Just throw out whatever comes to mind; sure, you'll cross out the nutty ones pretty soon. But at first, just invent; you'll scale back later.

Of course, this doesn't mean you don't try to come up with actual workable solutions; it just means you're keeping all your options open. And while you are trying to come up with workable solutions, you are now able to take into account not only your own concerns but your spouse's as well. Those concerns need to re-main an important factor in your thinking. Now that you've gone through em-pathic dialogue, you understand what your spouse desires, needs, and worries about in this situation. If the solutions you're suggesting address *your* desires, needs, and worries but not your spouse's, you're not really being genuine as far as working together as a team; you're still just focusing on yourself. At the same time, if you propose solutions that take *only* your spouse's concerns into account and not yours, you're not being real with *yourself* either. There are two people on this team. You need to keep both of them in mind.

When I worked with Johnny and Benita some years back, it was pretty light fare – they just needed a marriage tune-up, no drastic issues. We had wrapped up couples counseling when they felt their marriage was back on the track they wanted. I was surprised to hear from them a few years later requesting to book a session. It sounded urgent. It turned out that Johnny had been having an affair with his office manager, Kareen – for years. All through the time we'd been in counseling together. Benita, of course, was devastated. But they both wanted to rebuild the marriage. It took some time and a lot of grit.

It didn't take long for Benita to bring up the question of what would happen with Kareen. She couldn't stomach having her still working with Johnny; the idea of them being in the same office together was unthinkable for her. Johnny understood this. They had done a lot of empathic dialogue and had shared a lot of raw feelings. Al-though Johnny wanted to be fully supportive of Benita, he didn't know if he could run the business without Kareen. He proposed a solution: he wouldn't stay late at work anymore. This more or less shut down conversation for the day. It was obvious that his business concerns were foremost on his mind, and Benita's (very understandable) dis-

comfort with Kareen and Johnny being in the same office didn't factor into his "solution" at all.

Keeping your needs in the conversation doesn't mean that you cannot or should not sometimes give up on something you want for the sake of your spouse; it just means that when you do that, it should feel like you're giving a gift to your spouse, not like you're bottling up your own needs and brewing resentment. If you are squashing your needs to avoid conflict or make a problem go away, it is probably just going to hurt the marriage in the long term.

Once you've got a whole bunch of ideas on paper (or screen) – and perhaps have had a few laughs along the way – you can start evaluating them. Scratch out the ones that it's clear (to everyone) are just fantasies – playing the lottery to win enough for a renovation; moving to Greenland for a year to avoid another holiday get-together with Uncle Ethan. Then go through the decently realistic options and begin to assess and tweak as needed. It can be helpful here to use a similar format as in your exploration conversation, where one person gets to speak and the other one reflects what they're hearing, to make sure you're on the same page.

Of course, I can't tell you exactly how to weigh out the best option for any given problem; it depends on so many factors that are unique to you, like your personalities, your histories, your values, etc. For a discussion on the science of problem-solving itself we'd need a whole book in its own right. The point here is not to teach you how to arrive at the solution, but rather how to make the journey towards it possible.

Simon and Letitia were an intelligent and influential couple who were frustrated by the state of their marriage, especially in light of their demonstrated professional competence. Things improved steadily as we got their communication patterns dialed in and learned to recognize the emotional sensitivities each of them had. One of the frustrations we discussed was Letitia's indecisiveness. They would need to make a decision about any number of things, and though they could discuss the pros and cons of any approach, the decision never seemed to get made until they often had to wing it at the last minute. Simon wanted to know how to address this, given that empathic dialogue seemed to feed right into that problem – they could understand each other's feelings around the issue, but the needed decision still did not materialize.

I counseled him as follows: go through the process of empathic dialogue; discuss the options; and then, if she is still vacillating, go ahead and make the decision yourself. She won't be angry at you. Simon was surprised and skeptical. He turned to Letitia. "Absolutely," she confirmed. The point was this: Letitia had her own issues to work out regarding decision-making, and she knew that. Were Simon to deal with this with a dictatorial and unilateral approach, it would be a point of conflict between them. But because he would take the time to hear out and understand her perspective, she would not experience his finally taking the reins as dictatorial but as supportive and responsible – especially if he would do a good job of taking her concerns into account in that final decision.

Like an exploration conversation, don't expect a resolution conversation to wrap up in one go. That might happen sometimes, but probably not for the really big issues you're going to face in your life. And many of the challenges we come up against will develop and change over time – central issues like your financial situation, your children, and so on. Expect to have a series of conversations over time for juggernauts like those.

Expect also that resolution conversations *still* won't be purely about facts and numbers. Sometimes things will get heated during the resolution conversation. What this means is that someone has some feelings about the situation that haven't been brought to light, that haven't been heard and validated. This doesn't at all mean that someone was hiding something (though that's also possible); it's commonplace for us to discover we have feelings about an issue only as we talk about it. Perhaps new feelings are coming up now ("I'm getting frustrated because it seems we keep running into the same obstacles with our budget").

You have surely had seemingly empirical discussions with your spouse in which one of you developed an unpleasant edge in your tone. This should be taken as a clue that there are unheard feelings afoot and a directional sign guiding you to put the resolution conversation on hold and go back to the exploration phase. (A timeout may be advisable here as well. And just as with timeouts, anyone can call a return to exploration if they feel it's necessary.) What's the feeling that came up? What's going on for you? Explicitly acknowledge that you need to go back there. Don't try to push through with finding a solution; it won't work. Well, it might work as far as coming out with some semi-adequate decision if you bulldoze your way to the end, but you will almost certainly both be left feeling frustrated with the process and disconnected from each other. Short-term win, long-term loss.

Note that some of the problems you will face in life actually won't have a good solution at all. You may simply never be where you want to be financially. You may have a disabled child who will need extra care and attention for years or decades. I don't promise answers to these kinds of larger-than-life challenges. But I do promise that if you are vigilant about practicing empathic dialogue, you can still live a happy life in a loving marriage despite such challenges. Nothing bonds people together like shared adversity. Empathic dialogue helps you share it rather than fight over it.

APOLOGIES

You may recall that apologizing, like solving, is a Category B activity, and indeed, we are at the point where this action might be relevant. Remember, though, that validation and empathy are of far more importance than the words "I'm sorry." They convey your love and care far more meaningfully; and without those as a preface, an apology orients the conversation around a right-or-wrong axis. Even if you are the one accepting responsibility for some wrongdoing, you risk making this a conversation about fault rather than about mutuality and connection. Still, if you have indeed done wrong – even partially, in some small way – an apology might be appropriate and appreciated. You avoid the pitfall of faultfinding by preceding it with empathic dialogue.

I want to focus for a moment on the value and possibility of an apology even where you don't agree on the substance of the alleged offense. Recall that there is explicitly no requirement or expectation of agreement in empathic dialogue. How then do you handle your spouse being mad at you for something you don't think you did?

"I'm really hurt by the way you spoke to me yesterday when we were discussing the proposal I wrote. I felt belittled. I kind of got the impression that you don't think I'm very smart."

You are totally blindsided by your spouse's comments. You thought the proposal was pretty good, and you only meant to offer helpful feedback (as you had been asked to do!). Maybe you were a bit tired last night, but belittling? Not smart? Hard for you to fathom. But that's okay; you know that empathic dialogue is a great tool anyway. You reflect, validate, and empathize:

"You're hurt because of the way I spoke to you yesterday – you experienced my comments as demeaning and you think maybe I'm looking down on you."

"Yes."

"Well, I can definitely understand how hurtful and unpleasant that must have been. You really worked hard on that proposal and you felt dumped on, and that really stinks."

This may well be the end of the conversation. But you may also find your spouse still looking at you expectantly... waiting for an apology. So I want to propose what I call the "midway apology," which keeps us out of the rough waters of judgmentalism and sticks to love and empathy. It looks like this:

"If I somehow communicated to you that I don't think you are very bright, I am really sorry about that. I actually think really highly of your writing abilities, and I apologize if I communicated anything other than that."

This approach has been maligned in other writings (sometimes called the "non-apology" or the "ifpology.") Certainly it can be misused simply to mollify one's critics while deflecting blame (the kind of verbal misdirection that is used all the time in politics). In a relationship it might sound like "I'm sorry if you felt hurt," or worse, "I'm sorry if you think I did something wrong." What you are really saying is, "It's not my fault, and it's too bad you feel that way because you are incorrect."

But remember that we are not in a court of public opinion here, and we are trying to stay away from any discourse around blame or fault. Still, we are stuck with the problem that you may really not think you were being critical or disdainful, yet your spouse feels a certain way. The point then is that *you do not have to agree that you said it, but you have to feel bad that your spouse feels it.* And if you can accept that you may have played even the tiniest role

> You do not have to agree that you said it, but you have to feel bad that your spouse feels it.

in their feeling that way, then an apology is possible.

The midway apology accepts the possibility that maybe you are not 100% all-knowing. Can you be absolutely certain that you in no way communicated any-thing, verbally or nonverbally, that could possibly, in any way, have been miscon-strued for any reason? (A: No, you cannot.) All I am suggesting with this paradigm is apologizing for *possibly* having *unintentionally* hurt your spouse. If you acci-dentally conveyed the message that you think they're dumb (and if you were tired last night, there's all the more chance that you inadvertently said or indicated some-thing ambiguous), for that you can and should feel bad and apologize.[1]

The other component of making this work is your tone. If you speak genu-inely, if you really feel bad for possibly having caused your spouse pain and your tone is indicative of such, then the "if" statement won't come off as a deflection. On the other hand, if you really think your spouse is totally out of touch with reality; if you are more concerned about the appearance of accepting responsibility than about how they feel; if you sound annoyed, patronizing, or self-righteous – then yeah, your not-really-sincere apology may fall flat and make matters worse. You've got to be honest with yourself if you're going to give this a shot. If you fell short and were being mean on purpose, own up to it and apologize. If you *accidentally* hurt your spouse's feelings, that's worth an apology too. And if you really don't think either is true, the midway apology is still a helpful approach you can use. Consider the possibility that you are not infallible and that perhaps you unwittingly fell short of perfection. You don't have to apologize for not being perfect. You just have to apologize for possibly, in your imperfection, having hurt your spouse. Nothing wrong with that.

* * *

Kai: *I was thinking maybe this year we could go to the beach again over summer vacation since it was such a hit last year.*

Tanya: *I don't know, maybe let's try something a little different this year.*

Kai: *Different? Like what? It's so hard to find something everyone will enjoy.*

---

[1] Of course, if you *intentionally* communicated something derogatory, then there's no ques-tion an apology is called for, even if you believe what you said is justified. Intentionally causing pain to your partner has no place whatsoever in a marriage.

Tanya: Yeah, but I think the kids got a little bored at the end last year and it got a little crazy.

Kai: Well, that's going to happen no matter where we go!

Tanya: Wait wait wait... this is getting a little tense. Maybe we need to explore a bit how we feel about the various options.

Kai: I FEEL like we need to go to the beach!

Tanya: Okay, but you seem pretty irritated about it. What's bothering you?

Kai: I AM irritated, because... uh... I'm not even sure why.

Tanya: That's fair. Let's take a little break and check in in 20 minutes.

Kai: *HUFF.* Fine. Yeah. Let's do that.

Chapter 10

Mindsets That Help

Wilson: *Hi Honey, I'm sorry I'm—*

Val: *Where have you been??? You were supposed to be home an hour ago! I've been dealing with the kids on my own and they've been awful tonight.*

Wilson: *I know, I'm sorry, I—*

Val: *You always find a way to avoid helping with bedtime again.*

Wilson: *No no, it's not that – there was terrible traffic and then halfway home I realized I left a USB drive at work that I have to have tonight to work on some documents...*

Val: *You forgot.*

Wilson: *Yeah, I know, I'm really sorry.*

Val: *Well maybe try not forgetting!! I'm home alone with three kids, and you go and forget your work. Nice job. Oh, and you could have called, you know!*

Wilson: *Well, uh, I did. But it went straight to voicemail.*

Empathic dialogue is a skill that needs learning and practice like any other skill. It takes time and effort to develop. And like many other skills, there are some mindsets you can embrace that will make the process easier and/or more effective. For example, when you're learning to drive, it can be helpful to start with the mindset that not everyone else on the road knows what they're doing. This means you need to be prepared for the people in the cars around you to do strange things (no doubt you have had many such experiences). You still need to practice the skills of driving, but having this perspective can make a big difference for your safety. Below are some mindsets that will help you succeed at empathic dialogue and in your marriage overall.

1. NOBODY CAN READ MINDS

We've brought this point up a few times already, but Mr. Rogers may have said it best: "Nobody knows what you're thinking or feeling unless you share it."

> You need to tell your partner how you feel and not assume they will know without you saying it.

This leads us to two important points: firstly, *you should not assume that your partner knows what's going on inside you if you don't explicitly tell them.* And secondly, *you should not assume that you know what's going on inside your partner if they don't explicitly tell you.* Let's do a little recap here as we discuss the mindsets you want to have for optimal marital success.

You need to tell your partner how you feel and not assume they will know without you saying it. When I encourage clients to share how they're feeling, sometimes they respond with, "But it's obvious that I feel _____ about this!" I promise you it is not obvious.

> *Evan and Carrie sat dejected and deflated on my couch, neither one looking at each other. Carrie was weeping as she told me about her discovery of Evan's infidelity. She was shocked and deeply hurt. For his part, Evan clearly felt terrible about it. Whatever his reasons and justifications for having done what he did, he was now facing the hurt he had caused and his regret was palpable. When Carrie tearfully wondered aloud whether he still loved her, he burst out with, "Of course I love you! I wouldn't be here going through this if I didn't!" He thought it was obvious. He thought Carrie should be clear on that point. She certainly was not.*

Your partner does not live in your head. There is no reason for them to know what you're feeling without you telling them. Sometimes this may be hard to believe, but it's honestly true. Things that make you angry do not make everyone angry: I know many people go nuts when someone cuts them off in traffic; personally, it just doesn't bother me terribly. Things that make you anxious don't make everyone anxious: I get antsy when I'm late for an event; my wife just doesn't mind that much. One of the hardest parts about being a human among other humans is trying to grasp that our experience of the world is different from that of other humans.

Sure, sometimes you have experiences that are pretty universal and your partner has a decently good idea of what you're going through (or maybe they just know you really well). But it is very wise not to assume that this is the case. Even when they do have a good read on what's going on inside you, there are almost certainly nuances and details they aren't fully aware of. It is important for you to tell them clearly what you are experiencing and how you are feeling, not to assume they already know.

The flip side of this is that you also don't know what's in your partner's head until they tell you. You are not a mind reader any more than your partner is.[1] You may *think* you know; you may even be right. But you cannot be certain that you really get it until they tell you straight out. It is easy to misinterpret body language. It is *certainly* easy to take a text message the wrong way. It's also common to interpret nonverbal signals correctly but get the source of them wrong – your partner may be snippy not because they're mad at you for overcooking the vegetable souffle but simply because the receptionist at work was extra unhelpful today.

Even when they do tell you straight out, you have to check and make sure you got the message right (see chapter 6 on reflecting). It's so easy to filter what you hear through your own personal biases and take your partner's comments the wrong way.

Remember as you go through this process that you simply cannot know what someone else is thinking or feeling until they tell you. Sometimes it may turn out that what you suspected was correct – but often you will find out it really wasn't (or at least not entirely).

2. PEOPLE USUALLY MAKE SENSE

Everyone does what they do for a reason. And almost always, that reason makes sense on some level. It's true that there are people who have severe mental

---

[1] Mind reading is actually the name used in cognitive behavioral therapy (CBT) for a cognitive distortion that many people tend to employ and that leads to a lot of misery.

illnesses, to the point of being out of touch with reality. Probably your partner is not one of these people. Sometimes we colloquially refer to people as acting "irrationally," but even then it's usually possible to discover a reason that makes sense. For example, a person on a diet who strongly wishes to lose weight gets angry at themselves for slipping up and eating too big a portion of dinner; in their distress and impulsivity they grab a pint of ice cream and polish that off too. It's easy to think, *This makes no sense! They're just hurting themselves more!* It's true that they're just further thwarting their own goal – but let's consider where they're at. They've been trying so hard, for a long time. The diet is hard, but they've really been sacrificing to make it work. They mess up and overdo it at dinner. They feel terrible – regretful, ashamed, hopeless. The emotions overwhelm them and they're totally overloaded. Instinctively they reach for something loaded with fat and sugar to provide a sense of satisfaction and reduce their distress. Sure, in a calm and controlled moment they would logically choose otherwise. Ice cream is not a great pick for a dieter. But *it makes sense that they chose it* if you understand how they were feeling in the moment and what the ice cream did for them.

In our vignette above, Val is furious with Wilson, but his actions make sense when you consider his perspective – he may well understand the importance of being home, but he could not afford to leave the USB drive at work. Her anger also makes sense (though I do not advocate dealing with it in quite the same way she did): she's stressed and struggling and even though Wilson has a good explanation for what happened, we can understand why she's upset! Hopefully Wilson does too, although perhaps he hasn't taken the time to really see things from her point of view. Maybe he *doesn't* yet understand what she's so upset about.

Likewise, your partner will do things you don't understand. That doesn't mean it doesn't make sense in some way. Remember the "help me understand" approach (see sidebar "The Three Most Important Words" in chapter 2). Before you reach that point of understanding, you would be wise to assume your partner has some sensible reason for feeling and behaving the way they do. You may not get it yet – you may never 100% get it – but that doesn't mean their perspective has no validity. It's so common for both partners to think their perspective is the right one and their partner is just being unreasonable, when in fact they are *both* right, because, as we have discussed, there are different ways of seeing and interpreting a situation, different ways of reacting, different values and preferences, etc.

Once I was making some food for myself in the kitchen. This is an extremely rare and somewhat risky event. Chana was a little worried. She hovered a little bit, but I was in some kind of reckless mood and I was determined to do it myself. I indicated that I did not want her to get involved, but she was still hovering. Then I made it explicitly clear that I did not want her help, so she excused herself. Moments later she came back and began offering her help again. I got very snippy with her. I could not believe she stuck her nose in my "cooking" after I very clearly asked her not to. And I was even more annoyed that she walked away angry at me! All I wanted was to tackle the project myself, and I had said so. I could not understand what on earth she was thinking.

When we talked about it a few days later, we were able to hear out each other's perspectives. And we were both quite surprised at what we heard. Chana, somehow, had gotten the message from me that I was actually asking her to help! And then I went and got snippy at her! No wonder she was upset. From her perspective, her behavior certainly made sense; she was receiving mixed messages. I may have thought I conveyed a clear message to her, but, rightly or wrongly, that message didn't get across to her.

And she was equally surprised to hear that I was certain I had clearly communicated my wish to be left to my own devices. That was definitely not what she understood at the time. But she could understand why I got snippy, seeing as how I was pretty sure I had made my wishes clear! Both of us were originally baffled at the other's reaction; and both of us came to see how the other person's behavior made sense, despite what we had initially thought.

(Did we go back and argue over what I did or didn't say and whether I did or did not make a clear request? We did not. We validated the other person's position: "Of course you'd be annoyed if you're getting mixed messages from me!" "I get why you were so snippy now – you thought you'd told me what you wanted." And that's all that we needed.)

3. ASSUME GOOD WILL

In the absence of conclusive evidence to the contrary, assume your partner means well in any given situation. It is much easier to deal

> In the absence of conclusive evidence to the contrary, assume your partner means well in any given situation.

with a painful situation if the person responsible just missed the mark or otherwise messed up somehow than if they are deliberately trying to stick it to you. If you believe your partner deliberately avoided coming home because they didn't want to help clean out the garage, you are going to be a lot angrier than if you think they simply forgot because of a crisis at work or an urgent call from a friend (or any number of plausible explanations).

A related practice is giving the benefit of the doubt. If there are multiple ways to interpret or explain a situation or a comment your partner made (and there almost always are), choose one that supports having a good marriage rather than one that damages it, until it is impossible to explain it any other way. If you see your significant other running out of a bank holding a gun and a bag with a big dollar sign on it – that is pretty incontrovertible evidence. Short of something like that, consider the possibility that it's not what you think. Maybe your partner really *did* get an urgent call from a friend. Maybe there *was* terrible traffic. Truly there are many reasonable explanations for a lot of situations we find ourselves in. I have seen countless times in my own life and the lives of my clients that the explanation that seems most obvious to an observer turns out to be incorrect.

Bonus Tool: What Did You Mean by That?

As we've noted repeatedly, every individual has their own way of interpreting the world, their own filter through which every bit of data passes. It is easy and common for people to take offense at something someone says to them when truly no offense was meant. When your partner (or anyone else) says something hurtful, it can spare a lot of hardship to simply ask them, "What did you mean by that?" It will give them a chance to restate themselves in a way that changes your understanding of their comment.

Maya comes out of her room sporting a new dress that she wants to show off to Ari.

Ari: *You don't look good.*

Maya (wants to say): You moron! Can't you say anything nice?

Maya (actually says): What did you mean by that?

Ari: I mean, you look a little pale. Are you feeling okay?

Maya: Oh. Actually, I am feeling a bit lightheaded. Could you get me some
           water?

Ari: Sure.

Of course, if your partner *did* intend to be hurtful, then they'll simply insult you again more clearly, and you will have the certainty that they are being spiteful instead of accidentally hurtful.

Some people worry that this approach means they'll be taken advantage of because they are always turning a blind eye to negative behaviors by assuming their partner really meant well.[2] This is not what I am recommending. First of all, this is only meant to apply where there is a reasonable possibility of positive interpretations. If your partner calls you a nasty name in a fit of anger, you don't have to assume that in their family the word "idiot" is actually a term of endearment. Sometimes there's no positive explanation available. But you will be surprised at how often there actually is.

Secondly, after you assume good will, you can still clarify what happened afterwards. If you presume that your partner had good intentions and in fact they had *bad* intentions, you can always respond accordingly when that becomes clear: you can express your feelings; you can act to protect yourself (e.g., "since I can't trust them with my phone, I'll have to change the password"); you can leave the marriage if the transgression was serious enough. By contrast, if you assume they had bad intentions when in fact they really had good ones, the results aren't so good. Let's

---

[2] Ironically, the people who are likely to assume good will for too long are the ones who genuinely have good will towards their partner, and the people who are more likely to peg their partner's actions as malicious or manipulative are the ones who are willing to act in those ways themselves.

say they make some comment which you take the wrong way, so you think all these nasty things about them, get angry, perhaps yell at your partner, which only causes them to become defensive and/or yell back, things escalate and maybe turn into a major fight – and then you find out they didn't actually mean what you thought they did. But the damage to the marriage is already done, possibly totally for nothing. The example in the sidebar above could have gone exactly that way, but for Maya's wise decision to question her interpretation of Ari's words. In Val and Wilson's conversation, on the other hand, Val's initial accusation that Wilson's lateness was intentional definitely inflamed the situation.

Thirdly, if you repeatedly assume good will when something goes awry but the same thing keeps happening, at some point it becomes clear that something isn't right. For example, there's only so many times you can assume that your partner "forgot" to wash the dishes before it makes sense to suspect there is some ill intent at play that needs to be addressed.

That said, the reality is that being in a relationship means taking some level of risk. Relationships don't work well when there is no vulnerability and no trust. If

> **Being in a relationship means taking some level of risk.**

you are more concerned about looking like a sucker than in growing a relationship, you may keep your image intact but not your relationship. If you have had experiences in the past that make it scary for you to trust someone else, or that leave you feeling like everyone in the world is waiting to take advantage of you, it certainly makes sense to be more guarded and cautious. It might be a good idea to seek out therapy to heal from those experiences.

Just like most people are not crazy and make sense on some level, most people do not enjoy being cruel, and it is generally reasonable to assume good will and to give the benefit of the doubt. (If you truly believe your partner is being cruel for the sake of it, you probably need something other than a communication book.)

4. PEOPLE MAKE MISTAKES

Everyone messes up. Frequently. It's a normal occurrence and we should expect that some things will just go wrong. We all know this, but somehow when our spouse goes ahead and actually does make a mistake, we forget and we get all upset at them, as if "sure, *some* mistakes happen, but *this one* shouldn't have." Ah, but it did. Not only do mistakes happen, but you don't get to choose which ones it's gonna be.

The upshot of this is that when your spouse flubs something, you should take it in stride. That doesn't mean you can't be angry, if it's the kind of thing that could have been avoided, or sad, if they broke your very favorite porcelain cat statuette. As you know by now,

> Not only do mistakes happen, but you don't get to choose which ones it's gonna be.

feelings are what they are and I don't recommend pretending they aren't. But chewing your spouse out, berating them, putting them down – these are uncalled for and certainly unhelpful. Remembering that mistakes are a part of life can help you get through these moments.

It is also worth remembering that you too make mistakes (and probably not fewer than your spouse). Have you never forgotten something at the office? *How would you like to be treated when you do?* This happens to me all the time – Chana will be looking around for her car keys and I will fight back my annoyance, try not to roll my eyes, and just shut my yap and help her look. And then, minutes to hours later, I'm looking around for my Bluetooth earpiece, bereft and desperate for some help, feeling very glad that I did not make any snide comments when Chana lost her keys. Even if you are the kind of person who is very hard on yourself and you tend to be very self-critical when you mess up, you probably don't want your spouse to be harshly critical of you as well.

"Ah," you're saying, "but I'm not like that. I try to be very organized and on top of things. I don't lose my stuff. I don't forget things. I'm *responsible*." Very well. That could be. But what *other* kinds of mistakes do you make? Do you have a short fuse and lose your cool on people quicker than you should? Do you have trouble locating items in the fridge? Again, let me put the question to you: *how would you like to be treated when you make a mistake?* Think about that next time your spouse messes something up.

If you are saying to yourself right now, "Yeah, but honestly my mistakes are totally normal, and my spouse's mistakes are just stupid and careless" – I recommend you do some serious

> How would you like to be treated when you make a mistake?

self-reflection. If you believe that you are always totally reliable and your mistakes are excusable, while your spouse is unreliable and their mistakes are inexcusable, then either you are fooling yourself stupendously and need a good dose of humility, or you should really consider whether your spouse is someone you ought to be married to.

5. YOUR PARTNER IS AWESOME

I mean, aren't they? You got together with your partner, stayed with them, married them, because they are awesome in some way. Probably many ways! Aren't there all kinds of reasons you love this person? Maybe they're kind, or sociable, or deep, or open-minded, or creative, or dedicated. Maybe they know how to have a good time, how to cheer you up, how to mobilize social change, how to fix the computer. Every human being has many, many positive qualities and skills and strengths in addition to the faults and weaknesses and shortcomings that are part of the human condition. Where are you putting your focus?

Imagine if in the conversation above Val had been able to hold on to the knowledge that Wilson is generally a caring and reliable person. Val probably would have been able to stave off angry theories as to why Wilson wasn't home yet (see point number 3 about the benefit of the doubt). We can all do this too. Draw up a mental (or written) list of the great things about your partner. Next time they show up late, or forget to do this dishes, or whatever everyday infraction it might be – pull out that list and think hard about it. Weigh your (totally fair) irritation against how phenomenal they are with your difficult parents or how much their sense of humor adds to your life and let that guide what kind of energy you want to put into this marriage at this difficult moment. (Note that I didn't say ignore or squash your feelings of irritation. You can feel irritated and also choose how to react in a given situation based on a broader perspective. Context is critical!)

I have gotten myself into the habit, whenever I stub my toe, of immediately saying to myself in mid-wince, "Welp, the other nine are still working!" This doesn't mean that my toe doesn't hurt or that I don't get a Band-Aid. It just means that I can switch my perspective to recognize that 98% of my body is in fine shape at that moment, and that takes a lot of the negativity out of the situation. I try to do the same with my marriage and with my life. My wife has so many strengths that far outweigh the fact that she can't remember names (like, *at all*) that those little things don't get in the way of our marriage, even if I find them annoying at times.[3]

A similar way to take a broader perspective on a frustrating situation is to ask yourself "Will this bother me a year from now?" Odds are the answer is no. Again, contextualizing whatever you're going through – without feeling a need to squash it – can help get you back into a positive frame of mind.

> Ask yourself "Will this bother me a year from now?" Odds are the answer is no.

Let's see how Val and Wilson could have employed some of these mindsets to do things differently. In fact, the bulk of this happens before the conversation even starts:

Val (to herself): This is crazy. I can't believe he's not home yet. I canNOT manage these kids on my own anymore! [Deep breath.] Okay, probably some urgent matter came up or something's going on that makes sense [benefit of the doubt]. Or maybe he's just avoiding another awful night with the kids? No, that's not his style. I know him. He's been frustrated with bedtime too, but he's not the type to just flake out on me like that. He's not gonna just hang me out to dry on purpose [her partner is awesome!].

Wilson: Hi Honey, I'm sorry I'm—

Val: Where have you been??? You were supposed to be home an hour ago! I've been dealing with the kids on my own and they've been awful tonight.

Wilson: I know, I'm sorry, I—

Val: Is everything okay?

Wilson: Well, there was terrible traffic and then halfway home I realized I left a USB drive at work that I have to have tonight to work on some documents...

Val: You forgot. Sigh. Well, that's a real pain in the butt. For both of us. [People make mistakes.]

Wilson: Yeah, I know. I'm really sorry. I tried calling, but it went straight to voicemail. [People make mistakes!]

---

[3] I mean, we can spend five minutes just trying to identify who the person is she's trying to tell me a story about. "The guy with the big nose – you know, he said he once visited San Francisco? And he likes dogs?"

Val: *Ugh! Look, let's talk later. I'm a bit overloaded. I'm about to lose it with these kids. [Nobody can read minds.] Can you step in and take over?*

Wilson: *Sure. Go take a break, I'll see what I can do with these rapscallions.*

Chapter 11

Troubleshooting Common Issues

Let's take a look at some of the problems and objections that come up when people are trying to practice empathic dialogue. I promise that you are not the only one with questions and challenges! This is new for you, and any new skill has a learning curve.

1. WE STILL END UP IN A FIGHT WHEN WE TRY TO TALK ABOUT OUR ISSUES.

This probably means you are normal. If you've been getting into fights before now – and most couples, even happy couples, fight at times – then it will take some time to build new habits and break out of old patterns. If you are trying to change the way you and your partner communicate, it won't happen overnight. Remember to appreciate the small wins – if you usually have one blowup fight every week and next month you walk away from *one* of them, you're moving in the right direction.

> It will take some time to build new habits and break out of old patterns.

Hold fast to timeouts. They are your saving grace. Remember to pull out of a difficult conversation when it *begins* to get heated. If you are past that point and things are already hot, you can still take a timeout. Getting out of a conversation that has no chance of going well is always a wise move. If you aren't able to implement this when it's needed, you will likely have trouble implementing good dialogue skills too; it might be a good idea to look into working on your own emotional regulation, whether through self-reflection and meditation, self-help books or videos, or personal therapy.

Remember also that this is a team effort between you and your partner. Help each other succeed (take a look back at the sections on helping your partner out in chapters 3 and 5): redirecting your partner to get back on track in their role as speaker or listener is a form of teamwork – but be sure to come at it from a place of collaboration – polite and supportive, not angry or critical. Tone matters a lot here! You are working together to make this process succeed, not just to be right about the matter at hand or about the way you are discussing it.

Hang on to the mindsets from chapter 10 as well. When your partner bungles the communication, recall that you're likely to mess it up sometimes too, and have some compassion (which does not mean you stay put if one of you is getting angry – you may still need to leave the scene even while being understanding about your partner messing it up).

> The real value of this approach in the tough times is that you will develop the confidence that whatever the problem you are facing, you have a way to deal with it together.

I want to remind you that the value of this whole approach is not that it eliminates fighting. You will never be perfect, and unless your last name is Spock you will have feelings that derail your flawless execution of difficult conversations. The real value of this approach in the tough times is that you will develop the confidence that whatever the problem you are facing, you have a way to deal with it together, and you *will* deal with it together. The power of that level of security and trust in a marriage is life-changing.

2. I STILL KEEP GETTING DEFENSIVE.

Once again, let's start by acknowledging that this is difficult work, and you are trying to change old patterns. Keep up the effort, and don't be too hard on yourself when you inevitably fail sometimes. Note also that defensiveness is a normal reaction to being attacked, so if your partner isn't executing their role very skillfully, you may rightly be feeling defensive!

The first tool here is, of course, timeout. If you're feeling defensive, take a break and try again later. Clear your mind, or talk yourself back into the right mindset, and don't give up! It can be helpful to develop some self-soothing tools to use while in timeout or even just in the moment if you can (see sidebar "Relaxation Techniques" in chapter 1).

Be honest about what's happening when the defensiveness starts to creep in. You can acknowledge in your head that you're feeling this way, that you're having trouble with what you're hearing, and remind yourself that right now you're listening and you'll get your chance to share your perspective soon. It may help to even share this out loud with your partner: "Hang on a sec, I'm feeling defensive and I really want to listen." If they are reasonably calm, you can also ask for reciprocity to help you stave off the feelings of urgency to respond: "I want to listen to you and I could use some help here. I just need a little reassurance right now that later on you'll allow me to share my perspective too." (This tends not to work so well when your partner is in a very emotional place, though; it can come across as if you're really only going through the motions of listening in order to get to the part where you get to say your own piece. Which is something people do sometimes when they are not being genuine about the process, and you should not do this.)

Another helpful approach to solving this problem is to dialogue *about the dialogue* later on. Work together to find ways to communicate things that don't set each other off. "I think I had trouble back there because you said [blah], and when you say this, it feels to me like I'm under attack. Can we come up with a different way to say that? What if you said [yada yada] instead?"

3. MY SPOUSE KEEPS GETTING DEFENSIVE.

Hopefully your spouse is reading this book as well and is considering the above section. But even if they are not, you have a role to play here (and it's not pointing a finger and accusing them of ruining the process with their defensiveness).

First, check yourself earnestly. Are you doing your best to *not elicit defensiveness*? Are you using true I-statements? Is your tone inviting and not accusatory? Are you genuinely trying to be heard and not just to be right? You can't make your spouse change; you can only change yourself. So the first stop is always checking what you can do differently to shift the dynamics. You will never be perfect, but you can keep growing in the right direction.

If you're executing the speaker role as best you can (and even if you're falling a bit short of your best), you have the option of talking about the process later: "I'm finding these attempts at dialogue a little frustrating. I'm really trying to share things with you in a non-accusatory way, but it seems like I'm still triggering some defensiveness in you, and we're not really getting anywhere. I wonder if there's something I can do differently that would help?" Perhaps they are used to you blaming and accusing them in the past and they are having trouble believing that you really intend to hear them out and take what they say into consideration. Persisting kindly and patiently with the message that you really mean it and asking them to give it a try might get you there. If you can't seem to get past their defenses, the next step might be seeing a couples counselor who can help the two of you get unstuck.

> You can't make your spouse change; you can only change yourself. So the first stop is always checking what you can do differently.

What If My Partner Isn't Interested?

Obviously, the process of empathic dialogue works best when you have two people who are both engaging in it. But what if your partner isn't interested or motivated enough to learn the ropes? Fear not – there is still much you can do to move things in the right direction (that does not involve leaving this book out in conspicuous places for them to hopefully notice and pick up).

The key job here is to be a killer listener. LOVE your partner really well; give them the phenomenal experience of truly being heard and validated. This alone might be enough to turn things around in your marriage. It will take patience and effort, of course; you may have to hold on to your own stuff for a while before there is room for you to unload it. But the experience of validation and empathy is truly powerful, and might ultimately open their heart to try to get on board with the process themselves as well.

You will need to be prepared for your partner to do all the don'ts – chiefly, to talk about you and what you're doing wrong rather than about themselves. Remember the strategies we discussed for the listener to help keep the speaker on track (see the section "Help a Partner Out Again" in chapter 5): dodge any accusations and come back with "what's that like for you?" or "tell me how that makes you feel," then carry on with the process, focusing on their experience as much as you can and remembering that there is a legitimate feeling in there that needs empathy.

You can also try sharing your own feelings by prompting them into the process, using an extensive preface: "Hey, I just want to share something with you... **I'm not looking to solve a problem** or anything, just want you to know **how I'm feeling** so we can be on the same page. Can you just **listen** to me for a bit and **reflect** back what you hear me say so we can both know that we're there? I have a lot on my mind, but **I'm not even suggesting this is the absolute reality**, just the way some things look to me." See how I covered a lot of key points in that disclaimer?

If your partner is willing to play along, you might be able to slowly get into a good communication groove in your marriage. And of course, if things improve by using these strategies, perhaps eventually they'll be willing to formally pick up the practice of empathic dialogue. Oh, and don't forget timeouts – you can and should still take those unilaterally as needed (and you can explain that plan to your partner ahead of time).

All this said, it's also possible you have a partner who simply isn't willing to change the status quo – not by book, not by counseling, not by any which way – in which case, you may have a decision to make about whether the status quo is good enough for you to stick around for.

4. I'M NOT SURE HOW TO SAY THIS WITHOUT TALKING ABOUT MY SPOUSE.

This part can definitely be tricky at times. You certainly can't just erase your spouse from the scenes they play a part in. Yet it's important to keep the story about you as much as possible. Therefore, it's not necessarily a problem to refer to your spouse as part of the story. Just remember that when you're the speaker, you're the main character. Come back to talking about your own experience as soon as possible. So rather than, "You're on your phone too much and it's just rude!" try: "Sometimes I see you on your phone before bedtime, and I start to get angry because I'm feeling ignored." Instead of, "I feel like you're angry at me and you're just trying to punish me" – remember, "I feel like you" is really about you and not about me – try, "I'm *worried* that you're angry at me. And I feel angry myself, because *I see it as* you trying to punish me on purpose."

See how that second version is a lot more about me than it is about you? Rather than accusing your spouse of something, you can share your perspective (but remember, you can't know for sure what they're thinking unless they tell you!) and describe *your reaction to* that perspective.

5. WE'VE BEEN OKAY AT AVOIDING BLOWUPS, BUT WE NEVER CIRCLE BACK TO DIALOGUE ABOUT THEM.

This is a common and understandable experience. Once you're through the initial anger, who wants to go back and revisit a thorny and unpleasant issue? If things are calm again, the prospect of making waves isn't very appealing.

The solution to this is getting better at the skills of empathic dialogue, which will allow you to revisit a difficult issue with less discomfort and anxiety. Sure, it will still be hard to do; but when you have confidence that you and your partner will handle it well and come out the other side, it's less fearsome to give it a go. It's kind of like the famous walk across the coals: it's daunting to think about doing it, but you prepare as best you can, push yourself through, and after you've done it, it's surprisingly gratifying. I have witnessed many couples transform their marriages (and have experienced tremendous profundity in my own) by steeling their nerves and pushing forward into empathic dialogue around a sensitive issue.

The other part of this is making time for dialogue to happen. Life can get busy, and you may have the best intentions of revisiting an issue after calling a timeout, but somehow it just doesn't materialize. One way to approach this is to set a designated weekly relationship check-in time – e.g., a half-hour block of time over coffee on Sunday nights, or Friday evenings after the kids have gone to bed. (It's probably better to aim for later in the day, because if a conversation tanks over breakfast, you might end up spoiling any planned couple/family activities you had for that day.) With this approach it's important to (a) meet regularly even when you have no Big Issues to Discuss, and (b) start the conversation with things that went *right* over the past week and/or verbal appreciations of each other. (Some weeks, perhaps that's all the meeting will be!) If this check-in time is only ever used for complaints, you will both quickly come to dread it.

You can also be a little more fluid, if that's your style, by setting a time to discuss the issue as soon after an incident as you're able to calmly do so. You take a timeout, and then once the iron is cold enough, you ask to come up with a not-too-distant time to revisit the issue with empathic dialogue (without getting into the issue itself right then). This part you can even do by text while you're out cooling down. Then follow through!

You may be thinking that this is very stressful and will leave you anxious for the entire time until the appointed conversation hour. Fear not – again, once you get the hang of the skills of empathic dialogue, the waiting period won't kill you. Sure, you may feel a little antsy – even seasoned actors can have stage fright, but the nervousness is manageable, perhaps even motivating; they can keep going rather than getting paralyzed or spending the week before opening night throwing up. You'll get there too.

6. WE HAVE SO MANY ISSUES THAT WE KEEP GETTING LOST IN THEM!

I totally understand! Life is so full of stuff. There's always plenty to talk about. So, first of all, remember to avoid kitchen sinking (see "Kitchen Sinking" in the section "A Few More Don'ts" in chapter 3). You won't get very far if you throw everything into one discussion. If there's something on your mind that you want to dialogue about with your partner, plan ahead of time what you want to address in that dialogue, and also note what you do *not* want to address. Having clarity on this point going in will help you stay on track. Maybe even write it down and have it in front of you, so that if you notice you are wandering too far afield you can recenter yourself.

Recall also that politely helping your partner stay on track is a valuable contribution to the process. If they have wandered onto a topic different from where they started, bring this to their attention. "Hey, hang on, I noticed you're talking about allowance for the kids, but you started off wanting to discuss shared household responsibilities. Should we finish that up first?"

> Politely helping your partner stay on track is a valuable contribution to the process.

You will find this intervention easier to pull off if you truly are trying to understand your partner. If that's where you're coming from, then when they shift gears in the middle and you haven't fully understood yet, you will naturally pin them down to the first topic because *you* want to hear it. "Wait wait wait, before you move on to allowance, you were in the middle of saying how you feel about our chores wheel, and I'm not really getting it yet. I'd really like to be clearer on this point!" When you really want to know how the show ends, you're naturally going to protest if someone changes the channel in the middle.

7. WHAT IF WE CAN'T COME UP WITH A SOLUTION?

You've gone through the exploration phase. You both totally get your partner and feel heard. Now you want to solve the problem – but no decent solution is presenting itself. This is not an implausible situation – some problems don't go quietly into the night.

First, a practical take on this predicament: what are your tools in general when you have a problem to solve? Probably you usually draw from some of the following options:

- Talk to a friend.
- Consult a professional (doctor, accountant, personal trainer, etc.).
- Consult a respected figure/mentor (clergyperson, teacher, community elders, etc.)

- Ask Google.
- Ask the latest AI bot.
- Read a book on the topic.
- Research what's worked for others.
- [Fill in the blank.]

Those are all good methods to try here as well. But, more fundamentally, this is not a question on empathic dialogue as much as it is a question on how life is. Life comes with challenges. Good communication doesn't mean you will magically have a solution for every problem you will ever encounter, just like having a high-end car doesn't mean you can drive from Chicago to Abu Dhabi.[1] But solid communication skills are still good to have, because at least you won't get waterlogged from trying. Meaning, keep at it. Keep the conversation going using your empathic dialogue skills. I can't guarantee you'll find the right solution, but I contend your marriage will be awesome nonetheless.

8. THIS PROCESS IS TOO SLOW.

I agree with you on this partially – it's slow. But it's not *too* slow. These days we are so used to instant results that anything that isn't lickety-split gets on our nerves. (I am as guilty of this as anyone – if it takes seven seconds to load a website I am already rolling my eyes.) The reality is that the good things in life take time. You do not become a banjo virtuoso in a day. You do not achieve financial security in a month. You do not build a deep, meaningful, and intimate relationship in a year. It's going to take time. More time than you want. But not necessarily more time than you need, or more time than you have.

If you're looking for shortcuts or quick fixes, there are plenty of people out there willing to sell them to you. (My website tends to get lots of spam comments supposedly from women who found an AMAZING African healer who cast a spell on their ex-boyfriend and made him fall in love again.) Feel free to try them out. In my opinion, they will not get you where you want to go (if where you want to go is a deep, meaningful, and intimate relationship). I always tell my clients that I don't work in miracles. I work in small steps. That's the only change that sticks, anyway.

---

[1] As of the time this book goes to print, you cannot.

WHEN IT JUST DOESN'T FEEL RIGHT

Sometimes you have something you want to share with your partner, and you're doing all the right things: you're really trying to implement empathic dialogue and speak from your own perspective and use I-statements and all that, and somehow their responses as the listener just don't feel *right*. The words are all there, but your partner simply doesn't strike you as fully genuine or empathetic. Now what?

There are several reasons you might be having this experience.

- **Their Listening Needs a Tweak**

The first possibility is that your spouse isn't being genuine or empathetic. Maybe they're just going along with things but don't buy into the process, or aren't actually that invested in the marriage, or are hopeless about fixing it and are already planning an exit. If you suspect that one of these is the explanation, it might be helpful to just ask them if that's the case. They may give you an honest answer. If it's not one of these, and they sincerely do want to work with you to improve the marriage, then we can continue to work on tweaking the process to get it right. And if they acknowledge that they think this approach is garbage, that's okay; this is not the only path to success. Trying out a different communication book or seeking out a couples counselor would probably be the way to go. Of course, if they're not interested in the marriage anymore, there may be a limited amount you can do to change the course of things (although couples counseling can still help if your spouse is willing).

On the other hand, you may *not* get an honest answer; you may get smooth lies from someone who has bad intentions, in which case there's unfortunately not much a book can do to help. I hope this is not the situation you find yourself in. You may also get defensiveness and anger in response to such questions; if you have asked without anger or accusation, but sincerely to find out where they stand, such reactions probably do indicate that they're not being honest (perhaps not even with themselves). These are all complicated scenarios beyond the scope of just communication issues, and again, getting outside help is a good idea.

There is also a less nefarious way in which your spouse might not be completely genuine in their role as listener – even if they do care, they do want to work on this marriage, and they do see the potential in this process. This happens when the listener is honestly trying to LOVE but is still holding on, just a little bit, to their own point of view; they haven't quite relinquished their own thoughts and feelings, and those are creeping into their responses to you. It's kind of like they're giving you a hug, but one hand is still behind their back holding onto something, so it's not an outstanding hug. They *intend* to be there for you, but really there's also a little *them* in there; they're not 100% in your world.

This is a normal roadblock people face – you are likely to do this at times too; it's really hard to let go of our own stuff to be there for our spouse! Again, you can ask about this, with empathy and understanding, not accusation: "Hey, is it possible you're still holding on to some of your own stuff while you're trying to listen? I'm kind of getting a feeling of frustration – it seems like maybe you're not 100% in my world when you reflect back to me."

If you are the listener, and your spouse is complaining that you're not being genuine, consider whether you might be hanging on to something in this way. If so, don't try to just brush it off and forget about it; if it's important to you, it will keep coming back and buzzing around your head like a mosquito when you're trying to sleep. Notice it, admit to yourself that you haven't let go of it yet. You can also admit it to your spouse! Remember, we are trying to be genuine here, not win the Listening Competition. Then mentally put it down, or you can even write down the point on a piece of paper or an app so you know you won't forget to bring it up later. Remind yourself that you'll get back to it when it's your turn. Maybe you feel anxious that it's going to get buried and not dealt with – that's fair! That's another feeling to disclose. "I'm really trying to listen, but I realize I'm feeling nervous about not getting my own chance to speak. Can you reassure me that I'll have my turn sometime in the future – doesn't have to be right now – and I think that will help me put down my own stuff and really listen?"

By the way, even once you get good at empathic dialogue, you're likely to make mistakes or fall short from time to time. (The reason for this is that you are human.) The good news is that when an attempt at empathic dialogue goes awry, you can always take a break – and you can dialogue about the dialogue too: "I'm feeling dismissed and kind of angry because of the way our dialogue went last night. I tried to be genuine and you sort of got this sarcastic tone which to me meant that you weren't really taking me seriously."

- ### There's a Problem with Their Listening

Another possible explanation for your sense that they're not being genuine is simply poor execution in their listening. Maybe they really do care about what you're saying but the way they are listening is sending you nonverbal messages that they don't. And that could be to *you* specifically, because people are different, and there are different ways of paying attention. In the Western world we tend to expect eye contact when someone is listening, but in, say, Japan, they definitely do not. Similarly, studies have shown that Western women are more likely than men to look directly at each other when conversing; men may stare straight ahead but equally register what's being said.

As always, this is not about right or wrong; it's about what works. There are many ways to listen, and you can ask for what feels best to you. Maybe you want them to look at you when you speak; maybe you want them to face you with their body instead of reclining on the couch. You know well by now not to accuse them of wrongdoing, but simply to share where you're coming from: "Hey, would you mind sitting up and looking at me? That would help give me the message that you're really listening and help me feel more heard." Much better than, "How can you possibly be listening if you're not even looking at me?!"

> There are many ways to listen, and you can ask for what feels best to you.

Of course, there are things your spouse might be doing that are pretty universally understood as signs someone isn't really taking in what you're saying – they're on their phone; they've got their arms crossed and they're sneering; they're rolling their eyes. In this case you can still address the situation – and using the same tools is a great way to do it: "I'm having a hard time continuing. I get the impression you're not really listening because your arms are crossed and you look kind of angry. Should we keep trying, or take a break and come back to it later?" You're using I-language again – you refer to your spouse's behaviors (noting a specific action), but you are fundamentally talking about you, your perception, and how you feel about it.[2]

---

[2]   The benefit of the doubt is also a great mindset to call upon here. Rather than assuming your partner doesn't care about what you're saying, consider that maybe they're just preoccupied because of work stress or any other large number of possibilities.

You might still get pushback from your spouse if they've been emotionally triggered: "*I'M NOT ANGRY!!!*" In which case you'd probably carry on with the tools we've been discussing: "Well, since now your voice is getting louder, it just kind of reinforces that impression for me. So I guess I'm not sure how you feel inside, but at this point I really need a timeout. Let's come back to this after dinner."

Or, it might be less emotional than that: "I'm not angry; I just disagree with you." And you can answer, "Okay, well, I don't need you to agree with me. I just want you to hear where I'm at. Should we keep trying?" If a timeout is needed, that's fine. If they are okay to continue, you can make a request: "Okay, so it would really be helpful to me if you could uncross your arms and look at me so I can feel more heard." Of course, you might also get agreement: "You're right, I think I am feeling kind of angry." A good extension of that might be, "Let's take a break and come back to it later," or "Can I have a turn to share what's going on for me right now?" (You can of course agree to that or not, depending on how you're feeling.)

If you are the angry spouse in this scenario, do pay attention to what's going on inside; if you're getting worked up, you have a couple of options: a timeout is always available if needed. You can also talk yourself down by reminding yourself that your spouse's perspective is just their perspective, and you'll have your own chance to speak soon. It might also be helpful to say this out loud – "Yeah, I think I'm feeling angry hearing your view of the situation. Can we remember together that this is just your view and it may not be the reality, and that I have my own view, which might also not be the reality?"

If, however, you get called out for an angry demeanor and you don't actually feel angry (or insulted, or bored, or whatever), there's no need to turn that into an argument. It's certainly possible that your body language is communicating something unintentional (or that you actually are getting a bit angry but haven't realized it yet). Try to modify your nonverbal messages; ask your spouse what you can do to demonstrate that you're listening and take their suggestions. "Sorry, I didn't mean to look angry. I want to hear you out. Is there anything I can do to convey that better?"

- **They Keep Bringing Themselves into It**

Maybe you're trying to get your feelings heard, but your spouse can't seem to stay in your world and they keep bringing themselves into it, perhaps even just tangentially. This is not a capital crime, but it can definitely water down the power of the empathy they are trying to communicate. It is a natural mistake for people to make, especially as you learn the skill of empathic dialogue (but even once you're pretty good at it, it's hard to be on point 100% of the time).

The first answer to this problem is simply practice. You'll both get better over time if you put in the effort. Don't get too frustrated with each other for messing up; just redirect and try again. Beyond that, you can always do a meta-dialogue about your dialogue, as we noted above: "You know, we had a failed attempt at talking earlier, and it was very frustrating for me. When you share your own opinions during my turn as speaker, the message I get in those moments is that you don't really want to hear what I'm saying, and that's hurtful to me."

The truth is that talking about our feelings – especially the vulnerable ones – can be hard. Like with any skill you want to develop, it can be helpful to have a coach. Someone who does relationship coaching or couples therapy can help you grow and improve in this area. And having an objective third party there to call you out when you fail to listen, fall into Category B activities, etc., can certainly benefit your marriage.

- **You're Just Not Feeling the Empathy**

Assuming your spouse isn't being fake or displaying conflicting body language, which we dealt with above, it's still possible that the message just isn't landing. It seems like they get what you're talking about, but you just don't feel the love and caring there. Now what?

The question I ask clients when they express this concern is, "How would you know if your spouse really *did* care?" Think about it for a moment. As we've asserted, you can't know what's inside their head. All you have to go on is their verbal and nonverbal communication. So pause for a moment and think about what you're experiencing. Is there something they're doing that's spoiling the empathic message they're trying to send? We've discussed different communication styles; maybe you're sitting side by side and they're looking forward, and you really need some eye contact to back up the message. Maybe you'd feel better if they were holding your hand. You can make a request for them to share their empathy in a way that feels best to you. Remember that people are different; what you expect and need might not be what your spouse expects and needs, so there's no need to criticize or shame them; simply ask for how you'd like them to do it.

If there's nothing your spouse is saying or doing that is missing the mark, consider if there's some blockage in your own mind.[3] Are you perhaps insisting to yourself that they don't care because you are attached to your own narrative ("Obviously he doesn't care if he could just forget to call me for three days")? Are you reluctant to change your mind about where they stand (because that would mean you were wrong about your perception, and being wrong is Totally Unbearable)? Check in with yourself and see if maybe you're keeping out the empathy somehow. It makes sense to have mixed feelings about this – wanting empathy but also wanting to hold on to your anger at your spouse. Don't get down on yourself about it; notice it, share it, and put that part of yourself through the same dialogue process as all the other feelings you're putting out there.

When Your Partner Needs Therapy

Experiencing and conveying empathy is not easy for everyone. Some people may be disconnected from their own emotions, which sure makes it hard to connect to others' emotions. If you feel a lack of affection and empathy from your partner in general in your marriage, one possibility is that this is something they need to explore in themselves. (That's ONE possibility – don't go assuming off the bat that if your marriage isn't on track it's because your partner is the problem!) Individual therapy can help them do this kind of thing, and if they're interested in that, more power to them.

If you think your partner could benefit from therapy, you can certainly suggest it (especially if you do have a solid marriage already). Obviously you want to do this in a calm time, not when you're angry or as part of an argument you're having, at which times an exclamation like *"you need therapy!!!"* is more likely a form of putdown than a helpful suggestion. What that statement really

---

[3] It's also possible that they're acting in a passive-aggressive way (intentionally or unintentionally) that's so subtle you can't quite put your finger on what the problem is; a couples counselor can again be helpful in catching the issue here.

says is, "You're messed up, this is all your fault, and it's your problem to fix this, I'm not taking any responsibility." Not a great contribution to the marriage.

The only way you can legitimately bring up the idea of therapy for your partner is out of care and concern for their well-being and the well-being of the marriage. This does not happen in the context of an argument or even a discussion about some other topic. It is something you bring up as a conversation of its own in a loving and concerned manner, with empathy and understanding, not with blame and judgment, or demands and expectations.

Note that apart from just the need to get in contact with one's feelings – which is a common need and use of therapy – mental health problems are pervasive: over half of the population will qualify for a diagnosis of a mental illness or disorder at some point in their lifetime. Obviously, mental illness can seriously impact a marriage. That doesn't mean it will destroy it; it just means it needs attending to. If your partner has problems with anxiety, depression, addiction, if they have a history of trauma or abuse, or if they struggle with any other mental or emotional issue, a conversation about your concern for their well-being is a good place to start as far as helping them get potentially needed professional intervention. If you or your partner are having suicidal thoughts, speak to a professional immediately.

Of course, you don't need to be mentally ill to seek therapy. Individual therapy is great to help with less acute concerns like emotional awareness, assertiveness, self-esteem, and other very normal and common issues. And, needless to say, couples therapy is a great way to improve various aspects of your marriage as well.

Note that you can still have a good marriage even if your partner isn't able to be 100% empathic with you. Not everyone needs the deepest levels of intimacy to be happy in a marriage. But for many people, real intimacy is a key part of what they want from a marriage. The lack of connection on that level may be a real obstacle for you. This is a personal decision that you have to figure out for yourself; there's no right or wrong answer here.

"BUT NOTHING HAS CHANGED!"

Warning: don't confuse genuine empathy with the problem being gone. It's possible that an empathic dialogue session will eliminate a problem by shifting perspectives: maybe you have a better understanding now of why your partner needs to call their mom every day, and so it bothers you less. Maybe they realize they misunderstood your intentions when you said that thing you said the other day and they aren't angry about it anymore.

> Don't confuse genuine empathy with the problem being gone.

But it's also certainly possible that dialogue alone won't cause the change you are hoping for. Meaningful change rarely happens in the blink of an eye. If you want your partner to stop smoking or start doing the dishes or moderate their social media usage, the odds of them making a firm commitment on the spot are slim, and the odds of them being able to stick to such a hasty promise are even slimmer. Communicating well doesn't make the situation automatically different. But it does actually make it automatically better.

The question you should be asking yourself in empathic dialogue is not whether your partner has agreed to do what you want, but rather, *Do they mean it in this moment?* If your partner truly understands your problem and truly cares about your problem, *now* we're actually in a position to *try* to change things. Without understanding and empathy, change isn't really on the radar. If your partner has no idea why you want them to spend less time on Instagram and doesn't care that it bothers you, but deletes their Instagram account just to stop your complaining – well, not only has your marriage not gained anything, but the change is unlikely to last (or even be implemented in a meaningful way – maybe they'll just switch to Snapchat, then argue, exasperated that you're still not satisfied, that they did what you said already by deleting Instagram).

On the other hand, it's very possible to care about a problem even while it is still unresolved. I may love Instagram dearly and not want to give it up, and at the same time still sincerely care that it's causing you distress. If we are clear on this, if we are sharing the problem that I love Instagram and you want me off it, then we are in relationship with each other. The actual solution will come later. But don't disregard your partner's empathy because the situation hasn't changed; empathy is meaningful even before change has happened.[4] This relationship is about love and care, not about the resolution of any one specific problem.

WHEN YOU'RE REALLY STUCK

There are many good reasons you might get stuck in this process. It is new, it is challenging, and you're learning it from a book. Books are great; they can be helpful, and they can make a real difference for you (which is why I just wrote this one). At the same time, actionable skills can often be hard to pick up from books alone. I strongly suspect that nobody ever became a great rugby player, public speaker, or prosthodontist from reading books alone. There's trial and error that goes into it, of course, but there's also great value in getting guidance and feedback from a coach, mentor, or advisor.

If you're not seeing improved communication and better connection in your marriage by using the skills described heretofore, consider reaching out to a professional couples coach or therapist to help you get on track. A couples counselor can help you and your significant other in ways that a book cannot (as described in the sidebar "How Is Couples Counseling Going to Help?" in chapter 6).

There's no shame in going to couples counseling. It is not an admission of failure or incompetence. How exactly is anyone supposed to be competent in skills that nobody has ever taught them?[5] If you think all your friends are somehow doing fine in their marriage and you're the only ones who can't figure this out, I assure you that's not the case. You are probably aware that about half of marriages in the US end in divorce. And that doesn't mean the other half are thriving ecstatically in their marriages! Think about times when you might have been struggling in your marriage (perhaps that's now) and how you present when you are out with others. You probably try to make it look like things are okay. Lots of other people are doing

---

[4] On the other hand, if someone professes empathy but *refuses* to change, then something isn't adding up: "I really care that you don't like my drinking habits – really I do! – but I'm not stopping, so take it or leave it." This is very superficial empathy (if it can even be called that). The response ought to be (after empathic dialogue has taken place) something like, "Gee, you really want X and I really want Y. This is a toughie. I'm not sure how we're going to figure this out, but we're definitely going to come up with something – together."

[5] I don't know about you, but I learned a lot of things in high school that were totally useless and not exactly vital to my living a successful life. Trigonometry comes to mind as an example.

this too. And this is because we have all been missing critical skills to make our marriages work well.

It is absolutely worth seeking out professional help if you need more support in getting your communication on track. Your intimate relationship is the most important relationship in your life. Don't let pride get in the way of making it the best one too.

Finding a Couples Counselor

The good news is, there are plenty of good couples counselors out there (or marriage therapists, or relationship coaches – the particular title doesn't matter all that much if they're able to help!). The bad news is, there are also plenty of bad couples counselors out there (I've heard some horror stories...). How do you find the good ones?

Well, you can always start by asking around. Certainly if you're having marital trouble it's not everyone's business, but perhaps there are friends or family you can trust with such a question. You can also ask your doctor, clergyperson, mentor, or other trusted person in your life if they have providers they like to refer to for couples counseling.

You can also, of course, hop online and do a search in your area; you'll get plenty of results (unless maybe you're in a rural area – in which case you can opt to meet with a counselor online, a perfectly viable choice whether or not there's anyone local you could meet in person). Read what they've written about themselves or their work and see if it resonates with you. If they have any online reviews, those can be a helpful guide too (but ought to be taken with a grain of salt – I have had my fair share of disgruntled clients (and non-clients) say nasty and untrue things about me online).

All that said, you really can't know whether a counselor is right for you until you try them out. Different people need different things and respond to different personalities and approaches – your friend's positive experience with a counselor is not a guarantee that you will have one too. By no means should you give up if the first one you meet doesn't work out! You may have to try more than one before you find a good fit for you (and, of course, for your partner at the same time).

Note also that there are many effective, validated couples counseling modalities; different counselors will use different methods. Not all of them will use an approach like the one described in this book. If what I've been describing speaks to you and you'd like more help with it, ask potential counselors if they can help you with your communication and listening skills. On the other hand, if you're not vibing with empathic dialogue and need help with your marriage, shop around among some of the other approaches out there. Help is available!

(Oh, and please do yourself and the counselor a favor – give counseling a shot sooner than later. Don't wait until the situation is dire! Your marriage will be much easier to set on the right path if you haven't been off it for years or decades.)

Chapter 12

Positive Communication

Most of this book has focused on communication around feelings, "issues," and conflict resolution. That's usually what people are referring to when they say that communication is a problem in their marriage. We've discussed at length the process of empathic dialogue that will help you improve and see success in that area. But I wanted to add in a chapter about a different aspect of communication that is also vitally important to a happy, thriving marriage, and that's what I call "positive communication." I'm referring to all the positive inputs you add to your marriage in the absence of any friction or conflict.

This is in no way meant to imply that empathic dialogue is only for when something isn't right in your marriage! Empathic dialogue is also a great tool for when things are going well – if you got a promotion at work, had a good talk with a friend, enjoyed a movie – these are all positive experiences you can share with your spouse, and having them listen, reflect, validate, and empathize is surely a meaningful and connecting experience.

When something is bothering you, you feel a push to say something, to deal with it, or else you squash it and keep it inside. But when things are going well, unless you make an effort to notice and speak up, you'll likely just carry on without paying attention, and you'll miss opportunities to feed needed positivity, energy, and connection into your marriage.

GRATITUDE

Gratitude is a key quality for a happy life, let alone a happy marriage. At any given time there are many things in your life that are going right. Remember my toe-stub reaction? When I walk into a piece of furniture that has moved into my path, I immediately remind myself that 9 out of 10 toes are feeling fine. At this very moment, a number of things are almost certainly true: you can read; you can see; you can breathe. You do not suffer from psychosis or dementia. There are many people for whom some of these things are not true. Taking pleasure in what you do have is a reliable way to generate more happiness in your life.[1] Certainly this can be applied to your marriage.

The problem, of course, is that it's easy to take things for granted. We can get used to just about anything, whether it's an annoying car alarm going off right outside or a super-comfortable pair of high-end shoes. Positive or negative, we just stop noticing. So the job here is to pay attention to those positive things in your life – and here we'll focus on your marriage – and develop gratitude and appreciation for them. *And then you express them to your spouse!*

> **Pay attention to those positive things in your life – then express them to your spouse!**

To be clear, just thinking about the good things about your spouse and about your marriage will bring great benefits to both of you.[2] But letting your spouse in on those yummy thoughts you're having doubles the profit! It's a fairly low investment, too – all you have to do is say, "Thanks for ____." If you pay attention, you will surely find things to appreciate every day. You can say thanks for doing the dishes, walking the dog, making you coffee just the way you like it, taking care of the broken closet door, finding you the perfect pair of socks on Amazon, bathing the kids, planning a vacation, spending all day at work to support the family, taking a timeout instead of yelling, buying the right kind of tuna (the one with the pop-top so you don't need a can opener), taking the guinea pig to the vet – you get the idea. Seek and ye shall find – don't just

---

[1] Research has demonstrated that people who keep a gratitude log – writing down three things they are grateful for every day before going to bed – score better on a wide range of measures of happiness and well-being, including meaningful relationships and even physical health.

[2] It is especially helpful to have a thick stack of things you're grateful for to turn your mind to when you're irritated with your partner. Remember Mindset #5 – your partner is awesome! Yes, they're running late *again* – but if you set this annoyance in the context of their many strengths and positive qualities, it helps you get some perspective. Having a broad palette of things you appreciate about your partner helps you see something that bothers you as part of a bigger picture.

wait for these things to show up in front of your face! Actively look for things to appreciate. It's an easy way to boost your marriage.

Don't skimp, either. Say "thank you" and "I appreciate" more than you think you need to. Your partner will tell you if it's enough, and then you can always dial it back. But we tend to underestimate how much is needed and overestimate how much we actually convey to our partners what's in our heads. And don't stop with a mere "thanks." "Thank you" is nice, but "Thank you for getting the grease spots out of my shirt" is better. And even better than that is if you also mention the *impact* their actions have on you: "Thank you for getting the grease spots out of my shirt! I'm glad to have one less thing I have to worry about before this big meeting tomorrow." In fact, you can approach this the same way you do in empathic dialogue: "I really feel loved when you make my favorite dessert. Thanks, dear!"

Pay attention to areas where you can express *partial* gratitude as well. Things may not be perfect, but there's always something you can appreciate. If your spouse burned the chicken, *you can still thank them for making the meal.* Isn't it valuable to you that they spent their time and energy preparing your dinner? Isn't it meaningful that they care about you in that way? Just because the chicken is extra-extra-crispy doesn't mean that their efforts aren't of value in your marriage. Similarly, you can thank them for getting the groceries even if they did get the wrong tuna, for fixing the closet door even if it did take them four weeks to get to it, and for taking a timeout last night even if they lost their temper the night before. *Things don't need to be perfect for you to cultivate and express gratitude.*

> If your spouse burned the chicken, you can still thank them for making the meal.

Chana once made a cauliflower-chickpea stew that frankly just tasted off. It was too sour, maybe from the tomato sauce or something? Who knows. I had a few spoonfuls, thanked her genuinely for making dinner, and found some leftovers in the fridge to warm up for myself.

This perspective is not one I've had too much trouble cultivating. The year after I graduated from college was the first time I had to plan and prepare my own meals on an ongoing basis. I'd guess that about 85–90% of my meals were comprised of some combination of toast, tuna, spaghetti, and Morningstar Farms Chik'n Patties. (This was one of the year's many tribulations, including, for instance, the fact that I was living with nine roommates in a three-story townhouse that was around twelve feet wide, and from which I could literally almost touch the Brooklyn-Queens Expressway.) I've never forgotten that experience. I am so genuinely happy every time my wife prepares a meal that even if it's totally inedible I am teeming with gratitude that I didn't have to make it myself.

A good way to ruin an expression of gratitude is to follow it up with a "but": "Thanks for getting the tuna with the pop-top, but I prefer it in water, not in oil." As with the skill of reflecting, putting in a "but" clause takes you in the wrong direction. It essentially wipes out whatever was said before.

More insidiously, be careful here not to sneak in criticisms with your gratitude: "Thanks for not burning the rice too!" "Thanks for finally getting around to fixing the closet door." "Thanks for not blowing up again like a total jerk last night!" – these are passive-aggressive comments that are actually meant to highlight the negative and not the positive, and they will not take your marriage where you want it to go. Be genuine in your gratitude and watch your marriage flourish.

You are of course free to be angry about the burnt chicken or the delay in fixing up the house, but there are better ways to express it (see chapter 3). Recall that being passive-aggressive means you stick the message in indirectly, under the radar. This is quite the opposite of empathic dialogue, isn't it? Instead, give a full, genuine thanks for the part you can appreciate, and use empathic dialogue to express your concerns and frustrations (you can feel grateful and frustrated at the same time!). Don't lump them together, though. You're better off focusing on the positive first – "Wow, thanks for taking care of the shopping all this week – it's really been a relief to be able to focus on this paper I need to write." – and later on coming back to address your frustration: "I really appreciate your help with the shopping. At the same time, I'm feeling frustrated that you got the wrong tuna after I've asked you many times to please get the one with the pop top."

Sharing your gratitude and sharing your frustration are not opposites. They're both contributions to the marriage, in different ways.

COMPLIMENTS AND ENCOURAGEMENT

Saying nice things to your spouse doesn't have to happen only when they do something nice for you! Just as there are innumerable things in your life to be grateful for, there's no lack of targets to compliment in your spouse. You've got simple, everyday things like "You look nice in that shirt" and "You really know how to find the best deals online!" But you've also got many opportunities – especially as a marital partner – to see parts of your spouse that others don't get to see.

You're around to see them when the baby wakes up at night and they silently drag themselves out of bed without complaining, or when the cat throws up on the rug (again) and they just take it in stride and go get the Lysol. So when they somehow manage to pull off a tight deadline at work *and* catch the middle school graduation ceremony, you're in a unique position to notice: "You really worked hard to pull that off!" And when they navigate the third preschooler tantrum in one day, you can praise their parenting skills with, "I love how you handled the twins so smoothly! Very creative."

Not only do you see your spouse more frequently, you also see them more *deeply*. You likely know your spouse better than anyone else does (especially if you've been together for years or decades), and you have a better view of their amazing positive qualities. That means that you can get really granular in what you're complimenting. A good compliment is specific: "Wow, this is a great hamburger! It's perfectly pink in the middle, and you got the texture just right!" has a much greater impact than "Mmm. Burger good." Not that you have to write a sonnet every time you want to say something nice, but when you spot something that really deserves a good compliment, flesh it out all the way!

On the flip side, of course, you are also probably the person who best knows your spouse's *negative* qualities. And what this means is that you recognize better than anyone that your spouse can, for example, have a short fuse; so when they hold it together during an especially trying family dinner, you have the clearest view of what an accomplishment that is. "Wow, I can't believe your mom said that. You really held it together under fire there!"

It's in those challenging moments that encouragement can be a real boost as well. A compliment says, "I value you." Encouragement says, "I believe in you." Statements like "You can do it," "You're going to be great out there tonight," and "You got this!" tell your spouse you know they have what it takes to succeed at whatever they're trying to do. And after

> A compliment says, "I value you." Encouragement says, "I believe in you."

the fact, comments like "That was incredible," "Way to go," and "You nailed it!" tell them you are a witness to that success. Compliments and encouragement are easy ways to draw you and your spouse together, and they won't cost you a dime. On the other hand, criticism and discouragement are reliable methods for driving you apart. It's easy to see what's wrong in life. As they say, nobody notices the janitor until the day he doesn't show up for work.

Thus, as with gratitude, it behooves you not just to try to catch the right moment for a compliment but to *look* for things to compliment and encourage. What skill did your spouse demonstrate today? What virtue do they possess that shone? What difficult task did they accomplish (or try to)? Be on the active lookout for positive qualities and behaviors in your spouse, and then mention it to them!

Also as with gratitude, avoid giving back-handed compliments – the kind where you are outwardly saying something nice but subtly (or not-so-subtly) you are actually being critical. "You got a nice haircut!" is a cute compliment. "You *finally* got a nice haircut!" is much more of a complaint about your spouse's appearance until now (and if part of you actually meant to be complimentary, I can assure you that message is all but drowned out by the critical one). You don't even have to change the words to scuttle your positive message. "Wow, you handed your paper in on time!" will convey a very different message depending on tone – imagine ending the sentence with an upwards inflection (the end of the sentence going up in pitch) vs. a downwards inflection (the end of the sentence going down in pitch). The first way is supportive and encouraging – "You did it!" The second way sounds sarcastic and diminishing of the accomplishment. You want the first way.

> Be on the active lookout for positive qualities and behaviors in your spouse, and then mention it to them!

On Receiving Compliments

Some people find it hard to receive a genuine compliment. It can feel uncomfortable, embarrassing. This can be a result of their beliefs about themselves, about relationships, about the world; it can be a product of their histories, their experiences, their families of origin; it can come from any number of places. We all have a story. But when you reject compliments that are genuinely given, it breeds disconnection. If your partner reaches out to say something nice and you deny or turn away from it, it sends the message that their contribution to you and to the marriage isn't wanted or valued. And it makes it less likely you will receive further compliments, which drains from the marriage the positive focus we're endorsing here.

So for starters, if you can't think of what you're supposed to do or say in response to a compliment, a simple "thank you" will do just fine. You're also allowed to enjoy the compliment! It doesn't mean you are conceited or arrogant to feel good that someone has appreciated something about you – especially if you put work into it. If your partner tells you they really liked the onion soup *au gratin* that you made, a great response is, "Thanks! I put a lot of time into getting the cheese to melt just right."

If you do feel uncomfortable with giving such a reply, or with receiving compliments in general, guess what I recommend for addressing that? It's called empathic dialogue. Conversations that explore how you feel will lead you to more closeness and, very possibly, more clarity about yourself as well.

TALKING ABOUT THE BIG STUFF

As we pointed out before, you didn't get married to solve conflict. Nor did you commit your life to someone so that you'd have someone to do the laundry or take care of the car when it breaks. Marriage is about building something bigger than yourself.

> When Chana and I were first discussing getting married, we both had a long list of questions we wanted to ask, things we wanted to know about each other. I warned her that I'm pretty incompetent in the kitchen; she had no problem being in charge of that arena. She shared with me her wish to go to South Korea one day and see the place she was born. As we got deeper, she asked me what marriage meant to me. I probably stammered a bunch of ideas, but the vision I finally proposed remains etched in both

of our minds: two people sharing one life. We remain committed to that ideal to this day.

Building that kind of team mentality doesn't happen by itself. Yes, it involves managing conflict when it comes up. But it also involves sharing who you are so that you can make room for each other, adapt to each other, meld with each other in such a way that you become one unit without losing your individual selves. And because you don't live inside each other's heads, the only way to do this is to communicate about what's in there. This includes the day-to-day ups and downs we all go through. But more fundamentally, it means talking about who you are – what makes you *you*.

What do you like? What do you dislike? There are plenty of game shows and party games that center around asking people what their mate's favorite movie or band or ice cream flavor is and seeing how well they know each other. Do you and your partner know each other that well? When is the last time you talked about your preferences, your interests, your yums and yucks? And don't think you can get away with a set of static facts about your partner – these things can change and evolve over time. (When I got married, olives were strongly on the yuck list.[3] Now I love them. Go figure.)

Talking about Sex

Yikes! This is a super sensitive topic. Many couples unfortunately go through a lifetime without having a frank conversation about their intimate life. Sex just kind of happens – or it doesn't. This, of course, is totally understandable. For many people, talking about sexual matters is massively taboo. And for even more people, while it's not officially taboo, it's simply not something we grew up talking about – at least, not in a personal and vulnerable way. Sure, we all talked about sex constantly in high school and college, and the media has always been full of off-color jokes and innuendos. But how many people would be comfortable getting up in front of an audience and sharing details

---

[3] There actually was a physical yuck list.

about their sex life? About their sexual preferences? About what turns them on? (Some readers might *not* be all that uncomfortable doing this. If you are in that group, this sidebar might not be so relevant to you. Consider, however, that your partner might belong to the other group!)

> *I used to work extensively in child sexual abuse prevention. At one conference I attended, the dynamic and relatable speaker was discussing why it's so rare for children to disclose their abuse. After detailing a few aspects of this troubling phenomenon, he asked us to do a short activity. He instructed us to turn to the person sitting next to us and pair up, then introduce ourselves if we didn't know each other. Then he said, "Okay, great, now every pair please select one person to be the speaker. Got it? Okay. All the speakers, please turn to your partner and I'd like you to tell them about the first time you had sex." There was nervous laughter all around, and the point was made.*

So to start, set yourselves up for an empathic dialogue – i.e., one person is going to speak and the other is going to listen, and you'll switch roles as needed. Acknowledge the feelings of discomfort going into this. Perhaps the first dialogue is a conversation about just that – how awkward and difficult it is to talk about sex with each other:

> *"This is hard to talk about."*

> *"I'm nervous you'll think I'm weird."*

> *"I feel embarrassed about some of the things I want to tell you."*

You may also want to talk about what words you're comfortable using, whether it's nicknames for certain body parts, scientific names, slang, or whatever feels most comfortable (or least uncomfortable) for both of you.

One of the best ways I think you can start off the discussion of the intimate stuff is with the listener making a clear and explicit statement to the effect of "I won't laugh at you." (And then they have to make good on that promise, of course!) Continue in small chunks – you don't have to cover your entire sex life, past, present, and future, in one discussion. And at the end of every conversation, big or small, thank each other for being supportive, for not laughing or cringing or running away, and for being willing to talk about this critical topic. Congratulate yourselves as a team for any successes – and for any efforts you make, even if they don't end in success! You can always try again tomorrow.

If you need help with this conversation, a competent couples counselor or sex therapist can help. Yes, it can be even more uncomfortable to bring a total stranger into this discussion; but is it better to have no sex life to talk about? If your intimate life isn't on point, it is super worthwhile to push through the fear and discomfort and get the help you need. You'll be glad you did.

What are your personal values? What's important to you? Sure, your partner probably knows you're a vegan or a conservative or a Buddhist. But your deepest values can't be conveyed in one sentence or even one conversation. Talking about your values can foster deep connection. (Note that it's important to avoid turning such conversations into political arguments. Use empathic dialogue tools to make these discussions productive: one person shares, the other person simply tries to understand.) See where your values are aligned and where they are less aligned. Develop *family* values together. You don't have to agree on everything, of course, although hopefully you agree on the values that are most important and integral to who you are. Those will also become integral to who you are as a family, especially if you have/will have children. "In this family, we believe..." is a strong rallying cry for a team.

> **What are your goals in life? What's on your bucket list? Support each other in working toward them.**

What are your goals in life? What's on your bucket list? Support each other in working toward them. If your partner has always wanted to see the fjords, you can work to make that happen, or, if that's way out of reach, just dream about it together. But you can only do that if you know that's on the bucket list to begin with. Do you want to learn to play the piccolo?

Become a motivational speaker? Start a nonprofit to end homelessness in your city? These dreams and goals, the big and the small, are a part of who you are as a unique individual. And to the extent that you talk about them with your partner, they become a part of who you are as a couple. What moves you? What do you want to achieve? And why? What meaning do you take from the piccolo, the stage, the street? Learning about each other in these deep ways, using the skills of empathic dialogue, will open up new worlds for you in your marriage. Those are the worlds you will inhabit together, hopefully, for the rest of your life.

Conclusion: Hope and Optimism

You got this.

Truly, I believe in you. If you've come this far – you bought this book, you read through it, you're serious about getting the communication in your marriage on track – then you certainly have the wherewithal to take it all the way. Yes, it will take work. Yes, there will be setbacks. You will still have misunderstandings, disagreements, and fights. You will still get your feelings hurt at times and you will still get mad at each other.

But you will also have a mechanism to deal with all those unwanted events. You will have confidence, in due time, in your ability to communicate about anything – *anything!* – that comes your way, and to do so in a way that leaves you and your spouse closer, stronger, happier together. You will have a marriage characterized by collaboration instead of antagonism, by optimism instead of anxiety, by security instead of doubt, by closeness instead of distance, by teamship instead of self-interest, by real, *real* love instead of the superficial stand-in that so many people, sadly, learn to live with their whole lives. Is that what you're looking for?

I thought so.

Don't let go of the skills you've learned in this book, the skills you are hopefully putting into practice already with your significant other – maybe with your friends and family too. Remember:

1. Strike when the iron is cold. If it gets hot, take a break.
2. Explore first, resolve second.
3. Speak about your experience and your feelings, not about your spouse.
4. Listen, Reflect in Your Own Words, Validate, and Empathize.

That's a lot of information I just redacted into a little summary; I encourage you to review the details in depth as needed, and practice, practice, practice. Your relationship will thank you for it.

And now, I want to push the envelope a little bit further. What if... what if you didn't stop there? What if *we* didn't stop there? What if you and I agreed we would take these skills and generalize? We could use them not just with our husbands and wives, our boyfriends and girlfriends, our partners and fiancés and lovers, but with our parents and our children, our siblings and our in-laws; we could listen to our friends and colleagues, reflect to our neighbors, validate our coworkers and bosses, even empathize with our exes! Can you imagine a world in which people really *communicated* with each other? Really *heard* each other? Really *cared*?

And then... what if we kept going? What if we pushed beyond our families and our neighborhoods and all our one-to-one interactions and brought this worldview to our social, political, and religious groups? What would it be like if instead of unending partisan combat there was openness and understanding – without, of course, requiring agreement? Just think what kind of progress could be made if progress were allowed – and not just allowed, but fostered!

And – forgive me for being a hopeless idealist – what if we took it even farther than that? What if we could bring this kind of dialogue to nations and peoples? What would international conflicts look like if, despite conflicting versions of the same historical record, people from this tribe and that tribe, from that country and the other country, could get together, hear each other's perspectives, experiences, and feelings, and genuinely encounter their empathy for the Other? What could this world truly be like?

Look, I know – we're a long way off from that. But perfection was never the expectation. Only effort. All we can ask for is the effort. And it starts with you.

The world needs dialogue. The world needs *empathy*. And the world needs you to be a part of the movement to make it happen.

Epilogue

Rob was at the kitchen sink finishing up the dishes when Denise got back from her yoga class. She dumped her bag on the chair by the door and joined him in the kitchen. "Hey," she chirped, giving him a peck on the cheek. "Thanks for taking care of that." "No problem," replied Rob. Denise cleared her throat. "Um, so, can we have one of those... you know, one of those feelings talks when you're done?" Rob glanced at her over his shoulder. "Yeah... that's a good idea," he mumbled. "Great," she declared. "I'll make us some tea and meet you at the table in five?" "Sounds good," agreed Rob.

Four and a half minutes later, they found themselves face-to-face over two steaming cups of chai.

Rob: *So... who's gonna go first?*

Denise: *Um, I think you're more upset about this than I am. Why don't you start?*

Rob: *Yeah, I kind of have some stuff to get off my chest.*

Denise: *I know. Okay, tell me how you're feeling about it.*

Rob: *Yeah. Well. Okay, let me just talk about how I'm feeling, and you're listening, right?*

Denise: *Right.*

Rob: *Okay. Um. Well, I'm glad we salvaged last night and enjoyed the movie. But I'm really bummed about how mad you got at me over the dishes. And over what we did or didn't agree about them. And then you called me selfish or something, and that really hurt.*

Denise: Okay, so you're sad that last night went poorly – well, happy that it ended up okay, but it nearly went poorly – and you're hurt that I got mad at you for not doing the dishes right away and called you selfish or whatever I said.

Rob: Right. I mean, I can't think of any specific examples right now, and maybe I'm wrong, but in my head it's like this situation has happened so many times before, where the slightest misstep gets treated like a major crime.

Denise: It feels... unfair.

Rob: Yeah. But also, I feel bad that I reacted harshly and I wish I'd done a better job in the moment. I feel like I let myself get pulled into the old, dysfunctional dynamic we've had and I'm disappointed in myself.

Denise: You feel bad that you didn't handle things better. Sounds like you don't want to get stuck in the same cycles of fighting we used to have?

Rob: Right. I really don't want to go back there. But also, I'm really annoyed at you for starting that up again in the first place. I really thought you agreed that it was fine if we watched the movie first. Is it possible I misheard you? I guess. But the reaction you had was so big and so harsh... man, that was rough.

Denise: You're really bummed about my reaction. It felt harsh and unfair.

Rob: Totally.

Denise: Anything else?

Rob: Yeah. I mean, the whole thing, it's just like – it's like I can never do anything right. I really want this marriage to work. I'm really trying. You say nice things when I help with your parents, you appreciate that I do most of the cooking, all that stuff, but then one little thing goes wrong and I'm back in the jerk box and it seems like none of the effort I've put in makes any difference.

Denise: Wow. Yeah. You feel... defeated?

Rob: Um, kind of. Not exactly. That sounds kind of final. Maybe more like... discouraged. Like really discouraged.

Denise: Yeah. Wow. That really sucks. You're putting in so much effort to make this marriage work—

Rob: —and to make you happy!

Denise: And to make me happy, and then over a few dishes, maybe, it's like we're back at square one. I can understand how that's so discouraging. And sad.

Rob: Exactly. It's like, what's even the point?

Denise: That's a really crummy place to be.

Rob: It is.

Denise: ...

Rob: [heaves a sigh]

Denise: I'm so sorry you're feeling like this.

Rob: Thanks.

Denise: Am I getting it?

Rob: You are. Thanks.

Denise: Anything else?

Rob: Um... well, I'm really hoping we can win this together. I don't want to fight anymore. I want us to be happy together. So I'm feeling – well, not optimistic exactly, but... hopeful. I'm hoping we can do this.

Denise: You want things to get better – you're not feeling totally confident, but you really want to get there.

Rob: Yeah.

Denise: I am really hopeful for you to get what you want too.

Rob: Thanks. [Smiles.] Okay... I'd like to hear from you now.

Denise: Ready to move into my world?

Rob: Yeah. Gettin' on my space suit. Let's go!

Denise: Okay great. So, again, we're not trying to make anything different right now. Just working on getting where each other's at.

Rob: Right.

Denise: Okay. So, first of all, I feel totally bad and ashamed of how I acted last night. I lost my cool and I made things worse and I'm really embarrassed. And sorry.

Rob: You're embarrassed at how you acted last night and you feel bad that you yelled at me.

Denise: I do. I really want this marriage to work also, and I feel awful awful awful when my own behavior puts that in danger.

Rob: You feel bad about damaging our relationship.

Denise: REALLY bad.

Rob: REALLY bad.

Denise: And at the same time, I really am very mad at you about the dishes. Well, not the dishes. The dishes – who cares about the dishes? But when I saw the full sink, I really do think I'd asked you to take care of it before the movie, and I know you disagree and that's fine, but when I was standing in the kitchen staring at the mess, it just put me back in this place of "nothing I say matters around here."

Rob: Yeah, but if I actually thought we said—

Denise: —wait wait – my world, remember?

Rob: Right right right sorry. So... you get this message that what you say doesn't matter... um, how do you feel when that happens?

Denise: Like, totally crushed. Like all I ever wanted from a marriage was a partnership of equals, where I matter and you matter and we both matter. And you know I never got that as a kid; with my dad it was always like, "I didn't ask for your opinion," and really it didn't matter what I thought. I want to have

a voice in this relationship, and if my voice isn't being heard, even on some-
thing as stupid as a few bowls and spoons... it just feels so bad.

Rob: Yeah. I hear that. It's like if I'm not even taking you into account when it comes to some cutlery, then of course in your mind, with the bigger stuff there's no chance.

Denise: Right.

Rob: And so that just feels totally, um, alienating to you. And you feel horrible.

Denise: [tearing up] I do. I really do.

Rob: I can totally understand that. You've told me about the not being heard thing before and I'm so sorry that button got pushed again. That really sucks.

Denise: Yeah. Thanks.

Rob: Am I getting it?

Denise: I think so.

Rob: You're not sure though?

Denise: Well... I don't know. It feels like there's something missing. I'm not sure I even know what it is.

Rob: I think... is it maybe this feeling of frustration you've mentioned in the past? Like you're just sick of this issue always coming up and ruining things for us, and you're worried we'll never get over it?

Denise: Yeah, that's definitely there too.

Rob: Yeah. It's hard. [He takes her hand in his.]

Denise: ...

Rob: ...Can I have a turn again to share some more stuff?

Denise: Yeah, go for it.

Rob: Well, I'm also frustrated by this tendency you have to go to this place of "he doesn't listen to me." I mean, I try so hard to be a good husband, to be attentive—

Denise: —you ARE a good husband!

Rob: I know I know, but hang on, stay with me, yeah?

Denise: Yeah, sorry, go on.

Rob: I try so hard to be attentive and to take care of what you need. It hurts that you would look at me and have these thoughts like maybe I don't care. And at the same time I get it. I understand why you feel that way sometimes, especially because, hey, I'm not perfect, and sometimes I'm sure I do tune you out. And that does suck. So it's kind of both feelings there.

Denise: So on one hand, you hate that I keep putting you in this he-doesn't-listen box, and on the other hand, you really get it and feel bad for me and feel bad when you actually don't listen.

Rob: Right. And I'm not blaming you at all. I have my stuff, and you have yours. And that's okay. And we'll get through it all together.

Denise: You're not blaming me. You sound more optimistic now. You're optimistic that we'll figure this out somehow.

Rob: I am. I want us to work.

Denise: Me too.

Rob: Yeah...

Denise: ...

Rob: Um, can we have a hug?

Denise: I'd like that.

[They hug.]

Rob: *I really love you, Denise. We're gonna make it. We're gonna make it together.*

Denise: *I love you. I know we will.*

Did you find this book helpful? Help others find it too by leaving a review on Amazon!

* * *

Have more questions? Send them my way, and find more tips and info at www.TheCommunicationBook.com.

About the Author

Raffi Bilek has been working with couples across the globe for over a decade. He has helped hundreds of couples improve their communication, boost their connection, recover from hurts and betrayals, and, in many cases, save their marriages.

Before that, Raffi earned a degree in computer science from Brown University, but never much enjoyed it because the computers wouldn't laugh at his humor. Besides being a couples counselor and a computer programmer, Raffi is a dad to four girls, a former swing dancer, an Orthodox Jewish rabbi, and a nationally ranked Scrabble player.

Raffi speaks English, Hebrew, French, and Spanish, has seen the fjords (they really are that good), and enjoys playing word games and telling good (and bad) jokes. He deeply loves his wife, but frankly wishes she got more of his jokes.

www.ingramcontent.com/pod-product-compliance
Lightning Source LLC
Chambersburg PA
CBHW011228120626
46549CB00008B/3186